THE BARTHES FANTASTIC

THINKING LITERATURE
A series edited by Nan Z. Da and Andrea Gadberry

The Barthes Fantastic

LITERATURE, CRITICISM, AND THE PRACTICE OF LANGUAGE

John Lurz

The University of Chicago Press
Chicago and London

The University of Chicago Press, Chicago 60637
The University of Chicago Press, Ltd., London
© 2025 by The University of Chicago
All rights reserved. No part of this book may be used or reproduced in any manner whatsoever without written permission, except in the case of brief quotations in critical articles and reviews. For more information, contact the University of Chicago Press, 1427 East 60th Street, Chicago, IL 60637.
Published 2025
Printed in the United States of America

34 33 32 31 30 29 28 27 26 25   1 2 3 4 5

ISBN-13: 978-0-226-83997-4 (cloth)
ISBN-13: 978-0-226-83998-1 (paper)
ISBN-13: 978-0-226-83999-8 (e-book)
DOI: https://doi.org/10.7208/chicago/9780226839998.001.0001

The University of Chicago Press gratefully acknowledges the generous support of the subcommittee on Grants-in-Aid of the Faculty Research Awards Committee at Tufts University toward the publication of this book.

Library of Congress Cataloging-in-Publication Data

Names: Lurz, John, author.
Title: The Barthes fantastic : literature, criticism, and the practice of language / John Lurz.
Description: Chicago : The University of Chicago Press, [2025] | Series: Thinking literature | Includes bibliographical references and index.
Identifiers: LCCN 2024046666 | ISBN 9780226839981 (paperback) | ISBN 9780226839974 (cloth) | ISBN 9780226839998 (ebook)
Subjects: LCSH: Barthes, Roland—Criticism and interpretation. | Fantastic, The, in literature. | Literature—History and criticism—Theory, etc. | Critics—France—Biography.
Classification: LCC P85.B33 L87 2025 | DDC 801/.95092—dc23/eng/20241127
LC record available at https://lccn.loc.gov/2024046666

♾ This paper meets the requirements of ANSI/NISO Z39.48-1992 (Permanence of Paper).

TO ARTURO, WHOSE DIFFERENT LANGUAGES
CONTINUE TO BEGUILE AND RILE ME.

IN MEMORY OF HELIOS, OUR HAPPY,
FRATTY, BRINDLED SUNDOG.

Proust is a complete world-reading system. This means that if we accept this system in the slightest degree, if only because it is so seductive, then there is no incident of daily life, no encounter, no trait, no situation which doesn't have its reference in reading Proust.... The pleasure of reading Proust—or rather of rereading him—is like consulting the Bible: abstraction made of the sacred and the respect it demands: it's the encounter between a present and what must be called, in the complete sense of the word, a wisdom: *a knowledge of "life" and its language.*

ROLAND BARTHES, interview in *Le Figaro*, July 27, 1974

So that the fact of writing, of the possibility of language as such, is the miracle, the fantastic.

STANLEY CAVELL, "The Fantastic of Philosophy"

Contents

A NOTE ON QUOTATIONS x

FORE-WORD xiii

INTRODUCTION: On the Fantastic, in Barthes 1

CHAPTER 1: Magic Lessons 31

CHAPTER 2: How Notation Works 53

CHAPTER 3: The Value of Literary Reflexion 77

CHAPTER 4: Citation and Its Image 102

CONCLUSION: The Wisdom of Criticism 128

ACKNOWLEDGMENTS 145

NOTES 147

BIBLIOGRAPHY 163

INDEX 171

A Note on Quotations

Quotations from English translations of Barthes's works are documented using parenthetical citations in the text, identified by the following alphabetically ordered abbreviations. When it is necessary or productive to include the French, I do so in square brackets and add the volume and page number of the *Oeuvres complètes* published by Seuil. For full details on all these publications, see the bibliography. In a few places, I deviate from the published translation, which I mark in endnotes. If no translation of a French text is cited, the translation is my own. Italics are original unless noted otherwise.

Album	*Album: Unpublished Correspondence and Texts*
China	*Travels in China*
CL	*Camera Lucida*
Contemporary	*"Simply a Particular Contemporary": Interviews, 1970–1979*
Critical	*Critical Essays*
Criticism	*Criticism and Truth*
Eiffel	*The Eiffel Tower and Other Mythologies*
Empire	*Empire of Signs*
Fashion	*The Fashion System*
Gide	*"On Gide and His Journal"*
Gift	*"A Very Fine Gift" and Other Writings on Theory*
Grain	*The Grain of the Voice*
IMT	*Image-Music-Text*
LD	*A Lover's Discourse*
Leçon	*Lecture in Inauguration of the Chair of Literary Semiology*
LF	*The Language of Fashion*

MFN	"Masculine, Feminine, Neuter" and Other Writings on Literature
Michelet	Michelet
Mythologies	Mythologies
NCE	New Critical Essays
Neutral	The Neutral
Pleasure	The Pleasure of the Text
PN	The Preparation of the Novel
Préparation	La préparation du roman (Transcription des enregistrements)
Racine	On Racine
RB	Roland Barthes by Roland Barthes
Responsibility	The Responsibility of Forms
Rustle	The Rustle of Language
Sarrasine	"Sarrasine" de Balzac: Séminaires à l'École pratique de hautes études
Semiology	Elements of Semiology
Semiotic	The Semiotic Challenge
SFL	Sade, Fourier, Loyola
Signs	Signs and Images: Writings on Art, Cinema, and Photography
Sollers	Writer Sollers
S/Z	S/Z
WDZ	Writing Degree Zero

and read'. He had begun it by citing Macrobius: 'In this Book all is mine, & Nothing is mine. Omne meum, nihil meum.' Pastorius meant that by assembling bits of the old, he had created something new. It took considerable intellectual discernment – and long, cramped hours of reading and notetaking – to create a masterpiece that was at once his own and a compilation of others' writings.

Phonics, in the words of the reading researcher Reid Lyon, is "nothing more than a relationship between sound structure and a print structure." It's breaking down the word "cat" a spoken hard k sound, follow short vowel a, and finally p tip of your tongue on the fr of your mouth and letting go that little burst of t. Phonics teaches

1. Untitled (June 2023). Author's handmade collage.

Fore-Word

From the very start—or, as the Gospel says, "in the beginning"—there was a word: *fantastic*. And if the opening of a critical book is expected to concisely announce the claims to come, it is the word *fantastic* that, as the Alpha and Omega of my thinking here, incarnates and gives shape to this book's argument. Less coded than the stagey "fabulous" of homosexual camp and less loaded than the "imaginary" of psychoanalytic schemas, *fantastic* shares aspects with both but adds further literary and philosophical associations that will, I hope, transfigure it as a term and give it some new analytical glory in discussions of literature, theory, and criticism. More than anything though, it is a word that I like and that I like thinking about. I like its sounds: the easy softness of the *f* and *s* set off by the aspiration of the first *t* and cut short by the hard "-tic" that will make a very real difference for this argument. I like its sense of excellence bordering on the magical, its unfounded echo of fannish worship, and even the space it makes for the menace of the grotesque. In fact, I can't swear that this obsessive verbal excoriation has not been worked up in order to work with this word, to weave it more soundly and more meaningfully into the fabric of my everyday experiences. To admit this is also to tender a provisional instance of the fantastic that this book aspires to discern, which is to say, the liaison where language and life light into each other and where the world finds itself quite literally fashioned out of words.

Here might be an ideal place to insert a personal anecdote, a sliver of my sensuous experience that received fantastic form and legibility from this word—if doing so didn't threaten to distract us from the linguistic register that this fore-word wants to foreground. What the fantastic indexes is as much the experience of the world as it is the—impossible, illusory, unreal—experience of language itself, which might surface from a sense of coincidence with our "extra-linguistic" life but is by no means dependent on it. Quite the reverse, in fact. For that reason, we will purposefully approach the fantastic as a so-called textual phenomenon, through the discursive reflexions of a writer whose entire oeuvre involves the practical exploration of a linguistic mode of existence: Roland Barthes. Indeed, the second (though not secondary) aim of this book is to engage Barthes's writing not as an attempt to turn his life into literature but rather as an extended effort to turn literature into his life. Expanding on the recent efforts to explicate and exploit the marvelous lecture courses and novelistic ambitions from the last years before his untimely death, this discussion ranges over and over across the entire sweep of his varied career to assemble a kind of literary living that Barthes never stopped trying to practice.[1] For his late attempt in the 1977-1978 course on *The Neutral* to "live according to the nuances literature teaches me" is only a more meticulous articulation of the sentiments he pens in his 1944 essay "Enjoy the Classics," in which he claims that "nothing forbids me from thinking that this sentence of La Bruyère's, this verse of Racine's has been written to double very exactly my present bitterness or passion . . . [the writer] has seen all of it, felt all of it, and still other things that I did not see or feel" (11, 1:57). In both cases, literature provides Barthes a medium in which to encounter and even embellish his own life, a linguistic register of experience that we will see the word *fantastic* eccentrically but insistently figuring in his discourse. Barthes's close friend Phillippe Sollers puts it resonantly when he writes that, with him, "we have literature as practice, process, proper experience. . . . A material world subject to differential development."[2] In this book's elaboration of the fantastic, we will thus be plotting a readerly practice that draws on the real values of language in order to draw out a "proper experience" of lived textuality.

This investment in the text is what keeps me from locating something like the degree zero of the book's animating idea in the less personally focused argument about tragedy that Barthes mounts as a student in 1942: writing in an explicitly Nietzschean vein, he proclaims, "In the grand epochs of tragedy, humanity knew how to find a tragic vision of existence and, for once maybe, it was not the theater that imitated life, but life that received from the theater a dignity and a truly grand style" (1:29-30). Instead, I turn to the world-shaping role that Barthes repeatedly finds in the writing of Proust, which he describes in an assertion that is effectively a reworked citation of these early lines. "Proust has given modern writing its epic," he writes in the famously overcited essay "The Death of the Author"; "by a radical reversal, instead of putting his life into his own novel, as is so often said, he made his life itself a work [*une oeuvre*] of which his own book was the model, so that it is quite clear to us that it is not Charlus who imitates Montesquiou, but Montesquiou, in his anecdotal, historical reality, who is only a secondary, derived fragment of Charlus" (*Rustle* 51, 3:42).[3] Singling out the novelistic character (Charlus) as the source of our understanding of the historical personage (Montesquiou), Barthes describes a situation in which "real life"—both individual and collective— is itself a literary phenomenon, a textual tissue woven out of linguistic formulations. No surprises here: sixty-plus years from the advent of structuralism and its ensuing controversies, we know this much is true. But Barthes's treatment of this idea in a short piece that precedes his death sentence will help me resuscitate some overshadowed implications of this line of thinking. Reviewing George Painter's Proust biography in 1966, Barthes once again claims that when we turn to this life narrative what we find there is nothing other than Proust's work: "To read Painter's book ... is not to discover the origins of *À la recherche* but to read a duplicate of the novel, as though Proust had written the same work twice—once in his book and once in his life" (*MFN* 73). The emphasis is less on the infinite postponement of meaning and the inescapability of imitation that Barthes uses to challenge a traditional understanding of authorial agency than it is on an expansion of both the terms "writing" and "life". This presents the actions of Proust's life (which of course include his scribal activity) as an effort of existential articulation only made legible in the explicitly linguistic labors provided by the novel or biography and opens up onto what I am suggesting is the fantastic framework of Barthes's entire intellectual project.

What is more, when he continues, the writerly dissolution of the boundary separating life and literature extends beyond Proust the author to also encompass his readers in a way that repeats his youthful claims about reading literary classics. He asserts that "each of our individual lives may open itself up to receive Proustian essences. Hence the constant feelings of running into Proust's world in our own lives" (*MFN* 74). In the same way that Proust's work informs his life and draws out the latter's own particular textuality, his novel can also have resonances and echoes with the reader's experiences, conferring on them an open legibility otherwise unavailable (or otherwise filled in by dominant cultural mythologies). The specific operations that might constitute this conferral is what this book's fantastic reading of Barthes explores. For while the unending complexity of this legibility has come to be a major strain of Barthes's critical reception, one that will certainly feature in my discussion, he never abandons the "real life" implications of literature that Proust makes so perspicuous for him. We thus find him anchoring the preparation of his novel at what would be the end of his work with an all too concrete example of the knot between reading and reality that my argument tries to inspect. Continuing the willful embrace of the personal and the pathetic that characterizes his late writing, Barthes appeals to the death of the grandmother in *The Guermantes Way* to illustrate, in the devastating wake of his own mother's passing, a "Moment of Truth: that which, in my reading, happens *to me*, a subject in the literal sense: which means I can only make sense of it by referring to my own experience" (PN 104).

At first glance, it looks as if Barthes is using his "own experience" to make sense of his reading rather than the model I've been introducing, where it is the linguistic engagement of reading that helps to make sense of and give shape to experience. But the exact relationship between the two categories isn't so easy to parse. In this case, reading *is* an experience: it is something that "happens" to him, that presses on him and makes him "a subject in the literal sense." What characterizes this "Moment of Truth" is precisely the indistinguishability between the text and his life, the way that they intertwine with, collapse into, and assign significance to each other. (Indeed, if we read the sentence again, we can see how the "it" he is making sense of here is the very "happening" of this collapse itself.) Marielle Macé takes this indeterminacy as the topic and driving force of her 2011 book *Façons de lire, manières d'être* [*Ways of Reading, Manners of Being*], which works to reconceptualize reading as "one of the behaviors by which, quotidianly, we give a form, a flavor, and even a style to our existence."[4] Through wide-ranging discussions centered around Proust, Sartre, and Barthes himself, Macé rejects any stark distinction between literature and life, resisting a fundamental "*face-à-face*" that would need to be overcome. Rather, she writes, there is only "at the interior of life itself, the forms, the urges, the images, and the manners of being that circulate between subjects and works, that expose them, animate them, affect them."[5] Positing a kind of originary chiasmic relationship between the individual reader and the works that form them, she picks up on Barthes's play with the word *subject* and explores what she calls "the pragmatic duplicity of *sub-jectum* / support and subject-agent" performed in reading.[6] In this subjective duplicity, we see the mutually constituting dynamic that Barthes finds in Proust, the way the shape that one's lived experience receives from reading a literary work is fantastically bound up with the shape that one's own particular reading imposes on that work.

Macé's spirited commitment "to consider reading as a behavior" is where my discussion both coincides and diverges from her argument. Distancing herself from "semiotic or narratological models (which have the tendency to describe the activity of reading as an operation closed on itself, as valorized as it is separated, and which thus struggle to make reading enter into life *afterwards*)," she approaches reading as "a comportment rather than a deciphering."[7] I, too, approach reading as a lived and living "behavior" and want to resist isolating it into some kind of autonomous or idealist sphere. For me, however, "deciphering" isn't opposed to but rather *constitutive of* this "comportment," so where I see myself building on her innovative work is with the central place that the functioning of signification holds in my account of living literature. Putting this distinction in terms of the "bovarism" she works to revive and revalue, I could say that my argument tries to imagine the fantastic situation in which Emma Bovary had read and enacted Barthes's texts rather than romance novels. (*Quel fantasme!*) In this, I am actually coming much closer to an earlier discussion of Macé's, where she explores "the novelistic" in Barthes's work as "a system of perception before being a modality of writing."[8] Rather than just describing the formal decisions and lyrical gestures by which Barthes tried to imbue his theoretical writing with an ambiguous textuality, she argues that "the novelistic" also names "an approach to life" that is linked to "a manner of cutting up the real."[9] As we will see, this kind of cutting up is what an emphasis on signification allows me to elaborate in a readerly dynamic I am calling "the practice of language," which is to say, the animated and imaginative engagement of the words we receive from our books. This phrasing not only allows me to parry any clear distinction between an actively determining and a passively determined relationship to language but also avoids any suggestion that I'm calling for everyone to necessarily become literal writers: as Macé puts it, "this is decidedly not about turning reading towards literary creation to make a writer-to-come out of every reader."[10] Rather, its plainspoken pragmatics should orient my exploration of the fantastic, for all its theoretical abstraction, toward the broader context of everyday life and activity.

Relatedly, my practical investment in language as such extends my discussion beyond Macé's tight focus on subjectivity, which she draws from Foucault's late interest in the "care of the self," to the textual construction of the world that exists independently of that self. This is also, in part, why I began to flesh out my account of the fantastic by way of "The Death of the Author," whose end might "birth" a reader but only one that "can no longer be personal"—can only be "the very space in which are inscribed, without any of them being lost, all the citations out of which a writing is made" (*Rustle* 54). This "space" of inscription is, in fact, what we find when Barthes attempts to explicate the "Moment of Truth" further. Circling around the role played by affect and a resistance to interpretation that recalls the haiku, his explanatory comments remain closely tied to the local specificities of the grandmother's death in Proust's novel. In a desultory attempt at a more conceptual explanation, he ultimately admits the "extreme impudence in speaking of truth outside of a system that tells us how to ground it"—as if to gesture toward the alternative, even baseless logic that is informing his thinking here (*PN* 107). And the ideas he goes on to glancingly offer do little to buttress the discussion, leaving the Moment of Truth hovering over the void of its own sense.[11] At what could be considered the pinnacle of Barthes's analytical appeal to his own subjectivity, we thus find ourselves aloft in the emptiness he announced via the author's death: "a field without origin—or at least with no origin but language itself, i.e., the very thing which ceaselessly calls any origin into question" (*Rustle* 52).

In this way, the book's argument seeks to take the intersection of these two intellectual currents seriously, to think the identification of a reader's experience and a literary text through the baseless functioning of linguistic signification. As experienced readers of Barthes will recognize, however, nothing fissures the operation of identification as soundly as the irreducible instability of the signifier. In reality, I realize this project is an impossible one; the approach to reading and criticism I develop here cannot be said to exist. And yet: Barthes also shows us how to inhabit those impossibilities, how to speak them *as* impossibilities, so that the readerly experience to which this book is devoted can perhaps *only be said* to exist, can only exist in its saying. It's for this reason that my argument insists on beginning with a word, one that not only signifies illusoriness itself but that also flickers across Barthes's oeuvre to obliquely name the shifting, real-world intertwining of literary and lived experience. Following this fore-word, the introduction continues to probe the unreal experience of language by tracing the course of *fantastic* through Barthes's texts and charting some of the forked paths it opens up into larger literary and philosophical domains. As this carves out a new perspective on a writer we thought we knew, it also helps us begin incorporating the articulating energy that language, in Barthes's hands, fantastically imparts to the world and those of us in it. The chapters that follow lay out a set of linguistic practices that bring this unreal phenomenon to life, mapping out the space of literature and literary criticism's "practical application" in ways that expansively delimit the very value of literary study.

The Barthes Fantastic thus engages and extends recent efforts to reconsider what it is we learn as students of literature. Less an abstract intervention into the forms and styles of critical discourse that have sought to make space for different modes of analysis, my argument strives to saturate that space by repeatedly reiterating the fantastic work of words.[12] In doing so, it joins—and joins together—an eclectic and otherwise unrelated set of critics writing today in what we could call a renewed field of practical criticism. In addition to Marielle Macé's pathbreaking work in France, Pheng Cheah's *What Is a World?: On Postcolonial Literature as World Literature*, Anna Kornbluh's *The Order of Forms: Realism, Formalism, and Social Space*, and Karen Zumhagen-Yekplé's *A Different Order of Difficulty: Liter-*

ature after Wittgenstein all engage, from different angles and with different theoretical and literary archives, the "real-life" effects of reading—what Cheah calls "the normative force that literature can exert on the world" and Kornbluh styles as "building in criticism."[13] Rita Felski's *Uses of Literature* and Joshua Landy's *How to Do Things with Fictions* might be the inaugurating examples of this nonexistent field, and the latter's attempt to explore "formative fictions" as "texts whose function it is to fine-tune our mental capacities" is perhaps most directly connected to my endeavor here.[14] Appealing to the notion of "spiritual exercises" that we will encounter again in Barthes's discussion of Ignatius Loyola, Landy seeks to "reinvigorate the pragmatic outlook [on literary art] in its broadly ethical, rather than narrowly moral, dimension" and discusses how a set of texts ranging from the Gospel of Mark through Beckett's first Trilogy "*train*" us in particular ways of thinking or particular mental habits.[15] Peter Sloterdijk leaches the lingering religiosity from even this "ethical" vocabulary in his rousing and wide-ranging *You Must Change Your Life* by insisting on "forms of practice" as the key to understanding secular modernity, the titular reference to Rilke's "Archaic Torso of Apollo" suggesting the Hellenistic philosophical model we will also take up in the introduction.[16] Pursuing this kind of formative project through Barthes's writing not only allows me to more deliberately explore the role that the operation of language as such plays in cultivating a kind of aesthetic asceticism (Sloterdijk discusses how language games "constitute the perfect impregnation of everyday life through artistry") but also gives me the resources to map, under the rubric of the fantastic, the distinctive register of experience in which all these practical efforts unfold.[17]

I have been convinced of the particular importance of putting a name to the experience of language that forms our sense of things—to name, we will see, the fantastic entailments of nomination itself—when I have encountered my students' resistance to and frustration with the lessons in the constructedness of their own beliefs and perceptions that the analysis of literary texts make available. Often responding with exasperated blanket dismissals that "nothing means anything" or, worse, emptily parroting arguments about "societal construction" (I am perhaps not doing my job quite right), my students have led me to think that I need to provide an additional perspective on and vocabulary for responding to and engaging with the textuality of the world—and with textuality as such. For the only thing more difficult than asking students to question their own thinking is perhaps getting them to notice the operation of language that both enables and exceeds it, to approach words themselves and not just their commonsense meanings. Though Barthes was only one of the figures who taught me how to access the fruitful affordances of such critical inquiry, it is to

Barthes I return because, as Françoise Gaillard has put it, he "loves things only insofar as they are intellectualizable"—insofar as they offer themselves to linguistic articulation.[18] What my investigation into the fantastic and its attendant practices ultimately aims at is a revaluation of linguistic mediation, a necessary if unattainable de-alienation of signification that would help me and my students resist opposing our experiences and the words we use to have them.[19] Going even further in her Barthes-inspired account of reading and literary study as "the gift of a practice" rather than "an object of knowledge," Tiphaine Samoyault effectively describes the utopian horizon of the new practical criticism I am trying to fantastically speak into existence.[20] "The reception [*l'accueil*] of a literary work must permit one to invent one's participation and to find a place," she writes in terms that gesture toward the active sign-wielding capacities that I hope to parse in the following pages.[21] Again, this is not to claim an unconditional and omnipotent sense of autonomous self-creation; routing this capacity for inventive signification through literary reading makes it, in fact, deeply and explicitly contingent. Putting this textual dependence more forcefully, she declares that "the available work, the hospitable work is that which not only does not exclude the reader (by intimidation for example, or by univocity), but that which transforms the reader into a producer, even into a creator" and describes my larger theoretical ambitions for this book's practical agenda.[22]

The insistent instability of the binary between theory and practice in Barthes's writing is perhaps the most compelling reason for turning to his work as a resource for thinking through an account of literature and language's formative relationship with lived experience. In the early, quixotic planning stages of this book in fact, I envisioned brief interchapters focusing on his amateur paintings and calligraphic exercises (sampled in *Roland Barthes by Roland Barthes*) as sites in which his semiotic theories took tangible, experiential form that attempted to expressly embody—rather than just performatively describe—the teeming effects of signification. I was looking for ways that Barthes took his intellectual project beyond the page, a set of illustrative examples to complement and concretize the impossible coincidence of language and life I wanted to theorize, and I thought I might find some in the rhythmic patterns of shapes and fanciful approximations of handwriting kept in the *Fonds Roland Barthes* (NAF 28630) at the Bibliothèque nationale in Paris. There is something fantastic in those paintings to be sure, the warp and weft of his sinuous lines and the mottled blocking of interleaved colors seeming to picture the very weave of textuality in ink and gouache; I hope to write on them one day still. But what of words themselves? What of the intricate phrasing, the novelistic lines, and the vibrant verbal images that had drawn me to Barthes in the first place?

2. Roland Barthes, Drawing 159 (December 15, 1971). By permission of Éric Marty. Photograph: Bibliothèque nationale de France (NAF 28630).

Wasn't it language—in all its literary coloration—on which I was trying to model the fantastic texture of my life? This realization was thrown into clear-cut relief by one of the few discursive comments he makes about his amateur hobby: "When I buy colors, it is by the mere sight of their name. The name of the color (*Indian yellow*, *Persian red*, *celadon green*) outlines a kind of generic region within which the exact, special effect of the color is unforeseeable; the name is then the promise of a pleasure, the program of an operation" (*RB* 129). The lesson here, which we will return to time and again, is that words lead the way; and that we can never quite know exactly where they will take us. Though Barthes is most obviously talking about "the special effect of the color," this is inseparable from, conditioned if not fully determined by, the "generic region" staked out by the name. Moreover, the "program of an operation" by which that region is outlined implies a practical signifying procedure that the name both stimulates and steers, a set of associations and connotations that it invites us to elaborate and explore as a supplement to our perception of the color.

As this interaction of sense and sensation plays out, in miniature, the fantastic dynamic Barthes's writing helps me to approach in particularly literary terms, it also informs the amateur collage art I am including as my own practical illustrations of this book's theoretical analysis. Certainly my most Barthesian gesture in a discussion that adheres much more closely to traditional academic argumentation than most of the writing for which he is beloved, these collaged divagations are, in part, my way of citing his critical élan, something like the "desperate plagiarism" he describes in *The Pleasure of the Text* as a way to approach the "text of bliss" (*Pleasure* 22). Begun in the depths of the COVID-19 quarantine, when my life consisted, in actuality, of little more than a steady stream of visual and verbal texts, this recreational practice developed as a rather literal application of the thinking I was pursuing while drafting early sections of my argument. In particular, and not by chance, it was the focus on the metaphors of cutting in *The Fashion System*'s arduous account of notation (see chap. 2) that had me taking a razor blade to my everyday periodical reading as I noticed words and images from this book's discourse in other, resonating contexts. Could this be one way, I wondered, to simulate the kind of readerly activity that would bolster literature and literary criticism in sculpting our perception of the world—a way, as Barthes puts it in his response to a questionnaire from the literary journal *Tel Quel*, "to see the world as it creates itself for a literary consciousness, to consider reality periodically as the raw material of a secret work" (*Critical* 157)? On the other hand, the surprisingly difficult task of pasting these snippets and excised images into meaningful compositions found its paradigm in the account we will see Barthes give in *Sade, Fourier, Loyola* of the linguistic pragmatics by which his titular figures fantastically formulate their living systems, their systems for living: not just their "mania for cutting up" the world into distinct signs but also the way these three authors "deduct, combine, arrange, endlessly produce rules of assemblage" for these signs (*SFL* 3–4). As the construction of the collages thus functions as a representative materialization of "the practice of language," the image-text relationships they stage dramatize the operation of the fantastic I am trying to describe. Resisting the possibility of straightforward or immediate consumption, the collages gesture toward the operative textuality of my own argumentation and insist on the vital place of *our own* interpretive reading in coming to terms with its claims about literature and lived experience. They could even be thought of as a physical, embodied execution of the critical approach I take to Barthes's work, driven as it is by the collection and methodical collation of textual citations that reflect and refract our understanding of his ideas. At my most unrestrained, I want to say that they extend and abstract my discourse from its focused consideration of one idiosyncratic twentieth-century virtuoso of French letters into, at least potentially, a more generalized intellectual stance or literary deportment through which to encounter the world.

These are big claims, maybe bigger than the crude cut-and-pasting of a pandemic pastime can really bear. But it's precisely the crudeness of the format and the amateurism of the production that is important to me. Because despite the elitist texture of my textual archive (not just Barthes's rarefied discourse but also the organs of the urban intelligentsia from which I've culled most of my collage materials), the practices I'm exploring and exploiting in this book are not limited to those of us with advanced degrees in literature and literary theory. Rather, they describe some of the ways that, as speaking animals, we all apprehend and give meaning to our experiences. Barthes's own image of amateurism is germane here. Focusing on the insignificant, inexpert artistic hobbies of the "middle-class maiden in the nineteenth century," he asks, "What is it which, in the practice of the middle-class maiden of those days, transcended her femininity and her class? What was the utopia of such activities?" (*RB* 52). He answers, "The middle-class maiden produced uselessly, stupidly, for herself, but *she produced*: it was her own form of expenditure" (52).[23] While the focus on producing obviously speaks to the practical framing of my project, the point here is also in the confusing mix of admiration and disdain that tries to loosen such production from any particular social position or political agenda and to make space for everyone, for anyone, to perform it. If this is also what the rudimentary character of my collage work is trying to imply, the stakes of the literary and linguistic emphasis that they share with the chapters proper have to do with the way that literature and literary study (which, we know all too well, do have distinct class associations) put this kind of productive practice into conscious action. Because, as Barthes fantastically writes, "far from being a copy of reality, *literature is on the contrary the very consciousness of the unreality of language*", it offers a sphere in which to examine and exercise the very processes by which a meaningful world is cobbled together (*Critical* 160). As I thus explore and variously perform the linguistic practices that are available for all of us—but especially literature students—to give meaning to our lives, I ultimately show how thoughtful and considered reading can build an effectual intellectual construction whose reality is, in a word, fantastic.

3. Untitled (March 2021). Author's handmade collage.

Introduction
On the Fantastic, in Barthes

An English-language study of a French writer that puts its interpretive faith so forthrightly into the specificities of a single word will sooner or later need to address the question of translation, a linguistic practice on which Barthes was largely silent except insofar as he expressed a "constant pessimism" and "confusion" in regard to it. This cynicism has to do with the fact that "so often [translators] appear to be ignorant of precisely what I regard as the very meaning of a word: the connotation" (*RB* 115). If wedded to the referential promise of denotation, translation imperils the multivalent workings of the text and potentially imposes a false, limiting objectivity onto its language that can inhere as much in the force of its rearticulation as in the retroactive authority bestowed on the "original." But this is not the only way to conceive of translation's textual effects. Translations can also be writing; they can also work as part of a text's infinite operation by, most simply, giving us more to read—which is by no means simple.[1] As we will see in the vagaries that the English renderings introduce into Barthes's writings, the supplementary language of these translations adds more sense, advances more meaning, to the extent that they slightly but significantly reword some of his diction. In other words—*in other words!*—the translations of Barthes's writing that brought the workings of *fantastic* to my attention are not, I found on further scrutiny, precisely consistent (though I would like to claim that they are, in their own way, consistently precise). While the French *fantastique* always receives its English cognate, there are places where the more psychological *fantasmatique* is replaced by what I will suggest is the greater generality of our operative term. The tension between the two, which judicious recourse to Barthes's French allows me to engage, indexes the complementary currents that this book's practice of language seeks to animate: the equal impact that language has on the construction of speaking subjects and spoken objects. The path of the fantastic that I trace through Barthes's writings in this introduction works to speak them both.

The depsychologized analytical framework I'm specifying here is part of the rationale for routing my reading of Barthes across his entire oeuvre and distinguishes it from resonant arguments about the place of fantasy and imagination in his thinking, which orient themselves around the teaching program he famously announces in his inaugural address at the Collège de France in 1977. Starting from Barthes's provocative proclamation that "at the origin of teaching such as this we must always locate a fantasy [*un fantasme*]" (*Leçon* 15, 5:445), Kris Pint thus looks to these late lecture courses as "an exploration of new possibilities of living" by way of what he calls a "phantasmatic semiology."[2] He develops this idea through extended engagements with Lacanian psychoanalysis and a Deleuzean reading of Nietzsche rather than through the overt semiological thinking from early in Barthes's career that we will see inform my account of the fantastic. What results for Pint is a thoroughly imaginary account of the literature-life interface that minimizes consideration of a text's signification to focus instead on its significations: accordingly, he enumerates "space, detail, time and the author" to describe the form and content of the new existential possibilities he's interested in.[3] Indeed, when he explains in more general terms how "the text does not destroy the subject's imaginary . . . but replaces it with the imaginary in the text," he helps me to stake out the specific space of the fantastic as a paradoxical and unrealizable imaginary *of* the text—if by that phrase we understand a dynamic repertoire of impersonal signifying operations on which any particular textual fantasy necessarily depends.[4] It is in this kind of a symbolic register that the following elaboration of the fantastic as an analytic term unfolds.

* * *

As we have seen, the fantastic intersection of life and text presents itself from the very beginnings of Barthes's work, and his 1942 commentary "On Gide and His Journal," which appears between the two earlier pieces I cited in the fore-word, revolves around an appearance of this very term. Taking Gide's journal as the occasion for a set of remarks that range over the entire corpus of his writing, Barthes makes claims for the continuity between the disorganized, confessional sentences of the personal document and the more explicitly crafted works by which the novelist was publicly known. In a kind of formulation that will already be familiar to us, he makes a reference to Gide's alter ego in *The Counterfeiters* and asserts, "it is not 'Édouard's Journal' which resembles Gide's; on the contrary, many entries in Gide's *Journal* have the autonomy of 'Édouard's Journal.' They are no longer completely Gide; they begin to be outside him, en route for some unspecified work in which they want to appear, which they summon into being" ("Gide" 4). The tension here between the "autonomy" or exteriority of Gide's diary writing and the "*egoism*" he claims for the journal a few lines earlier casts the relationship between lived experience and the reflective transcription of that experience as a form of self-detachment, but—importantly—one that remains synonymous with self-proximity. Macé describes the paradoxical dynamic that Barthes is finding here in terms of his later desire to have "life in the form of a sentence," which she formulates as an effort "to transport oneself energetically into artifice."[5] Though she is talking about the effort of the reader more specifically, Gide provides a writerly performance of the way a text offers, in her words, "verbal gestures that insinuate themselves in us and in which we, for our part, want to insinuate ourselves."[6] This mutual insinuation plays out explicitly in the place that "Édouard's Journal" has as a major structural component of *The Counterfeiters*; its echoes with Gide's own life and artistic ambitions serve, in this line of reasoning, less as a potted writerly biography than as a form of externalized, dissociated self-representation that he might work to realize—that he might realize, in part, by working. As Barthes puts it, "It is because at a certain moment he wanted to be someone that he summoned up Ménalque, Lafcadio, Michel, or Édouard, that Gide wrote *Fruits of the Earth*, *The Immoralist*, and *The Counterfeiters*" ("Gide" 12).

Macé helps us distinguish how the dissociation involved in such outwardly projected self-realization resists any uncomplicated or straightforward understanding of this practice, any sense that Gide is nothing more than a pen-wielding descendant of Emma Bovary. She writes that the "*task*" of subjectivation involves not the "'emanation' of a preexisting subjectivity" but rather "meeting oneself outside, that is, rejoining a possible identity in the concerted acquiescence to an exterior model."[7] Indeed, Gide's activity is not limited to what Barthes calls "fictionalization," a kind of unbridled fantasy in which "an equivalence between an abstract reality and a concrete fiction" produces an idealized, Bovarian "myth" of one's self ("Gide" 12-13).[8] Barthes also describes the complementary process that Macé is talking about, one in which concrete reality enters into the abstraction of fiction: "real episodes are inserted into the novel, without Gide's bothering to change the names: the episode of the old La Pérouse, George's theft, etc." At this moment, he veers away from questions of subjectivity and identity to think more generally about the name as the point of contact between fiction and reality; doing so, he introduces a new term that indexes—that names—their illusory correlation: "As in children's games," he writes, "reality suddenly spills over into the fantastic [*la réalité chevauche tout à coup le fantastique*]" (14, 1:43). Here, it is neither fiction nor reality that Barthes is talking about but rather the indeterminate boundary between them that constitutes the fantastic as its own category, which is to say, at once, the reality of the fictional and the fiction of reality. Exercising the more colloquial meanings of the French "*chevaucher*," we can begin to see how the fantastic is what results when one "overlaps" with the other and, even more tellingly, what occurs when reality "rides" the fictional like a horse—when, that is, it harnesses the energy and mobility of the fictional articulation for its own progressive comprehension. As it indicates the kind of verbal operation that informs Gide's textually mediated relationship with himself, the detachment that is impossibly coincident with proximity, this word imagines the fantastic as the fleeting and indeterminate experience of textual mediation itself.

When *Roland Barthes by Roland Barthes* returns to Gide and his journal over thirty years later, it approaches the novelist in terms that not only recall his relationship with his characters but also parse this fantastic dynamic with a bit more theoretical precision. Asking "Can one—or at least could one ever—begin to write without taking oneself for another?," Barthes describes Gide's position in his own formation as a writer and asserts, "For the history of sources we should substitute the history of figures. The origin of the work is not the first influence, it is the first posture: one copies a role, then, by metonymy, an art" (*RB* 99). Most obviously, the contrast between the performative vocabulary of "posture" and "role" and the concrete or substantive origin suggested by "sources" stages this imitation as one of practical actions rather than personal content. Barthes is acting out the same imaginative moves as Gide, relating to him in the same way as he related to his fictional characters. But, as the staccato progression of his phrasing emphasizes, the real, indeed the originary, activity at work here is the associative movement of metonymy itself. What Barthes is copying in this identification with Gide, this "taking oneself for another," is the slide of the signifier along the various chains of its related significations. The result is that he "establishes a secret system of fantasies [*fonde un système secret de fantasmes*]," which describes an unknown and even unknowable arrangement that takes shape according to the associations and connotations made available by words (*RB* 99, 4:677). Distinguishing the fantastic from fantasy as such, this "secret system" foregrounds the structural combinations and distinctions of language's operation as what the former really gives us imaginary access to.

When Barthes concludes these comments with the claim that "the Gidean *Abgrund*, the Gidean core, unchanging, still forms in my head a stubborn swarm," he offers his own verbal illustration of this fantastic relationship to language (*RB* 99). Effectively reconciling the contradiction between the vacuous term *Abgrund* (abyss) and the substantial solidity suggested by "core," the simultaneous suggestion of motion and stasis in the image of the "stubborn swarm" implies an empty space to which Gide's textual traces give teeming shape but do not wholly fill. Putting this in the semiological vocabulary broached by the previous lines, we could say that the image works as a metaphor for metonymic connection that allows Barthes to identify himself with the very motility of verbal relations. Similarly, the insistence on an originary, foundational language in the final statement that "Gide is my original language, my *Ursuppe*, my literary soup" is effectively synonymous with no foundation at all, the uncharacteristic and unexplained reliance on untranslated German—which is specifically *not* his "original language"—plunging him and us headlong into the very linguistic "abyss" he is using *Abgrund* to figure (*RB* 99). At the same time, the rhythmic repetition of "my" slides along an associative chain that liquefies even as it affirms the swarm of metaphors he is using to piece himself together.

As this utterly semiological core forms Barthes's self-conception out of nothing but the movement of signs, it abuts the literary genre that, not coincidentally sharing its name with the signal term of my analysis, might help us swallow this soupy linguistic structuration in all its thick indeterminacy. One of Barthes's most influential students, Tzvetan Todorov puts it tellingly if tautologically in his now classic study of the Fantastic as a genre, asserting that "it permits the description of a fantastic universe, one that has no reality outside language; the description and what is described are not of a different nature."[9] While this statement resonates with Barthes's own almost contemporaneous move to an increasingly writerly form of criticism that is not linguistically distinct from its object of analysis, the crucial point is in the way the fantastic offers a particularly perspicuous conception of what we might continue to call the *reality of language*, a phrase that refers as much to the real operations of signification as to the sense of reality they, so to speak, effect. Todorov expands on this paradoxical reality when he notes the close connection between the fantastic and explicitly figurative discourse, writing, "If the fantastic constantly makes use of rhetorical figures, it is because it originates in them."[10] His explanation involves the specifically supernatural aspects of the fantastic—"the devil and vampires exist only in words," he points out— but his larger claim is that "the supernatural is born of language, it is both its consequence and its proof."[11] And while chapter 1 will, in fact, be examining the magical terms in which Barthes figures language itself, I am more interested for now in exploring the way this vocabulary of linguistic birth and origination further explicates the moves by which Barthes, following Gide, rhetorically conceives of himself and the world.

These implications come out most clearly in Todorov's account of the reader-text relationship engendered by the fantastic, which can accordingly help us continue developing what something like the lived experience of this abyssal "reality" of language involves (while also tempering claims for the unclassifiability of Barthes's writing by providing a loose generic categorization for it). The main aspect that, for Todorov, characterizes this fantastic experience will be as recognizable to readers of tales by Poe or Hoffmann as to students of structuralism and poststructuralism: ambiguity and uncertainty. Opposing the readerly reactions of total belief or total disbelief, Todorov locates a third, intermediate space he describes as "that hesitation experienced by a person who knows only the laws of nature, confronting an apparently supernatural event."[12] This inbetweenness is in the service of framing the fantastic in terms of its difference from its neighboring genres, the uncanny (where we don't believe in the reality of the event) or the marvelous (where we do). As this literary situation plays out an indecision between two possible but irreconcilable options, it also dramatizes the kind of foundationless interpretive situation that results from the elaboration of differential structures or, more drastically, from the significant slippages and instabilities that Barthes and likeminded writers cultivate over the course of their careers. What Todorov's way of putting it adds, however, is the language of "hesitation" that sustains the reader's experience of ambiguity, that prolongs it as something *to be experienced*.

The content of this hesitating experience finds further elaboration when Todorov explains the narrative logic whereby the fantastic "occupies the duration of this uncertainty."[13] His general point argues that the basically linear unfolding of the plot holds off any explanation of the supernatural that would destroy the fantastic's generic specificity. But when he highlights the prominence with which this kind of plot marks its forward propulsion, he also describes the temporally extended mode in which the reader encounters its constitutive ambiguity: he writes, "the narrative of the fantastic, which strongly emphasizes the process of uttering, simultaneously emphasizes this time of the reading itself."[14] What is particularly significant about this expression is the way it links narrative and readerly time, the way time functions as the aspect of the text's action that it shares with or even draws from the real world of the reader. Todorov's discussion thus implicitly suggests the extent to which the fantastic stages reading as itself a lived experience rather than an immaterial or imaginary intellectual occurrence that takes place in some kind of elsewhere. It is in fact the very imbrication of the reader's real world with the narrative world of the text that this mutual temporality opens up, what Todorov describes earlier as the "integration of the reader into the world of the characters."[15]

Gesturing toward the kind of imaginative interpolation that breaks down the boundary separating the real and the fictional, Todorov's argument recalls the fantastic as Barthes finds it in Gide. He immediately goes on to specify that, similar to the strange combination of attachment and detachment we observed there, the fictional world into which the reader is integrated "is defined by the reader's own ambiguous perception of the events narrated."[16] Refusing any sense of independence for the world "of the characters," any sense that it exists outside the effect of linguistic signifiers in the reader's own mind, this specification suggests less her integration than her creation of this world. Furthermore, the phrase "ambiguous perception" also slyly, even surreptitiously gestures toward the particular—and particularly linguistic—mode of existence activated by this readerly creation. Most obviously, the phrase refers to the uncertainty surrounding the narrated events: Are they actually happening or are they imaginary? But the answer is, ambiguously, both. The events are imaginary *because* they are actually happening—to the extent that they are taking place through reading, in the operation of language. From this perspective, "ambiguous perception" describes as much the uncertainty over whether these events are really happening in the world of the narrative as it does the real instability, the real ambiguity of linguistic signification playing out for the reader in her world. To say this is to name language and textuality as parts of the readerly "experience" that the fantastic allows us to hesitate over and linger in.[17]

* * *

In this lingering, we also find the more general place that the fantastic has in Barthes's thinking, the way that, for him, linguistic signification establishes the literal fabric of experience as such. Indeed, Barthes has further recourse to this word in what is his most extended and exacting attempt to account for the material textuality of the broader world—namely, the analysis of "written clothing" that he published in 1967 as *The Fashion System*. Composed between 1957 and 1963, this signature if almost immediately disavowed foray into the à la mode semiology of the 1960s seeks to address "neither clothing nor language but the 'translation,' so to speak, of one into the other, insofar as the former is already a system of signs" (*Fashion* x). The scrupulousness of this statement makes it clear that his exploration departs from "the customary distinction which puts the real on one side and language on the other" and situates itself at the very site where the two indistinguishably and, we will see, fantastically interpenetrate (*Fashion* x). His examination is exhausting if not completely exhaustive and encompasses a thorough account of the science of signs as developed from Saussure and applied to clothing, including the denotative structures of signifier, signified, and sign that make up the "vestimentary code" and the systems of connotation that together comprise the rhetoric of Fashion as such. I will discuss the workings of this complex semiological organization with more detail in chapter 2, but Barthes points to the implicitly fantastic framework in which this signifying practice takes place when he describes what he calls "the paradox of Fashion" (*Fashion* 209). Though he asserts how "everything happens as if the Fashion lexicon were fake," he quickly goes on to acknowledge that "this lexicon seems to exist" (*Fashion* 209). The strange, ambiguous combination of falsehood and reality, appearance and existence, that Fashion puts on show echoes the fantastic as we've begun elaborating it—even as it also promises to explore this paradoxical linguistic category in terms that go beyond the readerly subject as emphasized in the discussion of Gide and Todorov.

But if Barthes's statement on Fashion here is only implicitly fantastical, his wording is much more explicit in an appendix that, examining the "history and diachrony" of fashion underplayed in his main discussion, details the dynamic by which a sign system like that of Fashion's works to come alive. Commenting on the way Fashion appears as unceasingly novel despite having clearly repetitive cycles, he writes, "in our society, what is new in Fashion seems to have a well-defined anthropological function, one which is bound to its ambiguity: simultaneously unpredictable and systematic, regular and unknown, aleatory and structured, it fantastically conjoins [*il conjoint fantastiquement*] the intelligible without which men could not live and the unpredictability attached to the myth of life" (*Fashion* 300, 2:1200).[18] A cursory reading of these lines would suggest that the fantastic indexes the kind of mythologization that cloaks the signifying processes of culture in the artful guise of an artlessly and immediately available nature. But grammatically it is Fashion itself, with its mirage of constant innovation, that performs the bait and switch, playing out the "well-defined anthropological function" of simultaneously producing and masking significations that Barthes classifies throughout *The Fashion System* as a specifically human practice. As its adverbial form suggests, the fantastic here refers not to the fact but *to the manner* in which the incongruous aspects of Fashion's regular rhythms and its appearance of novelty come together or "conjoin." This distinction connects the fantastic not to mystification specifically but to a more general mode of thinking in which two unrelated, even contradictory phenomena coincide and condition each other. While, in this case, such fantastic coincidence mystifies the processes of signification at work in the world, we have also seen it operate in the opposite way—to accentuate signification itself by coordinating reading and experience, fiction and reality, detachment and proximity.

In each example (this one included), the fantastic thus bespeaks the fundamental uncertainty of signs, the *essentially* ambiguous relationship they set up between the fabricated and the factual.

However hairsplitting this point may be, it allows us to find in the fantastic a way to map the articulation of life's concreteness and language's abstractions. This is to imagine a space of reading or interpretation where the "unpredictability" we mythically associate with "life" derives from "the intelligible without which men could not live," where the liveliness of experience itself stems from nothing other than our engagement of signification in all its ambiguity. The fantastic thus opens up an energetic, transformative interval that mobilizes the static, preestablished mythology compressed into the noun "life" into the active orientation of the verb "live." In doing so, it galvanizes what, in Barthes's account of the "dazzling and evanescent" effect that the "'speech'" of the fashion magazine has on the garment it is describing, he calls "the life of the sign" (*Fashion* 65). This is importantly an existence that cannot be reduced to the "myth" of pure spontaneity or even to human life at all. (As he pithily puts it a few years later in *S/Z*, "the fantastic designates and will designate what is outside the limits of the human"—a line that, as we will discuss in detail in chapter 3, takes its place in perhaps the densest network of expressly fantastic references in Barthes's oeuvre [*S/Z* 24]). Rather, this living vivaciousness is created and carried on as the unending if mostly unremarked generation of experiential meaning that he tries to make perspicuous by addressing the question of "*what happens when an object, whether real or imaginary, is converted into language? or rather, when an object encounters language?*" (*Fashion* 12).

As these lines make clear, *The Fashion System* aims to account not just for the subjective experience of a reader but also for an impersonal "encounter" between objects and words that materializes the abstract linguistic configuration of the world itself. Barthes affirms as much when he magnifies the implications of his focus on the ostensibly trivial "garment of Fashion" by admonishing us "to keep in mind that the same relation is established between literature and the world." Continuing with a clarifying question, he asks, "Isn't literature the institution which seems to convert the real into language and places its being in that conversion, just like our written garment?" (*Fashion* 12). His ontological word choice here is surprising, especially in a discussion so heavily influenced by structuralism's opposition to notions of simple or straightforward being. By locating this being in "conversion," however, Barthes offers anything but a simple ontology and instead affirms a process that could be said to prop up if not produce the animating abstraction of the fantastic. That is, the change in form named by "conversion" depends on a basic element shared by both language and reality that would allow them to be changed into and confused for each other, a speculative commonality to which we have no direct access except through the flux of textuality made available by reading literature. As Barthes's argument proceeds, the example of literature proper recedes in favor of a more technical discussion of linguistics and semiology, but when it reappears late in the work, it brings with it a suggestion of the fantastic that carves out the very space where this confusing conversion takes place. As we will see, moreover, the space Barthes describes here also accords with a recent metamorphic development in the philosophy of being itself.

Pushing back against the way Fashion masks its constitutive significations, he postulates that the "reality" evoked by its signs is "not a transitive reality" but rather "a reality experienced fantastically, it is the unreal reality of the novel, emphatic in proportion to its unreality [*un réel vécu d'une façon fantasmatique, c'est le réel irréel du roman, emphatique à proportion de son irréalité*]" (*Fashion* 266, 2:1164). The English translation takes a certain liberty here by rendering the more personal and subjective suggestion of "fantasmatic" by way of the more depersonalized category of the "fantastic" (whose generality we could think of as informing or underwriting the former).[19] In doing so, however, it also covertly and no doubt unintentionally gestures toward the particular implications of "fantastic" that we have been using the overt occurrences of the word to develop—namely, the imaginary coincidence of language and life, the interpretive intersection of reading and reality. To say this is also to posit, in opposition to the "unreal reality" that implicitly preserves a "real reality" underneath the veil of its fantasms, the possibility of a *real unreality* that situates the machinations of signification as the foundation or support, the very fantastic scaffolding of what Barthes will later call the "reality effect."[20] And this is, moreover, how we might read the "emphatic" functioning of the novel's "unreality" on which Barthes insists here: though a few lines earlier he explains "the postulate of 'realist' style, according to which an accumulation of minute and particular details accredits the truth of the thing represented better than a simple sketch," these "realist" details only accumulate on the basis of the vacant space held open by signification itself.

We will take a more concrete look at this valuably vacant space as it is sliced open by *S/Z* in chapter 3, but for now the real unreality to which the fantastic gives voice finds some more theoretical explanation in the philosophical work of contemporary thinker Catherine Malabou, to whom I briefly turn in order to position my argument more precisely in the history of literary theory and to clarify the specificity of my fantastically existential vocabulary (*reality*, *experience*, and *existence* being terms that the arguments of poststructuralism and deconstruction would seem to have foreclosed). It is Malabou's thinking that comes closest to offering a locatable "origin" for my engagement with the fantastic as it was first the name and then the analytical method of her book *The Heidegger Change: On the Fantastic in Philosophy* that inspired both the lexicon and the style of this study. As its titular terms suggest, her project is one of elaborating the role that change plays in Heidegger's philosophy of Being, a particularly thorny task since she points out that, like the "conversion" in which Barthes roots literature's own "being," change *is* not; change's status as mutability in itself logically requires that it not be a stable essence. As a result, Malabou writes, "*its reality is necessarily imaginary.*" She goes on to amplify the resonance between this point and the real unreality we've been exploring when she glosses "imaginary" as a "*modality of presence free of every reference and referent*," which is to say, a presence untethered from any concrete correspondence in the phenomenal world.[21] It's not that the reality of change is imaginary in the sense that it doesn't exist but that its existence or its particular kind of presence can only be accessed by imagining it—rather than conceptualizing or perceiving it from a point external to it. The imaginative reality of change's ungraspable presence is what Malabou baptizes "*the fantastic*," characterizing it as "the apprehension *and* regime of existence of *what cannot be presented.*"[22] While the refusal of presence speaks to the ungraspability of change, what is most telling about this definition is the way that, in order to fantastically approach such ungraspability, it tempers our understanding of both "apprehension" and "existence" by tenaciously conjoining them. That is, the correspondence of a "regime of existence" and the epistemological act of "apprehension" describes a particular kind of nonpresent being that is attributable to if not exactly manifested by imaginative thinking itself. For these mental moves to coincide with this nonpresent mode of being, they cannot simply "exist" and cannot be thought—cannot themselves be "apprehended"—in any traditional way. As Malabou puts it a page earlier, they are "only possible for the philosopher if she invents a manner of ensconcing herself in this hole or cavity in thought that always refuses itself to concepts."[23]

The method she devises to lodge herself in the conceptual chasm of the Heidegger change is where her argument opens into my less philosophical and more literary investigation of the fantastic existence of signification Barthes helps me to assume. For she mobilizes a set of arch linguistic tactics—the tone of her prose is as playful as it is proud—that route her analysis through a set of words related to change that Heidegger "frequently makes use of" but "seems not to *vest* [*investir*]," seems not to endow with power or particular significance.[24] Instead, they "keep at a respectful distance from the traditional, technical concepts of change" and "remain, from his oeuvre's start to its finish, *ordinary words.*"[25] The opposition of "concepts" and "words" tells us all we need to know about the way her refusal of what she calls Heidegger's "major philosophemes" allows her to transform our understanding of his thinking.[26] If "concepts" collect a diversity of particularities into the solid edifice of a traditional metaphysical abstraction and recall the "signified" of structuralist discourse, "words" approximate the role of the "signifier," working differentially in a way that can divide up an otherwise homogenous, overpowering intellectual uniformity. In other words—that phrase, again—words make space for thinking's (nonpresent) being. Or they at least mark the space of a certain kind of nonconceptual thinking by which language fantastically allows Malabou to approach the impossible, imaginary being of change. For my part, it is less the engagement with change specifically that draws me to Malabou's work than it is her broader attempt to pursue, by linguistic means, *"the intelligibility and the evidence of the never seen."*[27] Because, of course, it is to some extent her investigative technique that I am slavishly mimicking throughout these pages by rummaging through patterns of otherwise trivial, sometimes even denigrated words stippling Barthes's writing (*fantastic* itself being the most prominent) rather than the more well-known terminological vocabularies with which he is associated.[28]

And I do so with a similar aim in mind—namely, to recognize in the intensities of his language a mode of abstract intellectual experience that is not immediately present or even really observable but that is, nonetheless, an *essentially intelligible* phenomenon. For, in lines that echo Malabou's methodological discussion, Barthes himself gestures in the direction of just this kind of fantastic verbal existence in the self-commentary of *Roland Barthes by Roland Barthes*. Describing his own discursive reflexions, he writes, "Different from the 'concept' and from the 'notion,' which are purely ideal, the *intellectual object* is created by a kind of leverage upon the signifier: once I *take seriously* such forms as an etymology, a derivation, a metaphor, I can create a kind of *word-thought* [*pensée-mot*] for myself which will ferret through all my language" (*RB* 134–35, 4:709). What we have here is a kind of thinking-through-language that functions as my argument's ultimate master discourse in the sense that it anticipates and begins to exfoliate Malabou's account of the fantastic and her claim for its *"irreducibility to a genre or category of discourse."*[29] While "*word-thought*" speaks most forcefully to her fantastic work with Heidegger, it is the slightly oxymoronic phrase "*intellectual object*," which Barthes retools as "*word-object*" [*mot-objet*] in the next lines, that grabs my attention. By combining the abstract ideality of the intellect with the concrete materiality suggested by object, this collocation formulates something like an imaginary shape made by words, if by shape we understand, as the financial metaphor of "leveraging" invites us to, an open and unsecured process of signification that consists of its own mobile activity of verbal exchange. In the chain of substitutions evinced by the particular linguistic "forms" that Barthes cites here, we have the fantastic overlap of thinking and being that language provides.

While the fantastic allows Malabou to pitch her discussion at a wholesale renovation of the way we understand ontology itself, it has a somewhat more modest aim in Barthes's discourse that helps to position my rereading of his work as a contribution to the dynamic afterlife of a poststructuralism it also helped to inaugurate. As indicated by the focuses on the individual self and the cultural system of Fashion that we've taken up, his work remains in the real (or "ontic") world and seeks to recast and expand our sense of the everyday.[30] We can hear this clearly in his explanation of his choice to focus on descriptions of clothing rather than actual garments in *The Fashion System*: because it is "entirely constituted with a view to signification . . . the being of the written garment resides completely in its meaning" (*Fashion* 8). If the "being" he is talking about here is the "meaning" of the written garment as it signifies within a particular sociohistorical context, it also gestures toward the kind of fantastic existence broached by signification itself. To thresh his statement thus is to isolate the point where this particular instance of thinking-through-language yields what, in a later exploration of the fantastic, Malabou calls "a certain modality of the real—a real that, as we will see, exceeds the real and outstrips it."[31] When she goes on to more deeply explore this fantastic "in-excess-of-the-real," she gestures toward the larger theoretical fields of deconstruction and postdeconstruction in which I am cultivating Barthes's intellectual legacy, writing that "the fantastic thus characterizes the effect in the real of deconstruction (*Destruktion, Abbau*)."[32] As the Heideggerean terms in the parentheses here return to the textual traces that Derrida works over in *Of Grammatology*, they indicate the way her thinking seeks to advance deconstruction by going more deeply into it.[33] And while that is not my precise project, the resources that Barthes's writings offer me to open up the fantastic "experience" of language without assuming anything like a pure and immediate presence nonetheless allow me the courage to sow my own language-based thinking within that formidable textual nexus.

* * *

When Barthes assembles his own idiosyncratic nexus of texts in *Sade, Fourier, Loyola*, he illustrates—and comes close to explicitly naming—the fantastic experience of language in terms that elaborate it further by synthesizing the personal and impersonal, the subjective and objective currents we've been examining. In doing so, this peculiar and somewhat overlooked work in Barthes's oeuvre further activates a central term in this argument that has been lying quietly in wait throughout my foregoing discussion.[34] What Sade, Fourier, and Loyola allow Barthes to chart is a *practice* of language that, while not identical to the fantastic, nonetheless works to bring it about. Addressing the seeming "arbitrariness" of collecting these three figures, he maintains that they all exercise the same intellectual maneuvers, which he collectively calls "the same writing," to become "founders of languages" (*SFL* 3). He admits that these languages are "obviously not linguistic," not for "communication"—which would frame language as only a transparent and *insignificant* medium, a point to which we will repeatedly return (*SFL* 3). But the fact that the significance of language exceeds communication is just what is at stake here, and it is also what is at stake in the linguistic or, more precisely, textual practice that summons the fantastic.

Barthes explains further a few pages later when he offers an account of textual pleasure that has been overshadowed by his more famous 1973 book; here, in 1971, he writes, "at times the pleasure of the Text is achieved more deeply (and then is when we can truly say there is a Text): whenever the 'literary' Text (the Book) transmigrates into our life, whenever another writing (the Other's writing) succeeds in writing fragments of our own daily lives, in short, whenever a *co-existence* occurs" (*SFL* 7). While Barthes's appeal to "*co-existence*" to figure the interaction between text and life affirms the affinity that his thinking has with Malabou's, it also weaves the depersonalized thrust of "another writing" into the subjective fabric of "our life." As I parse with exacting precision in chapter 3's account of literary reflexion, the objective "Other" gives meaningful—if not, we will see, fully intelligible—shape to the existential "fragments" that nonetheless feel like our own. This is truly "another writing," one we have already spied with Proust, in the sense that this word takes on beyond its narrow, literal meaning of inscription to describe a broader practice or at least a broader process of experiential structuration. This is, in fact, what Macé describes when she writes that "the sentences of the text are immediately invested by the reader starting from an existential situation; they *resonate*, they reverberate in provoking a sudden sentiment of accuracy [*justesse*], that is, of new possibility of speech for an interiority that would otherwise be mute: 'that's it, that's me!,' exclaims Barthes."[35] Macé's citation alludes to *A Lover's Discourse* and is developed later in *The Preparation of the Novel*; however, Barthes formulates this kind of recognition in more general and more vital terms when he declares here that "the index of the pleasure of the Text, then, is when we are able to live with Fourier, with Sade," the phrase "live with" evoking "in the company of" as well as "by means of." (And there is a very real sense in which my argument is an attempt to add *with Barthes* to this litany.)

As the vocabulary of "pleasure" and "success" running through these comments indicates, Barthes seems quite sanguine about the intervention of an alien idiom in a way that distinguishes his analysis from the kind of ideology critique we will see him perform so masterfully and so anxiously in *Mythologies*. At that early moment in his career he seeks to unmask the semiological construction of what presents itself as natural, but here he is more interested in intensifying semiological construction itself, in "bringing into our daily life the fragments of the unintelligible ('formulae') that emanate from a text we admire" (*SFL* 7).[36] It is as if he actually wants to mask our lives with an arrangement of signs whose open "unintelligibility" incites the "co-existence" he is describing, extending the significations of this "text we admire" and forcing us to forthrightly decipher—*to read*—our own experience. (Macé helpfully phrases this task in terms of using a text as "the instrument of a figural reading of life," referring to Barthes's particular investment in Proust and the characters of the *Recherche* who also comport themselves in this way.)[37] The parenthetical "formulae" he refers to here will play a central role in this deliberate kind of textual mediation, which comes out even more clearly—indeed fantastically—when he stipulates that "it is not a matter of taking into ourselves the contents, convictions, a faith, a cause, nor even images; it is a matter of receiving from the text a kind of fantasmatic order [*une sorte d'ordre fantasmatique*]" (*SFL* 8, 3:705). Unequivocal in his rejection of "content" or the particular subject matter that would count as a work's signified (once again, I think of Emma Bovary), Barthes instead imagines identifying with the linguistic work of structuration that would produce a fantastic experience of living language. Like in the previous section, my operative analytical term is a way of indexing the combination of an impersonal "order" with the more individual suggestion of "fantasmatic" alluded to there. Moreover, as these lines also recall the nonconceptual intellectual maneuvers that Malabou helped us map, their implicit gesture to a text's formal functions extends this kind of thinking in a specifically literary direction, one that we can use to embrace our life as the fantastic effect of words.

The particularly practical sense implied by the word "use" here finds further clarification if we compare Barthes's statements with the work of his close contemporaries at the *École pratique des hautes études* and the *Collège de France*, Pierre Hadot and Michel Foucault. Hadot, who joined the Collège in 1982 on Foucault's nomination after almost twenty years at the *École pratique* where Barthes also taught, devoted much of his work to reframing our understanding of Hellenistic and Roman philosophy from a strictly theoretical discipline to a practicable set of exercises aimed at transforming all aspects of students' existence—not just their intellect.[38] In "Forms of Life and Forms of Discourse in Ancient Philosophy," his inaugural lecture at the Collège, Hadot puts it succinctly: "the work, even if it is apparently theoretic and systematic, is written not so much to inform the reader of a doctrinal content but to form him, to make him traverse a certain itinerary in the course of which he will make spiritual progress."[39] This "formative" account of philosophical schools like Stoicism, Epicureanism, and Skepticism is the kind of thinking that inspired Foucault's investigation of the "care of the self" in the third volume of *The History of Sexuality* as well as in his lecture course on *The Hermeneutics of the Subject*; it also describes the kind of practical intellectual energy that drives my account of the fantastic in Barthes. And this is not by chance: in her scrupulous examination of Barthes's lectures at the Collège, Lucy O'Meara has addressed the relationship between the kind of thinking he pursued there and the work of these other figures. Though Barthes does not seem to have been explicitly familiar with Hadot's arguments, O'Meara nonetheless asserts that "Hadot's work provides the scholarly elaboration, via a study of texts from the Greek and Roman philosophers through Montaigne, Rousseau and Bergson, of the ideas which Barthes seems to intuit with regard to the relation between the subject and its environment."[40] In the topics he chooses, the fragmented methodology of his lectures, and the unapologetic foregrounding of his own subjectivity, O'Meara finds a similar resistance to conceptualization and an orientation to lived experience that locates Barthes in this tradition of practical philosophy.

As I have been illustrating, however, it is not just in the late lectures that Barthes links his theoretical meditations to more existential concerns. Rather, my tracing of the fantastic through his earlier, more overtly critical work is meant to develop a persistently practical orientation to language, even—or especially—in its most abstruse and abstract workings. Accordingly, we will notice an important difference between the appeal we have just seen Barthes make to the "formulae" we bring from a literary text into our daily lives and the understanding of that word in Hadot's otherwise resonant account of "spiritual exercises." The latter explains the keeping of a philosophical notebook that was one of the central practical techniques in which students of ancient philosophy were schooled and describes how "when one writes or notes something down . . . one is utilizing formulae considered as apt to actualize what is already present within the reason of the person writing, and bring it to life."[41] "Formulae" here serves as a kind of preestablished set of actions or a specific mindset to be recalled and embodied in the service of "forming" the philosophical pupil.[42] For Barthes, however, "formulae" explicitly do not provide any kind of concrete or formative dogma: "To live with an author does not necessarily mean to achieve in our life the program that author has traced in his books," he avers (*SFL* 7). Indeed, we will recall that these "formulae" are linked not to the intelligible but *to the unintelligible*, as if to suggest that what is being formed here is nothing other than the empty relationship between symbols to which this word refers at its most general. If there is any formula or program to follow from a literary text, it is that of signification itself, which Barthes describes in the following, truly fantastic turn of phrase: "it is a matter of speaking this text, not making it act, by allowing it the distance of a citation, the eruptive force of a coined word, of a language truth; our daily life then itself becomes a theater whose scenery is our own social habitat" (*SFL* 7–8).

In these marvelous lines, the act of "speaking" receives an expansion similar to what "writing" underwent in the earlier paragraph and stakes out a space or, really, a spaciousness that resists any sense of immediate identification and, stemming from the differentiating effect of language, inheres instead in verbal formulation. This is what I think we can gather from the divisive violence of words' "eruptive force," the way the text opens up a "distance" that allows for some perspective on the particular situation we use its signifying operations to figure for ourselves. If this describes one effect of the "encounter" with language that we were discussing in the previous section, Barthes's nod to "citation" seeks to fantastically inhabit that situation and even give it a more sharply pronounced shape. While we will see citation come to function as the topical fulcrum of chapter 4, here it begins to explain why I am so intent on more or less explicitly aping the locutions of the many writers without whom I could not think—which might also be to say, as I hazard the hysterical, the writers without whose words I could not *live*. For though the dramatic imagery that concludes these lines stops short of promising the activity of life itself, the transformation of *notre vie quotidienne* into a "theater" does incite a fantastic linguistic experience within the real world where to speak *is* to act and where "our own social habitat" becomes "scenery" in whose imaginary production we might energetically participate through this sense of textual citation.

The citational activation of speech staged by Barthes's theatrical rhetoric finds its most literal illustration in Loyola's *Spiritual Exercises* and its work of Christian meditation that, according to Hadot, makes the founder of the Jesuits a direct philosophical inheritor of the practical Greco-Roman tradition.[43] It's not just that his "manual of asceticism" develops "another notion of writing ... antecedent to man, whom it traverses, founder of its acts like so many inscriptions," which could describe the other two logothetes in Barthes's study as well (*SFL* 40). It's also that it maintains a resolute and quite peculiar commitment to embodied experience as the active medium of the living language whose practice we are trying to diagram. In terms that echo his own performative identification with Gide, Barthes thus describes how, in the *Spiritual Exercises*, "a body [is] incessantly mobilized into image by the play of imitation which establishes a literal analogy between the corporeality of the exercitant and that of Christ" (*SFL* 62). The emphasis on the imaginary and the analogical should not suggest a fantasy of ineffable, mystical communion with the divine but rather a particular combination of the sensuous and the spoken that materializes the entirety of one's mental and physical space according to the differential distinctions of signs. Barthes insists on the "incessant, painstaking, and almost obsessive separation" that comprises the actions of the *Exercises* themselves, writing that "everything is immediately divided, subdivided, classified, numbered off in annotations, meditations, Weeks, points, exercises, mysteries, etc." (*SFL* 52). The expansive punctuation he uses to hone our sense of this constitutive "separation" describes a mental space produced by—made out of—nothing other than the activity of segmentation and division, nothing other than the work of cutting up that chapter 2 will explore as synonymous with the work of notation.[44] As such, it offers a verbal picture of what he calls the system's "prime originality," the way "Ignatius has linked the image to an order of discontinuity ... has thus made the image a linguistic unit, the element of a code" (*SFL* 56).

This is of course a dynamic that my collages also seek to mobilize on the visual level, and we will unpack the literal articulation of language and image in chapter 4. For now, we see how such interweaving enacts the etymology of "making visible" (from the Greek *phantazein* and *phantos*, "visible") that "fantastic" quite literally puts into words. And this is very close to the vocabulary to which Barthes appeals when he details how "in the isolated and darkened room in which one meditates, everything is prepared for the fantastic meeting of desire [*la rencontre fantasmatique du désir*], formed by the material body, and of the 'scene' drawn from allegories of desolation and the Gospel mysteries" (*SFL* 63, 3:755). If the translator once again depersonalizes the more subjective implication of "*fantasmatique*," it is in anticipation of the generalizing effect produced by this strange instance of identification. As "the material body" of the retreatant becomes an explicitly "fantastic" manifestation of a literary "scene," the retreatant does not affirm the individuality of his desire as much as he loses himself in the generalized procedures of signification. For what is manifested here is not just particular "allegories" but also allegory itself—whose ultimate emptiness is driven home by the bleak image of "desolation." In this we can see the foundation, the very structure, of the paradigmatic axis of language in which similar terms can replace each other, as if the substitution of Christ by the retreatant is only the most visible instance of this linguistic phenomenon. At the same time, the "Gospel mysteries," whose narrative character Barthes emphasizes on the preceding pages, prolong this empty allegorical space beyond one particular instant, organizing a progressive chain that plots its temporal extension. Like with "allegories," the plural "mysteries" figure this chain not according to any single set story from the Gospels but according to a broader sequential succession driven by a persistent enigma or unresolvable uncertainty that provides its own kind of operative emptiness. In doing so, they enact the syntagmatic axis of language in which different terms follow each other as nothing more—but also nothing less—than a process of continuing on.

When Barthes pivots back to his more emphatically dramatic imagery in the next line, writing, "this theater is entirely created in order that the exercitant may therein represent himself: his body is what is to occupy it," the empty space carved out by this fantastic staging of signification allows the exercitant's body to star as the sign itself, in all the permutations it can take on. As he puts it on the next page, "the Ignatian *I*, when it imagines itself in a fantasizing manner [*quand il imagine selon les voies du fantasme*], is not a person . . . : he is no more than the verb that sustains and justifies the scene" (*SFL* 64, 3:756). If the life of Christ is the "content" that comes to play out in this cavernous signifying theater, it is only because he is, in the mythology of the West, himself the word made flesh and speaks more to the infinite possibilities of signification that fantastically take place right here in our earthly world than to any single and fully determinate meaning. The limitlessness is what Barthes's own theatrical language is trying to designate, since of all the moves that Sade, Fourier, and Loyola exploit to construct their systems it is only "*theatricalization*" that allows them to "found a language *through and through*" by going beyond just setting up "a ritual; or, a rhetoric" (*SFL* 5). What he means is not "designing a setting for representation" but rather "unlimiting the language"—letting the process of expression interpenetrate with what it is expressing, or, more colloquially, by letting the act of its speaking become part of what it is saying (*SFL* 6). When he figures the "unlimiting" effect of this theatricalization, he gives some inadvertent justification for and a convenient elucidation of the terminological basis of my own argument. Working through the expansive echoes of an incisively meaningless suffix that resounds within as well as between French and English, he writes: "as the style is absorbed into the writing, the system disintegrates into systematics, the novel into the novelistic, prayer into the fantasmatic" [*le système se défait en systématique, le roman en romanesque, l'oraison en fantasmatique*] (*SFL* 6, 3:703). The last of these, of course, is what I am cutting off from its religious and psychological roots by unraveling *fantasy* into the *fantastic*.

* * *

The question remains as to how or whether we can actively, even intentionally, engage the kind of linguistic practice that generates the fantastic—without necessarily joining the Jesuits. If this was a priestly option that, coincidentally, I briefly considered after finishing my studies at Loyola High School in Towson, Maryland, my eventual turn to the slightly less ascetic profession of the literature professor has nonetheless allowed me to broaden the significance that the name Loyola has for me—to splice it into a different linguistic context that activates additional meanings and new connotations. This has given me a taste of the fantastic, the sense that the very word is somehow in my mouth as I face the text that is my life and find my experiences expanded by the delicious play of signification. A visit to that leafy suburban campus would now invoke a new combination of images, the empty Barthesian "formulae" substituting perhaps for the mind-numbingly doctrinaire lessons of my adolescent religion classes or the Ignatian investment in the corporeal linking back to the wet hours I spent training with the cut and chiseled bodies of the swim team. This is all to say that my argument allows me to construe my experiences according to or in terms of the differential linguistic structuration that give them meaning and to activate the paradigmatic and syntagmatic operations that give them—that continue giving them—sense *as* an experience. If this process of express semiotic articulation is what the forthcoming chapters mine through particular linguistic practices, it is in order to concretely engage the indeterminate and abstract construction of the fantastic I've been adumbrating. Barthes takes these efforts beyond the personal perspective I said I would eschew through a late appearance of this word in his work. Weaving together the various ideational currents launched in the previous sections, these verbal incidents erupt into the discussions of painting he pursued at the end of his career and give us a final picture of the way language invigorates our lives.

Barthes etches an outline of this invigoration in his penetrating comments on the portraits of the Habsburg painter Giuseppe Arcimboldo, whose composition out of fruits, vegetables, and other inanimate objects leads him to claim that "[Arcimboldo's] painting has a linguistic basis, his imagination is, strictly speaking, poetic: it does not create signs, it combines them, permutes them, deflects them—precisely what the practitioner of language does [*ce que fait exactement l'ouvrier de la langue*]" (*Responsibility* 131, 5:495). His point is that Arcimboldo's method of constructing an image out of other, smaller images mimics the "double articulation" of language: his use of visual features like lines and color to fashion objects like a peach, ears of wheat, and cherries that themselves combine

4. Giuseppe Arcimboldo, *Summer* (1572). Funds from Helen Dill bequest (1961.56). Photograph: Denver Art Museum.

to form a portrait of "Summer" mimics the way that language combines letters or sounds to form words (the first linking or "articulation") and then words to form a larger discourse (the second articulation). But this is not exactly how Barthes explains it: "Let us recall," he writes, "the structure of human language: it is doubly articulated: the sequence of discourse can be divided into words, and the words divided in their turn into sounds (or into letters)" (*Responsibility* 134). Placing the accent on division—

decomposition—rather than combination, he indicates the flipside of the linking or joining suggested by "articulation," the fact that, as we saw so authoritatively in the *Spiritual Exercises*, language cuts up our experience of the world *in order to* give it a graspable form or composition. In the same way that the emphatic punctuation in Barthes's sentence structure underscores its own constitutive divisions, Arcimboldo's portraits reveal rather more elegantly than my collage work how this differential dynamic plays out in the visual register.

As this kind of painting "constantly verges on graphic experience" on the basis of the cuts introduced by linguistic articulation, made sonically manifest in the hard *t* and *c* sounds shared among these words and our central analytic term, it brings us into the thick of the unreality whose fantastic contours I have been sculpting in my verbal itinerary through Barthes's career (*Responsibility* 135). If, as he writes explicitly, "Arcimboldo makes the fantastic out of the familiar [*fait du fantastique avec du très connu*]," it is in part because these paintings also evoke the other ideas we've been exploring (*Responsibility* 141, 5:505). Recalling our discussion of the fantastic's fundamental ambiguity and uncertainty, Barthes maintains that "the picture *hesitates* between coding and decoding" because "at first I do not see that the fruits or the animals heaped up before me are anything but fruits and animals" (*Responsibility* 137). He continues and, unpacking the transformative force of linguistic structuration, describes how "it is by an effort of distance, by changing the level of perception that I receive another message" in which a metaphorical "system of substitution" and a metonymical "system of transposition" allow us to make larger, more figurative sense out of what we are seeing (*Responsibility* 137). The enlivening effects of this systematization come out when Barthes reiterates his explanation of the paintings' double articulation, the fact that "Nothing is ever *denoted* [*Rien n'est jamais dénoté*], since all the features (lines, shapes, spirals) which serve to compose a head have a meaning *already*, and since this meaning is diverted toward another meaning, somehow cast beyond itself (this is, etymologically, what the word *metaphor* means)" (*Responsibility* 138, 5:500). His particular locution is meaningful, literally evacuating the literal meaning named by denotation—it is strictly "nothing" that is (not) "denoted"—and making space for the indirect operation of meaning mobilized by metaphor or connotation. The insertion or, better, excavation of this kind of emptiness not only lets our visual experience have a meaning or a signification but lets it *signify* and participate in the lively process of meaning *as such* (which is perhaps the Barthesian critical ambition par excellence).

With these arguments, Barthes comes closest to the final, which is also in its way the initial, intertextual instance of the fantastic: the social theorist Roger Caillois's investigations into the eponymous literary genre and the more abstract category of analysis he develops out of it. A member of the Surrealist avant-garde and one of the founders, along with Georges Bataille and Michel Leiris, of the College of Sociology in the 1930s, Caillois belonged to the intellectual generation just preceding Barthes's but had many interests, particularly into the social and imaginative life of signs, that overlapped with Barthes's work. In 1970, for example, he wrote Barthes a letter praising the recent publication of *Empire of Signs* and drawing attention to *The Writing of Stones*, which had also just appeared from the same publishing house and whose argument he elaborates further in an essay of the same year entitled "The Natural Fantastic."[45] In ways that anticipate Todorov and Malabou (who both make reference to his work), Caillois is concerned with the fantastic as "the disruption of a natural order that it is deemed impossible to disturb"; his initial examples are bizarre animal morphologies that seem to establish an impossible connection of resemblance between species that inhabit entirely different areas of biological taxonomy. As he puts it, "the fantastic cannot *exist*, properly speaking: it cannot be part of nature, of the attested universe . . . it has to be *imaginary*, that is, a deliberate invention of the mind, which recognizes it as such."[46] As he locates a realm of experience that is, explicitly and self-consciously, an "invention of the mind," he describes in more general terms the language-based dynamic by which something like the painting of Archimboldo exhibits an alternative or additional configuration that both departs from and coincides with their "attested universe."

Indeed, my intention in introducing Caillois at this late point in the discussion is to extend the signifying activity that Barthes is trying to make visible beyond the specific context of these works. As Caillois finds this phenomenon playing out in the panorama of "nature," he implicitly stages perception itself as a kind of reading or even a kind of speaking of the world. While his framing of the fantastic as an "invention of the mind" gestures in this direction—it is something we *do*, almost something we add—his more concrete discussion of the images or patterns that appear to form in the inanimate world of rocks pursues this perceptual articulation where one would least expect it. Despite asking "what order exists in the mineral kingdom, aside from the overly complicated geometry of crystals?" he proclaims, "In the kingdom of undifferentiated matter, we find a certain symmetry taking shape," an uncanny process in which a recognizable silhouette or a distinct figure seems to constitute itself out of this stony chaos.[47] Describing the introduction of this alternative, fantastic order in oxymoronic terms as "the emergence of a strict and unpredictable legislation," Caillois appeals to an exacting organizational structure that does not, for all that, guarantee a certain or scripted formation.[48] This is a "writing of stones," as the title of his book attests, that can always be read *otherwise*, a visible or a fantastic language that, in a kind of phenomenological example of connotation, lets us see in the world more than what meets the eye.

For him, this opens up a Baudelairean vision of correspondences and echoes across the diversity of the visual universe that would establish the "unity of the world," but I am more interested in the "mania for interpretation" on which the recognition and multiplication of these fantastic echoes rely.[49] Not only does this phrase indicate an animated and energetic practice of language that sees our experience of and in the world as something to be repeatedly rearticulated—that is, articulated *doubly* and also articulated *again and again*—but its suggestion of uncontrollable excess also dissolves any clear border between the texts we read and the lives we live. With this, we find ourselves rejoining the hybridity of Arcimboldo's portraits and, more specifically, the sixteenth-century discourse of the "monstrous" or the "wondrous" in which they participate. Using terms that could be said to explicate manic interpretation itself, Barthes explains, "the 'wonder'—or the 'monster'—is essentially what transgresses the separation of realms, mingles animal and vegetable, animal and human; it is *excess*, insofar as it changes the quality of the things to which God has assigned a name: it is *metamorphosis* which causes one order to collapse into another; in short, to use another word, it is *transmigration*" (*Responsibility* 147). There are several entangled claims being made here, entanglement itself being only the most fundamental of the forces at work. As the "monstrous" nature of Arcimboldo's portraits "mingles" the human with the nonhuman and "transgresses" the established taxonomic order of creation, it echoes Caillois's discussion of the fantastic in a way that emphasizes the possibilities for reconfiguration or recombination made available by the divisionary effects of verbalization. If the sense of reconfiguration is underplayed in the conjoining of the visible and the intelligible that Barthes maps so markedly in *The Fashion System* and in the practical imitation of articulation by which he illustrates the "transmigration" of textuality in *Sade, Fourier, Loyola*, it is nonetheless part of what is at stake in the "metamorphosis" of our embodied sensory experience into the inhuman functions of signification on which both Barthes's and Caillois's discussions insist. Moreover, taking us all the way back to Barthes's formative relationship to Gide and his language, these lines suggest that such creative, configurative possibility is dependent on the fantastic's most radical "transgression," which involves the collapse of the very axes of signification into each other as the metonymic, syntagmatic movement suggested by "transmigration" stands in metaphoric, paradigmatic relationship to "metamorphosis." In other words, the fantastic "excess" of signification from which any kind of meaningful reconfiguration would emerge involves, on the one hand, making available all the potential (paradigmatic) associations that could name or describe an experience by laying them out in a horizontal (syntagmatic) chain; on the other, syntagms themselves must be put into a paradigm to create an associative structure among different signifying chains that allows them to speak to and replace each other. (This is also, we will see in chapter 3, how Barthes understands the proper Name to work in Proust.)

My claim is that this is the kind of thinking that Barthes finds in the exteriorized, literary self-representation performed by Gide and Proust, the cutting up and rereading of their lives that are played out so explicitly in their novels. This is also the unrealistically existential orientation that this book seeks to cultivate, one that, as visualized in my collage work, would hail fragments of texts we read to supplement our lived experience. The result, as Barthes intimates here, would be that the "names" organizing our world are no longer divinely or permanently "assigned" but rather complexly and actively *signed*—able to take on lively associations and connections from our reading that themselves are by no means permanent or stable. If, as Barthes put it, "The principle of Arcimboldo's 'monsters' is, in short, that *Nature does not stop*," then we also need to learn how to act accordingly, how to let our reading of the world continue on with a similar energy and momentum (*Responsibility* 147). The distinct ways we engage what I am calling the practice of language are what the chapters that follow take up, the intellectual actions by which, often without knowing it, we fantastically realize and inhabit the dynamic field of language's operation.

The ultimate argument I am making here revolves around the possibility that one of the things we learn as students of literature, as readers who study how verbal texts create imaginative worlds out of nothing but words, might be how to know what we are doing, how to recognize the resonant processes of signification by which we fantastically impart meaning to our own "extra-literary" lives. This seems to be the general critical stance that Barthes is circling around when, referring to Arcimboldo's poetic painting toward the close of the essay, he writes that "the exercise of such an imagination relates not only to 'art' but also to knowledge" for "all knowledge is linked to a classifying order" (*Responsibility* 147–48). And it is just this imaginative, literary "knowledge" that these chapters aim to explicate by exploring (and, by necessity, also performing) particular linguistic practices that engage and expand on the features of the fantastic I've been introducing. As will become apparent, however, the practices I identify bleed into, depend on, and reprise each other; any suggestion that they occur in a linear developmental sequence is imposed on them by the successive format of the book and the closely related argumentative form of the traditional academic monograph—which I have chosen because it remains, at least at this point in my intellectual career, the only way I am able to give coherent discursive shape to the inchoate associations that the word *fantastic* causes to swarm in my mind. This is another reason why I have opted to include some of my decidedly nonlinear collages as punctuating divagations: condensing the book's overall argument into visual form, they act as a kind of rhetorical reset or a musical key change that allows me to begin again and reimagine my thinking in new words. I thus see my fantastic account of literary study's practical knowledge unfolding not on a straight line but in a spiral, for "on the spiral," Barthes writes in his essay on the painter and sometime collagist Bernard Réquichot, "things recur, but *at another level*: there is a return in difference, not repetition in identity" (*Responsibility* 218-19).

The same could be said for the picture of Barthes that this study pieces together. It should be clear that this is not an explanatory introduction to Barthes's thought or even really a critical exegesis of his arguments. Barthes's writing functions, for me, as an opportunity to put some of my intellectual fantasies to a textual test, to see if his words could help me to say some of the vital things I want to learn from literature and literary study. What I hope emerges as a by-product of trying to read my own literary desires in the arabesques of his articulations is a fantastic reconfiguration of a writer who nonetheless also remains comparatively familiar, a different Barthes who is also somehow the same. This may be, in the end, the best illustration I can give of the expansive, amplifying effect that careful, imaginative reading can have on our sense of the world, an aspiration that finds inspiration in the lines that conclude Barthes's comments on Arcimboldo's work: "to aggrandize or simply to change knowledge is to experiment by certain audacious operations, upon what subverts the classifications we are accustomed to: this is the noble function of magic, 'summa of natural wisdom' (Pico della Mirandola)" (*Responsibility* 148). Highlighting the most fanciful and even fabricated implications of the fantastic, the experiment in language that I've begun to undertake is an attempt to help us understand how we might magically make words work in the world.

Chapter 1 thus reformulates the theoretical focus of the introduction in more explicitly practical terms by developing Barthes's appeal to figures of magic in his conception of language's status as part of our lived experience. Intertwining his mesmerizing essays in *Mythologies* with his bewitching writing on the historian Jules Michelet, the chapter develops an alternative and notably less alienated vocabulary that approaches the cultural materials scrutinized by a critic or cultural analyst as a kind of fantastic reality. Focused less on a mediation of the real than on the reality of mediation, this alternative receives its most forceful formulation in the introduction Barthes pens for a reissue of Michelet's *La Sorcière*, which marks a conversion from his originally pejorative view of magic to something much more affirmative and even invigorating. Rather than just revealing the preestablished myths inherited from the ideology of one's culture, what the sorceress shows him is how to stage signification as an ongoing performative process that enchants the world with the kind of unstable and ultimately undefined meaningfulness associated with the literary. This has particular payoff for Barthes's relation to what, in "Myth Today," he anxiously calls "metalanguage" and lets him—and us—cut across the chasm assumed to separate critical from more obviously "creative" writing. While this addresses my decision to route my argument through a writer whose work asserts a shifting and willfully ambiguous relationship to literature proper, it also shows that what is so magical about language, in both its creative and critical employment, is the fantastic, dreamlike way it seems to put us in impossibly direct touch with the indirect operation of mediation itself.

This is not, however, to suggest that the magic of language is effortlessly executed—quite the contrary. Chapter 2 underscores the intellectual and perceptual labor entailed in such a practical conception of language and highlights the exertion entailed in the noting or noticing by which we activate the fantastic and actualize the world. It returns to *The Fashion System* to take up Barthes's extensive discussion of notation there, which boils down to borrowing language's fundamentally discontinuous composition to execute an articulated series of differentiating cuts that impart meaningful and, in Barthes's tailor-like hands, fantastic shape to a cultural object like a dress or sweater. As a central practice cultivated by literary and linguistic analysis, the incisive work of notation migrates into the more expansive attempts Barthes makes to characterize the textuality of the world in books like *Empire of Signs* and *Travels in China* as well as in the lectures he titled *The Preparation of the Novel*. What becomes clear, however, is not just that notation slices up our experience into units whose sense inheres in nothing but their difference from each other but also that such sense only exists by virtue of our unrelenting continuation of the constructive exertion of language use itself. Expanding on the stakes of my practical orientation to language and literature, this assertive examination of linguistic work serves as the enabling condition for cultivating the fantastic "transmigration" of the literary into our lives to which this book is finally dedicated.

Chapter 3 continues the argument about notation by compounding it into one about reflexion that also moves the practice of language in a more overtly literary direction. Plotting its course from Barthes's early discussion of literary language in *Writing Degree Zero* through his dazzling cut-up of Balzac in *S/Z* to end with his early essay on the textuality of names in Proust, it explores the common structure of signification by which the intelligibility of both verbal communication and lived experience is constituted. The homological reflexion between word and world that it schematizes hinges on the Saussurean notion of linguistic value, which names a sign's position in a shifting network of interdependent terms that determine its particular significance and moves us beyond the simple linking of signifiers and signifieds. As *S/Z* considers the way such a network functions in a literary text specifically, its cutting commentary on the famous indistinguishability between art and life in Balzac's story (that Barthes explicitly and repeatedly labels "fantastic") also offers an opportunity to develop the practice of reflexion as not only the recognition and exploration of this kind of signifying network but even its existential extension. While this finds its most striking illustration in Barthes's trenchant treatment of Anne-Louis Girodet's painting *Endymion*, which he discusses as both an image of the youthful castrato in the narrative of *Sarrasine* and as a real-world painting in the Louvre, the discreet appearance of the Proustian narrator in his explication of Sarrasine as a literary character helps him make a similar point in more verbal and more subjective terms that find their origin in his essay "Proust and Names." Bringing this selection of Barthes's literary criticism together allows me to dream up a way to really, which is to say fantastically, read one's life as a reflective and reflexive literary text.

Such readerly reflexion receives a more writerly cast in chapter 4, which takes up a second, complementary cross section of Barthes's illustrious literary criticism to develop citation as a practice that mobilizes fragments of particular texts to represent or express an experience or situation. Turning to two works that straddle *S/Z*—the early trio of essays he published as *On Racine* and the later collection of verbal figures he titled *A Lover's Discourse*—it formulates a literally imaginary relationship to language in which the energy of signification works to galvanize our conventional or mythologized sense of the world. This receives its most perceptible illustration in the essay "Racinian Man" and Barthes's curious handling of its footnotes (the rhetorical space of citationality as such), which sometimes take up over half of the page space as they separate and set off Racine's alexandrine verses from his own argument. As they describe the cultural confinement that Barthes takes to be the key to the Racinian universe, these citations also visually display a kind of formalized linguistic activity that he uses to recognize and even re-cognize these confined conditions. Effecting less a wholesale liberation than a more modest loosening, citation offers Barthes a way to open up space within confinement, a result that looks rather more potent when he turns from the social myths embodied in classical tragedy to the more subjective, interior stage of the lover "speaking within himself, *amorously*" (*LD* 3). As the place in which literary citations most obviously inform an account of concrete quotidian experiences, *A Lover's Discourse* fleshes out the fantastic freedom afforded by this linguistic practice. More than just affirming and activating the otherwise derided or disparaged language of love, Barthes's discursive "simulation" details the way in which love expands our sense of things by ardently turning the facts of the world into signs full of unspoken meaning. As citation is what gives legible, articulate form to this expansion of our consciousness, it offers a way to find agency and writerly empowerment in the kind of readerly projection or Bovarian identification that a text like Goethe's *Werther* famously sparked.

The book ends with a conclusion that focuses on criticism more broadly as the intellectual activity that implements and integrates the foregoing linguistic practices. At stake in this synthesis is what I call its "wisdom": the sharp, savvy way criticism exploits the linguistic operations we've been exploring to work out and work up the world's significance. Illustrating this wisdom by complementing my specific emphasis on literature with Barthes's commentaries on photography as especially lucid elaborations of a perceptual, if not entirely existential, engagement with signification, I turn in particular to the development of visual meaning through a verbal supplement as effected by the caption. This focus on image-text interaction takes me from the early semiological essays on photography's "rhetoric" to the mostly overlooked role played by the caption in *Camera Lucida*'s famous development of the *punctum*, where a singular reference to Virginia Woolf connects back to the book's literary agenda. The resonant argument Barthes makes about film in "The Third Meaning" (one of the *punctum*'s theoretical antecedents) ultimately mobilizes this account of criticism's wisdom as a practice for reading life itself, for approaching it as a discontinuous and combinatory phenomenon into which linguistic and indeed literary articulations can and do interleave themselves. In doing so, it draws the preceding arguments together with their collaged divagations and leaves us poised to realize the fantastic literary text written by our experience of the world.

Cezanne
at Tate Modern until 12 March

carriers into which the slides fitted. The projection involves a complicated choreography in the dark. One person must insert the new slide as the old one is removed to avoid the dreaded empty circle of light. This is part of the allure of the analogue: it's impossible to forget the human behind the illusion. In our show, the magic lantern occupies a table at the

centre of the room, flanked on either side by rows of spectators, with the mechanism in full view. Rather than detracting from the experience, the exposed machinery adds to the sense of enchantment.

5. Untitled (April 2023). Author's handmade collage.

Magic Lessons [CHAPTER ONE]

A little more than halfway through *The Pleasure of the Text*, Barthes returns to one of his classic arguments but also makes use of a noteworthy and rather equivocal explanatory term: "The stereotype," he writes, "is the word repeated without any magic, any enthusiasm, as though it were natural, as though by some miracle this recurring word were adequate on each occasion for different reasons, as though to imitate could no longer be sensed as an imitation" (*Pleasure* 42). The approach to the stereotype through the lens of "the natural" should be familiar, but it's the appeal to "magic" (or its lack) that stands out. Significantly, the focus on "repeating" places emphasis on an automatic, unthinking act of speech through which the stereotype takes place and against which magic defines itself. Indeed, the connection between magic and a fervent, even fanatical kind of linguistic activity is what this chapter investigates in order to bring out the practical perspective on language running throughout the fantastic theoretical explorations of the introduction. Though it might be surprising to find a magical linguistic practice running through the work of a writer whose vocation was in part to explore and explode the illusions and delusions of twentieth-century bourgeois culture, it nonetheless provides a characterization of Barthes's intellectual procedure that, as we see here, he comes to embrace. Tracking the traces of magic that write themselves across an oeuvre known equally for its demystifying power and its bewitching style ultimately portrays his superlative sensitivity to the operations of signification as an unexpectedly pragmatic orientation to language. As the name for a linguistic activity that presumes its own productive power, magic spells out what we will see is the very real trickery—the fantastic efficacy—by which the words of critical and creative writers alike do their work in the world. Accordingly, the various kinds of magical thinking that Barthes employs paint a particularly clear picture of the fantastic's occurrence, which is to say, they allow us to glimpse how subtle linguistic dynamics offer themselves as a fanciful yet factual part of lived experience—how they produce our actual sense of the world out of what actually seems like nothing at all.

Such magical manipulation of language finds an early if disparaging comment in a 1945 letter that the young Barthes writes to his close friend Philippe Rebeyrol during his multiyear recovery from tuberculosis in the alpine sanatoria of France and Switzerland. Inaugurating an image system that will persist in various guises over the entire itinerary of his thought, Barthes proclaims his intention to "exorcise Romanticism," a movement he characterizes in terms of its desire "to fuse magic and truth, to criminally suppress the sacred distance between the word and the idea, to socialize, Christianize, authenticate the magic, which immediately resulted in depreciating truths treated thus: the problem of Michelet's great hollow words" (*Album* 23). This presemiological Barthes (who retrospectively describes himself in this moment as "a Sartrean and a Marxist") enforces a distinction between "the idea" and the language used to express it, rather than foregrounding the system of verbal signification that his encounter with Saussure's work will inspire. Within this context, he figures magic as an agent of intellectual "depreciation" because of the way it allows linguistic mediation to stand in for "truth" (*Contemporary* 10). Comparing this very early proclamation with his very late assertion in *Camera Lucida* that photography is "a *magic*, not an art" indicates the endurance of this rhetoric and the thinking to which it gives form (*CL* 88). Yet, as magic at the end of his life refers to the way the photograph functions not as "a 'copy' of reality" but as "an emanation of *past reality*," it contrasts with the attitude toward linguistic expression in Barthes's youthful thinking and provides a kind of representational immediacy that he comes to cling to rather than cast off (*CL* 88). The difference has as much to do with the move from the verbal to the visual as it does with a more complex conception of magic's (and language's) operation. And while unpacking the development of this complexity is the task of this chapter, the emphasis on the past in Barthes's statement—his insistence, we will recall, that the "*noeme* of Photography" is the "That-has-been"—stages his eventual understanding of magic as nothing other than the immediate presentation of what is not immediate (*CL* 71, 76–77).

To say this is to see the seeds of his later perspective on magic in his earlier comments: his initial refusal to allow for language's contamination of thought's imputed purity functions, in a sense, as the inverse of his later stance in which representation works not as the corruption but as the fantastic foundation of thinking itself. We will see how one of the main agents of the reversal that the attitude toward language undergoes in Barthes's thinking is his closer engagement with Michelet and his "great hollow words," which begins to appear a few years later and continues both explicitly and implicitly until the end of his life. Accordingly, it is through Michelet that Barthes transforms his early condemnations of magical enchantment into the virtual commendation we find in *Camera Lucida*. In doing so, Michelet helps Barthes take his place in the larger historical trajectory of modernity's relationship to magic's powers. Most notably, in his account of the magical legacy that shaped modern culture as a whole, Simon During traces the transmutations that a premodern sense of magic undergoes in and after the Enlightenment and details a shift in emphasis from the enigmas of the occult to the dazzle of technique. While During's focus on technical craft emphasizes tricks that require manual proficiency and mechanical devices with poorly understood (but perfectly explicable) operational principles, Joshua Landy extends this discussion by turning to literary language as its own kind of technique for what he calls a modern re-enchantment of the world.[1] It's at this point that the emphasis on language and signification Barthes develops so methodically throughout his career intersects with this magical history, a junction that is displayed nowhere more clearly than in Barthes's commentary on the portrayal of the medieval European witch in Michelet's 1862 *La Sorcière* (provocatively translated into English as *Satanism and Witchcraft*).

Writing in a preface to the 1959 edition of that book, Barthes claims a connection with the medieval witch in terms that emphasize their analogously alienated relationship to society as well as their intentional engagement of a ritually illusory signifying practice: "in our present society, what best resumes this complementary role of the Micheletist witch is probably the mythic figure of the intellectual, 'the traitor,' sufficiently detached from society to discern its alienation, seeking a correction of reality yet impotent to effect it, directed towards *praxis* but participating in it only by the motionless mediation of a language, just as the medieval witch comforted human misery only through a rite and at the price of an illusion" (*Critical* 113–14).[2] The focus on complementarity here comes from Claude Lévi-Strauss's roughly contemporaneous discussion of indigenous witch doctors in *Structural Anthropology*, which describes the position of the sorcerer or shaman as outside a cultural system into which he nonetheless helps people to integrate themselves and their inexpressible personal feelings.[3] Accordingly, Barthes locates the witch and the intellectual in a "detached," almost paralyzed position that, as he famously bemoans at the end of *Mythologies*, is simultaneously inside and outside the social order. ("The mythologist is excluded from the history in the name of which he professes to act," he writes [*Mythologies* 157].)

Yet, as the comments on "correction" and "comfort" imply, Michelet's witch is at least as interested in creating a new reality as she is in reconciling her medieval brethren with the world as it is. What the witch's seemingly contradictory combination of practical activity and "impotent" speech shows Barthes is the forthrightly fantastic mode of being in the world comprised of language use itself. Instead of assuming a full and immediate real or an unalloyed intellectual truth from which her practice of language would divide her, the witch's power—which, via Michelet, Barthes learns from her—is to profess the possibility that language's "motionless mediation" constitutes its own kind of truthful reality. This is as much to evoke the fundamental mediation of the real familiar to us from all manner of ideological and deconstructive analyses as it is to signal *the reality of mediation*—which is ultimately what the magical rites and "illusory" comforts of the witch work to produce. As the fantastic designates this magical experience of what is not real, it anticipates the "emanation of *past reality*" that we've seen go by this same name in *Camera Lucida* and bestows a certain existence, a practical actuality, on linguistic activity itself. Touching in equal measure on the effects of both enchanting dogmatics and illuminating analytics, magic thus enacts the dynamic, oppositional functioning of language itself at the same time as it fleshes out the existential claim Barthes makes at the end of *Mythologies*' original preface to "live to the full the contradiction of my time" (12).

While *Mythologies* is the point in Barthes's oeuvre where this contradiction plays itself out most markedly (and as such will receive much of my attention, especially in the first half of this chapter), Françoise Gaillard has placed such a tension at the center of Barthes's entire intellectual project, describing how, in his work, "to render things all their substantial thickness, to even outstrip the materiality from which their flesh is made, is to multiply in them the layers of meaning."[4] As she refuses the divide between thoughts and things, meaning and matter that tears through Barthes's writing from that early letter to Rebeyrol through his famous work on myth, she gestures toward the synthesizing sorcery that we will see the witch's use of language act out. Moreover, when Gaillard continues and suggests that, for Barthes, "the properly human is the unlimited power to make things signify," she also appeals to a "practice" whose effect is that "the world finds itself re-enchanted."[5] The idiom of enchantment drops out of the rest of her compelling discussion, but the more purposeful attention I pay to the verbal traces of Barthes's self-identified witchcraft exemplifies as much as it explicates the epistemological and perceptual reserves of language itself that incite the fantastic. More than this, the magical through line that cuts across his deliberately varied intellectual activity shows us that it is not just in the aesthetic register that signification effects a fantastic reality, even if During, Landy, and a host of others convincingly show how literary discourse remains one of the richest sources for the kind of "self-consciously illusory" magic by which, in the long wake of poststructuralism and Theory more generally, so many of us understand our work with language.[6] Rather, what we can learn by examining the magic lessons Barthes receives from the sorceress is that what he calls the "metalanguage" of criticism partakes in equal measure of the practical world on which it seems only to comment.

* * *

Though the sorceress herself doesn't appear in Barthes's thinking until 1959, he begins to revalue magic and its place in intellectual discourse as early as a 1951 essay on Michelet, which he expanded into his 1954 book. Using evocative terms to explain the import of the great historian's work, Barthes writes, "what matters is that the man of History be presented in an amplified gesture, struck by an enchantment which transmits him through Time, neither living nor dead, in a third state of dreamed existence which enlarges and *imposes* him" (*Michelet* 97). Singling out amplification as one of the primary powers of Michelet's writing, Barthes asserts a certain "reality effect" for the enchantment that inaugurates the revision of magic in his thinking. The "third state of dreamed existence" that figures this effect augments our sense of what we consider reality, as the mental world of dreams and imagination receives its own "existential" status. In this, we can see what Patrizia Lombardo means when, in her now classic account of Barthes's early works, she labels Michelet's writing as "an alchemy . . . a chemical operation in which elements are mixed together" that offered an alternative to what she characterizes as the chilling severity of the intellectuals who immediately preceded Barthes (e.g., Camus, Sartre, and Blanchot).[7] Barthes expands on this alchemical mixing of imagination and reality, this magical production of thinking's own fantastic actuality, in his account of Michelet's relationship to historical documents, which he treated "as voices, not as witnesses," not as impersonal traces of an abstracted moment in the past but as fragments whose survival indicates the "quality of having been an attribute of life" (*Michelet* 81). Here, as the specification of "having been" qualifies any sense of immediacy that the idea of a "voice" or a "life" might insinuate, it maintains a kind of distance or detachment that also characterizes mental or intellectual "existence" more generally. What the historian experiences is the past's very pastness, its inescapable separation from him, as if what is immediate in intellectual life more generally is, in an early version of the magic photography brings to light in *Camera Lucida*, mediation itself.

The contradictory coincidence of proximity and distance by which

Barthes characterizes intellectual reality is elaborated in two explicit—and explicitly contradictory—allusions to magic. Referring to the voices that the historian listens to, Barthes describes the way he has the responsibility of "completing by a magical action what in their lives may have been absurd or mutilated" (*Michelet* 82). At first glance, magic seems to name a kind of idealizing reparation or restitution that would redeem the ravages of history. More careful consideration hints, however, at the possibility of preserving or "completing" absurdity and mutilation as such. In other words, magic might actualize nothing other than the damage and the lack of the incomplete, less the incomplete's completion or restitution than the realization of incompleteness in itself. Barthes intimates the mode by which this paradox might be accomplished when, using magic in what we might think of as a more straightforward way, he details how "there was always an obstacle to this magical incorporation . . . Speech" (*Michelet* 188). Here, magic refers to a kind of transcendent immediacy, an absolute comprehension whose impossibility would ally it more closely with deception and delusion. But the "obstacle" of Speech forestalls such seamless perfection and thus functions as the very medium that allows the historian to achieve the incompleteness testified to in the earlier quotation. While Barthes's appeal to speech specifically regards the social gulf between Michelet's own bourgeois language and that of "the People" he is trying to resurrect, it also signifies the more general gap by which language, so to speak, coincides with reality. More than this, taking the contrasting implications of these two metaphors of magic together offers an instance of the lexical self-contradiction that Barthes will later label an "enantioseme" and articulates nothing other than the divergence that constitutes the reality of linguistic operation itself (*RB* 45).[8] The language of magic, it seems, opens up onto a fantastic experience of the very magic of language.

These circuitous argumentative convolutions about the reality of intellectual life find something of a more tangible expression when we turn to the occurrences of magic in the famous "World of Wrestling" essay, which launched Barthes' most influential and concrete foray into cultural critique. Published in a 1952 issue of the magazine *Esprit* before his mythology column became an institution in *Les Lettres nouvelles*, this early piece intertwines its specific account of the almost mathematically simplified form of retributive justice embodied by the wrestling match with a more theoretical commentary on the general condition of mystification that anticipates the later programmatic essay "Myth Today." In this early moment, however, Barthes's reliance on a rhetoric of magic rather than a vocabulary of myth to scrutinize the match's ideological operation echoes and amplifies his commentary on Michelet. Explaining the "pure and full signification, rounded like Nature" by which the wrestling match strips the idea of justice of its complexity, he writes, "It is at every turn during the fight, in each new situation, that the body of the wrestler casts to the public the magical entertainment of a temperament which finds its natural expression in a gesture" (*Mythologies* 25, 18). As it names the way the wrestler's bodily physique "perfectly correspond[s]" to the role he is playing in the contest, magic here functions as an indicator of the kind of impossible immediacy and total transparency that Michelet could only dream of (*Mythologies* 17). The coupling with "entertainment" adds a valence of distraction and diversion to this use of the word, just as the term "temperament" suggests a spontaneity and natural authenticity that would relieve the spectators of the need for any deeper deliberation. More than just speaking to the mystification of the wrestling match's "perfect intelligibility," however, magic as a descriptive term includes in its connotations an alternative—even illusory—perspective that reintroduces some of the nuance and ambiguity whose absence Barthes's commentary is so committed to displaying. That is, the category of magic implies something other than the normal and mundane, as if this presumed naturalness of expression is consciously restricted to the space "in the ring" (to use the title that accompanies the essay in the latest editions of *Mythologies*). From this angle, the wrestling match would be an example of the kind of "real illusion" that the intellectual himself magically produces—to say nothing of the kind of acknowledged artificiality that Barthes proposes as the antidote to what he comes to call mythological discourse.

Barthes is careful to disqualify the possibility of this meaning when he comments on the way the audience "condemns artifice," the moral rule of wrestling being that "all signs must be excessively clear, but must not let the intention of clarity be seen" (*Mythologies* 20). The delicacy of this proviso only highlights the ease with which we might otherwise confuse the mystifying performance of the wrestlers in the ring with Barthes's own demystifying performance on the page, a potential confusion that presages the ideological resurgence Barthes faces when demystification itself becomes critical doxa.[9] This confusion comes through with its own force of clarity in the extent to which the further magical imagery Barthes uses to evaluate the dynamic of the wrestling match could also be applied to the project of his essay's commentary. In particular, he makes a comparison between the melodramatic spectacle of the wrestlers' acting and "the gesture of a conjuror who holds out his cards clearly to the public" (*Mythologies* 19). The magic trick being performed here is one in which not only is nothing hidden but what is exposed are explicitly the signs by which the trick is composed; however, the image is so closely coincident with an analytical method seeking to unveil the semiological structures of what seems unquestionably natural that it can barely be called metaphorical. Speaking to both the artifice of the match and the artfulness of the critique, the magic evoked by the figure of the conjuror bridges the two "intelligible spectacle[s]" and allows the "reality" of the match's illusion to correspond with the operation of the critic's language (*Mythologies* 20). In doing so, it verbalizes a realism of the symbolic that dispels the mystifications of immediacy without also succumbing to them, an effect of magic's essential ambiguity that Barthes will not be able to recognize until he is reminded of it by Michelet's sorceress.

In fact, once he begins to regularly produce his monthly column, the ambiguous language of magic falls almost completely from view in favor of a vocabulary of myth that will drive a wedge between the critic and the world. Overlooking the 1952 "World of Wrestling" essay altogether (which is nonetheless included in the 1957 collection), he opens the preface by stating that "the following essays were written one each month for about two years, from 1954 to 1956" and goes on to claim that "right from the start, the notion of myth seemed to me to explain these examples of the falsely obvious" (*Mythologies* 11). Replacing magic with the more fashionable terminology of myth, Barthes aligns himself with the influential ethnological work done in the 1950s by structurally focused researchers like Georges Dumézil, Claude Lévi-Strauss, and Edgar Morin. Martine Joly investigates the way that this intellectual context approached myth as a "psychological and sociological elaboration of symbols capable of engendering and organizing a mass of signs" that provides a "pragmatic chart of societies."[10] And this is certainly one way that myth functions for Barthes: as he puts it, "I still used the word 'myth' in its traditional sense," which is to say as a kind of collective imaginary that constructs an implicit or unspoken grid of intelligibility for everyday experience. "But," he immediately goes on to stipulate, "I was already certain of a fact from which I later tried to draw all the consequences: myth is a language" (*Mythologies* 11). Here, Barthes attempts to complement the ideological perspective of his contemporaries with a semiological perspective taken from Saussure that produces "the double theoretical framework" by which he characterizes his analytical strategy in the preface to the collection's 1970 reissue (*Mythologies* 9). In doing so, however, he cedes the self-implicating ambiguity that magic would have offered his methodological framework to what is effectively a preconstituted and stubbornly external conceptual vocabulary.

If I stop short of figuring this move as an instance of mythology's own mythological condition, it is to avoid the linguistic and intellectual impasse to which Barthes's adoption of this discourse leads him. For, at the same time as his terse assertion that "myth is a language" attempts to develop the analytical purchase of that term, it also gestures at the paradoxically *asymbolic* place that the word *myth* essentially occupies.[11] Despite all the semiotic energy animating his diverse examinations of particular myths—those enchanting analyses of cookery and cars, of children and chips—"myth" itself functions as a strangely monolithic or monologic term in his discussion. As the name of a semiological system, it receives decidedly unsemiological treatment, as is shown by taking a closer look at the infamous discussion in "Myth Today" about the difficult task of combating myth to which I have made passing reference. He describes how "the very effort one makes in order to escape [myth's] stranglehold becomes in its turn the prey of myth: myth can always, as a last resort, signify the resistance which is brought to bear against it. Truth to tell, the best weapon against myth is perhaps to mythify it in its turn, and to produce an *artificial myth*: and this reconstituted myth will in fact be a mythology" (*Mythologies* 135). The persistent repetition of the term here is telling: in the same way that Barthes proposes myth's inescapability, he seems locked into the single word, the neologistic imperative that he extolled just a few pages earlier reduced to minimal inflections on the same invariable morpheme. It is partly this kind of redundant rhetoric that leads Irène Langlet to judge the "prudently programmatic tone" of the collection's long final statement as "a far cry from what the small texts of *Mythologies* had already attained."[12] Society might speak in a language of myths, but, as the very principle of social signification, myth itself seems to be the place where semiosis stops—or at least stutters.

To observe this, however, is not to fault one of the great demystifiers for a kind of Homeric nod but rather to expose the persistent if disavowed presence of the witch's magic that keeps the world-making power of language on the tips of our tongues. What myth's verbal reverberation reveals is the operation of tautology, which Barthes defines in "Myth Today" as "this verbal device which consists in defining like by like" (*Mythologies* 152). Though he discusses tautology as one of the privileged rhetorical figures by which the cultural presents itself as natural, the mediated as immediate, in this case it has the opposite effect and underscores myth's own linguistic constitution—to the extent that it brings magic back to his discourse. Admittedly, the recourse to magical language is in an explicitly negative register. He qualifies tautology as a "magical behavior" in which one "takes refuge . . . when one is at a loss for an explanation: the accidental failure of language is magically identified with what one decides is a natural resistance of the object" (*Mythologies* 135). Here, even as magic names a kind of shelter from thinking, a dodge that denies any sense of complexity, it also very much speaks to a laborious practice of brute assertion that stands in for more nuanced forms of signification. This comes out a bit more clearly in the explicit emphasis on a kind of linguistic or rhetorical activity all the more vigorous in that it has only itself to say: unpacking the frustrated parent's retort *"just because, that's all,"* Barthes frames tautology as "a magical act ashamed of itself, which verbally makes the gesture of rationality, but immediately abandons the latter, and believes itself to be even with causality because it has uttered the word which introduces it" (*Mythologies* 153). The force in these lines is wholly on the side of the linguistic, as they refer to a world whose rational and causal structures are (for better and for worse) only an effect of words. That is, as much as tautology "testifies to a profound distrust of language," it is also, and in the very same measure, a concerted conviction in it (*Mythologies* 153). The "bad" magic of tautology turns out to be indistinguishable from the "good" magic of language itself that so enchanted Barthes in Michelet's work and that enlivens so many of his mythological analyses.

At this point, however, any functional work that magic's ambiguity might do is obfuscated by his commitment to the unary framework of myth. As Serge Zenkine puts it in one of the few explicit critical comments on magic in *Mythologies*, "the term 'magic' usually serves to summarize the structure of myths, but it never designates an activity aimed at producing an effect in the real world, which is the ordinary definition of magic." This is part of Zenkine's larger argument that, for the vast majority of Barthes's analyses, he focuses on "magical objects" rather than active practices (the histrionic conduct of the wrestling match being a notable exception), an observation that throws Barthes's disregard of tautology's performative effects into sharper relief.[13] When Barthes is momentarily able to consider (or, given *Mythologies*' prehistory, reconsider) the analytical room that magical language opens up, he shunts it to the literal margins of his discussion. Thus, in an oft-quoted footnote toward the end of "Myth Today," he writes, "Even here, in these mythologies, I have used trickery [*j'ai rusé*]: finding it painful constantly to work on the evaporation of reality, I have started to make it excessively dense, and to discover in it a surprising compactness which I savored with delight, and I have given a few examples of 'substantial psycho-analysis' about some mythical objects" (*Mythologies* 158, 1:868). As Barthes attempts to address the mythologist's own alienation from the "reality" whose dual ideological and semiological constructedness he repeatedly unveils, his language of "compactness" and "savoring" points to a conception of "reality" as a solid and firmly available presence that engenders much of this pain and anxiety. Indeed, preserving a rich and immediate real that parallels the pure ideal of thought we saw in his 1945 letter allows him to set up the opposition between its "savoring" and its "evaporation," a dynamic that he repeats in the paragraph to which this footnote is appended when he laments that the mythologist "constantly runs the risk of causing the reality which he purports to protect, to disappear" (*Mythologies* 158). While we will see how Barthes approaches this situation as a more general split between "language-object and metalanguage," it is to this kind of differentiation that his surreptitious "trickery" speaks—or, better, it is this differential that "trickery" itself speaks (*Mythologies* 145). In other words, his recourse to a Bachelard-inspired approach that draws out the significance of everyday phenomena like steak and wine by lavishing detailed descriptions on their physical composition unexpectedly shows him that the remedy for his intellectual grief is the same as its cause. Almost despite himself, Barthes seems to be saying that thinking through language and linguistic structures leads to reality's "evaporation" and to its "compactness" alike, a divergent condition that only the tricky "ruse" carried by his phrasing seems able to secure. What is most magical about this verbal sleight of hand is the way it practically resolves the contradictory position in which Barthes finds himself—not by offering him direct access to a real untouched by signification but, quite the opposite, by helping him rediscover the experiential or fantastically "real" effects of signs themselves.

* * *

If Barthes is not yet fully able to absorb this lesson by the end of *Mythologies*—or if he is only able to admit it in pejorative terms ("ideologism and its opposite are types of behavior which are still magical," as he writes in the book's closing lines)—the figure of the sorceress that he re-encounters two years later when writing the preface of the 1959 reissue of Michelet's *La Sorcière* helps him to recuperate magic from the shameful sidelines into which the analytical framework of myth had pushed it (*Mythologies* 159). Summarizing, for instance, Michelet's account of the witch's gradual formation as a response to the increasing estrangement he finds in pre-Renaissance France, Barthes portrays her actions as an emancipatory force in history: "magical rites," he declares, "being the one way a technique of liberation could be acknowledged by an entire alienated collectivity" (*Critical* 105). He is specifically talking about the sorceress's use of herbs and often poisonous plants as curative treatments for common ailments, but his point speaks more generally to magic's potential to spark an awareness of alienation and to allow, however meagerly, for its amelioration. The emphasis on "rites" recalls Zenkine's point about the rarity of mythological analyses of practices rather than objects and designates another affordance of magic that myth does not possess. That is, in addition to—perhaps as a result of—being a word whose meanings cleave along opposing lines, a framework of magic invokes a practical register, a stress on an ongoing process of doing and making that explicitly opposes the timeless, incontrovertible givenness with which myth presents itself.

Barthes makes this more explicit when he observes that "Michelet never distinguishes the witch from her activity: she exists only insofar as she participates in a *praxis*, which is precisely what makes her a progressive figure: as opposed to the Church, established in the world as a motionless, eternal essence, she is the world making itself" (*Critical* 112). With her "existence" framed as a result of repeated practices rather than a given state, the witch works as a counter to the cultural conditions elaborated in Michelet's account of the way cruelly sclerotic religious dogma and an incontestable feudal system create a sense of static inevitability in which, as he puts it, "everything is foreseen; no room is left for hope in the world."[14] Bearing a passing, if exaggerated, resemblance to the sense of immutable "'naturalness'" by which Barthes characterized 1950s French society, this social stagnancy wraps the medieval world in a "heavy, grey, leaden fog" out of which the sorceress emerges.[15] The story Michelet tells of her emergence proceeds in a series of complicated steps, but taking a look at a key moment in her development will drive home not just the experiential aspects of language as we've been examining them but, all the more importantly given the anxieties with which Barthes concludes *Mythologies*, the magical contribution that the "metalanguage" of criticism makes in this endeavor.

Accordingly, the incipient witch withdraws to the outskirts of the social order—"leagues away," as Michelet poetically puts it, "from any thoroughfare, on a desert heath all thistles and brambles"—where she encounters an enlivened environment quite different from the "wretched death in life" in which she had previously found herself.[16] Significantly, the agent of this animation is language itself: Michelet narrates how "nature itself seemed changed. The trees had found a language of their own and told her tales of ages long ago. The herbs were simples now. Plants that yesterday she kicked away contemptuously like hay were become beings that spoke to her of healing."[17] The sorceress here not only prefigures *Mythologies*' own exploration of the world's linguistic constitution but also extends the import of semiological analysis itself by unearthing language in the natural and not just the explicitly cultural sphere.[18] This is less to suggest an understanding of nature as itself the product of a cultural framework than it is to advance a kind of linguistic functioning not necessarily dependent on (though nonetheless in potential conversation with) the human world. What's more, Michelet's dramatization of the witch's discovery places the agency of communication squarely with the trees and plants rather than in the witch's interpretive acumen. These lines thus offer another image of what I have called the fantastic reality of mediation—what is magically transparent here is communication as such—and accentuate the practical aspect of language, its functional operation that also possesses its own special kind of empirical status.

In doing so, they intersect with and expand on the one preserve of the nonmythological that Barthes offers in "Myth Today"—namely, his discussion of "the language of man as producer: where man speaks in order to transform reality and no longer to preserve it as an image, wherever he links his language to the making of things" (*Mythologies* 146). Appealing, for example, to the woodcutter who "speak[s] the tree" he is cutting down, he contrasts this "operational" language that is "transitively linked to its object" with the mythologist's "second-order language, a metalanguage in which I shall henceforth not 'act the things' but 'act their names,' and which is to the primary language what the gesture is to the act" (*Mythologies* 146). Between these two options, in a convenient coincidence of arboreal imagery, stands the sorceress listening intently to the tree's own speech, its own magical language. Imparting the tree with a kind of emphatically enunciated existence, a new attribute of intelligibility, this language also offers her a point of contact with it that Barthes's dogged faith in a solid, immediate real keeps him from fully imagining. That is, the tree's speech about itself articulates a mediation of its own presence that the witch's speech about it can link up to, a way in which she might "act the thing" *by* acting its name. In this case, the kind of speaking *about* things that Barthes calls metalanguage can work out its own "operational" and "transitive" effects—not on the real thing itself but rather on its only available aspect: its linguistic mediation. The alternative conception of reality implied here is very much like Gaillard's account of Barthes's work in which the distinction between things and meaning dissolve: "Because things are forged of meaning," she writes, "he does not touch things, he touches the signs that serve as their skin."[19] To say this is to make good on magic's promise to provide a signifying gesture that is itself a productive act, if we insist on framing the magic of this productive signification as anything but a kind of immediate connection or seamless correlation. It is, rather, exactly the opposite: a magical language that works to underscore—to actively speak—the very mediation on which its expressive efficacy depends.

This is the ultimate understanding of magic that Barthes learns from Michelet's sorceress, an understanding that relocates the exasperating split between language-object and metalanguage into the fantastic heart of language itself. Michelet illustrates this idea early in *La Sorcière* when, employing a lyrical syntax whose performative resonance with his point will have major and lasting ramifications for Barthes's thinking, he characterizes her as the embodiment of such elemental divergence. He writes of "*the half-sane, half-insane madness, illuminism,* of the seer, which according to its degree is poetry, second sight, preternatural vision, a faculty of speech at once simple and astute, above all else the power of believing in her own falsehoods."[20] Even as the power of believing in falsehoods prefigures the "artificial myth" by which Barthes tries to undercut the mystifying effects of myth itself, the insistence on duality and contradiction in Michelet's phrasing points to the operation of opposition as the actual power in play. By personifying the split between sane and insane, simplicity and astuteness, faith and falsity, the witch practices what is truly magical about language—namely, the differential effect of contrast that creates meaning and significance. This is what my own attempt to explore the workings of magic in *Mythologies* has been meant to achieve: magic not only as itself an ambiguous, contradictory term but also as an oppositional complement to myth that opens a different way of understanding language's critical work in that text.

The magic of opposition finds its literary analog in Michelet's own writing style, whose "special boldness" Barthes avers by noting the way it "deliberately establishes itself in ambiguity" (*Critical* 103). The ambiguity he is referring to is the stylistic or generic question of whether *La Sorcière* is a documentary chronicle of a culture or a fictionalized narrative of an individual, a work of history or a novel. "But it is just this duplicity which is fruitful," he writes in phrasing that presages the writerly commitments that will increasingly come to characterize his own work (*Critical* 103). Beginning to perceive the opposition that the witch herself almost literally embodies, Barthes goes on to proclaim that Michelet "participate[s] magically in the myth [of the witch] without ceasing to describe it: his text is both narration and experience, its function is to compromise the historian, to keep him on the verge of the magical substance, in the state of a spectator who is on the point of falling into a trance" (*Critical* 111). While the thrust of these lines seems to suggest Michelet's identification with the witch as a mythological phenomenon, the emphasis on magic, phrased significantly in an action-oriented adverbial form, also opens up a space for analytical commentary—without severing the two from each other. Michelet's "description" of the myth—what we have seen Barthes call "metalanguage"—is here staged as a way for him to engage with it, a collapse of "narration and experience" that posits the language of his analytical commentary as a specific, "magical" mode of connection rather than framing it in terms of an unbridgeable critical detachment meant to evade the opposite condition of an uncritical embrace of mythological immediacy. In fact, Michelet's "magical participation" involves treating language as its own kind of experience, its own reality, with all the revisions of those terms that our discussion of the "reality of mediation" has established.

* * *

Though Michelet evinces this experiential approach to language most clearly in a kind of "novelistic" writing that Barthes also increasingly tries to develop as his career progresses, the ways the latter resorts to magic after his reacquaintance with the sorceress move us more explicitly from a consideration of enchantment's operation to the more general realm of the fantastic as such. In doing so, the magical thinking we've been tracing develops into what we might see as a kind of existential linguistic practice. Discussing gemstones and jewelry two years later, for instance, Barthes notes the dearth of "poetic reality" in gold as a physical substance and contrasts it with the literal enchantment it takes on when considered as a signifier. He declares, "But as a sign, what power it has! And it is precisely the sign par excellence, the sign of all signs; it is absolute value, invested with all the powers including those once held by magic: is it not able to appropriate *everything*, goods and virtues, lives and bodies? Is it not able to convert *everything* into its opposite, to lower and to elevate, to demean and to glorify?" (*LF* 55). While we can read these lines as a further index of his commitment to Saussure, the forthright reference to magic also indicates the added tutorial influence of the sorceress—as if his re-engagement with Michelet's work taught him a kind of trickery he could feel comfortable taking out of the margins and placing front and center. Going beyond the antinomy of immediacy and mediation to which, on the surface, he seemed wedded in *Mythologies*, he turns to the work of conversion to effectively animate the magical functioning of opposition that we've just seen embodied in the witch. This substitution should come as no surprise given that conversion comes straight from her spell book: as he affirms, referring again to the use of poisonous herbs as medicine, "witchcraft is a *reversal*" (*Critical* 106). In brashly enacting the transfigurative sorcery practiced by the witch, the glitzy power of gold to signify signification itself discloses the very immediacy of mediation entailed in the fantastic and brings this unreal experience of language quite literally to life.

Barthes's vocabulary of value here helps to begin unpacking the experiential aspect of this fantastic phenomenon since the materialization of this so-called linguistic experience occurs by way of the increase in the world's meaning effected by signification. It's not that signification makes the world more valuable in the strictly monetary or economic terms called up by the gold imagery but rather that signification enlarges the *range of the world's possible values*—not just what its value is but the ways it can have value in the first place. That is, as the emphasis on both "lowering" and "elevating," "demeaning" and "glorifying" indicates, the magical practice of language frees the world from having just one value or even just one kind of value. We will capitalize on this idea in more explicitly semiological terms in chapter 3, but for now Michelet's examination of the witch's "charms and love-potions"—creations he appropriately describes as "fantastic . . . often willfully fantastic"—offer a more elaborate illustration of signification's magical expansion of worldly experience.[21] Take, for instance, the witch's demand that the lover "filch some trifle the fair lady would never miss or give a thought to," such as "a fragment torn from a garment long worn and soiled which she had moistened with the sweat of her body."[22] The focus here is on the mundane and the purposefully insignificant, a feature of the world so familiar as to be invisible. When Michelet nonetheless goes on to posit that "one day or another, looking at the garment again, the keen-sighted fair one would notice the tiny rent, would guess its meaning with a tender sigh," he describes a "fantastic" situation in which the details of the world are no longer beholden to their commonplace status. Concluding that "The charm had taken effect!," he indicates the way this magic involves the conversion of what might normally have passed notice into something that carries profound but uncertain—perhaps, in the trivial fissure of that rent, even empty—import.[23]

A few pages earlier, when he offers another account of a servant seeking romantic assistance, Michelet further excavates the part that signification plays in these charms' conversionary revaluation of experience. He reports how the sorceress works her magic by simply speaking to the young man: "'It shall have our best consideration, young sir. Meantime return; you will already see [*tu verras*] that something is changed,'" she promises.[24] Observe that the imperative undertone of the "you will already see" implicitly functions as a command to pay attention, to look *at* rather than *through* his experience, in another formulation of the more general stance or attitude that potentially puts the servant in immediate, fantastic touch with signs themselves. This immediacy is constituted, however, out of nothing more than opposition as such, the difference between attention and inattention that the witch's simple statement institutes. And it's partly for this reason that, when Michelet continues, his own language delineates a negative, empty space around which his words swirl: "What is changed is himself. I do not know what hope troubles him; his deeply downcast gaze, crossed by an uneasy flame, let escape in spite of himself [*Ce qui est changé, c'est lui. Je ne sais quel espoir le trouble; son œil baissé, plus profond, creusé d'une flamme inquiète, la laisse échapper malgré lui*]."[25] The articulation of this change takes place through a refusal to substantively identify it: notice the use of the indefinite relative pronoun "*ce qui*" ("that which" or "what") that insists on a structure of reference without any definite referent—except the referential pronoun "*lui*"—as well as Michelet's forthright denial of his own ability to pinpoint the phenomenon taking place here. His incapacity to provide a definite formulation of the change that the young man is undergoing opens up a space of indeterminacy that is what essentially constitutes the possibility of change itself (what, in other words, Michelet also calls "hope"). Indeed, the only concrete description we receive is anything but concrete: with its concentration on the servant's "downcast gaze," Michelet's statement focuses less on his physical "eyes" than on the signs of an invisible transformation they involuntarily emit. In doing so, it clarifies and further dramatizes the effect of the witch's words by transmuting the servant's body into something like a living sign.

This transmutation does not stop here, however; rather, Michelet depicts an uncontrollable proliferation of signs that also influences and invigorates the world outside the servant. Not only is the lady's own attention piqued by the young man's change—she "is quick to note [his] symptoms before others"—but, just as quickly, "an undefined feeling of impending trouble haunts the castle. A voiceless tempest, without thunder or lightning, broods over it, like an electric cloud on the surface of a swamp."[26] As the insistently latent imagery in these lyrical lines implies, the whole world seems to receive a kind of charge whose fantastic power stems from approaching worldly phenomena not in terms of their supposedly natural self-evidence but rather in terms of their operation as a sign structure, one that promises the potential for something more—even, indeed especially, if this promise is never fulfilled. As my discussion of magic in general and of these magical charms in particular has repeatedly suggested, Michelet is less concerned with the impossibility of a fully present phenomenal experience than with the phenomenal experience of this very impossibility. To this end, consider how the presences on which Michelet remarks don't seem quite *there*—manifestations of "haunting" and "voiceless . . . brood[ing]" that nonetheless possess a kind of imaginary reality—which is what, in my argument, goes by the name of the fantastic.

When, over ten years after penning his introduction to *La Sorcière*, Barthes returns to Michelet in two essays from the early 1970s, he reformulates his earlier points in language developed from his work in what he "roughly characterize[s]" as "'structuralism' or 'semiology,'" which helps to further elaborate the fantastic through arguably more familiar theoretical terms (*Rustle* 195). Commenting on Michelet's investment in "what we today call the *excess of the signifier*," he seeks to explain why "for many, Michelet is a bad historian." As his historical discourse foregrounds its own enunciation, it makes him a "practitioner of writing, operator of the text" instead of someone who focuses on "simply 'reporting,' 'chronicling,' etc." (*Rustle* 198). Barthes describes a more specific aspect of this foregrounding in his claim that "what interests Michelet is the *predicate*, what is added to the event (to the 'subject')" (*Rustle* 196). The quotation marks around "subject" intimate the illusory, constructed status that Barthes discusses more explicitly in essays like "The Discourse of History" from 1967 or "Writing the Event" from 1968 and indicate the kind of outspokenly discursive space in which Michelet's practice of the predicate can release its fantastic reality effect. As this is also the space in which the magical operation of the witch's charms takes place, it goes beyond the simple avowal of the essential position that language has in Michelet's thinking and implies the witch's resolutely performative understanding of language, her almost embodied embrace of its imaginary actuality. It's thus not by chance that Barthes describes the functioning of etymology in Michelet's work as "a magical sign [that] commits the name's bearer to a fatal thematics" (which he exemplifies through the echo of "*la bonne part*," the first prize, in Bonaparte, an echo from which "the whole Micheletist History of the nineteenth century emerges") (*Rustle* 199). This magical background allows us to see how his strange assertion that, for Michelet, "language's being is not constative (thetic) but appreciative (epithetic)" partakes in the larger existential orientation that accompanies this practical approach to language (*Rustle* 196). That is, the thoughtfully distanced perspective in the qualifiers "appreciative" and "epithetic" help to flesh out the paradoxical—I am calling it "fantastic"—idea of "language's being" because they refer to an avowedly second-order commentary that assumes or imagines the world itself not as a preexisting, nonlinguistic reality but as, already, a kind of primary verbalization on which the language of the historian looks back and re-marks. This linguistic accentuation of language's own operation thus divulges "language's being" as the articulatedness, in the abstract, that allows for more specific or concrete articulations—the articulation of articulation as such that the fantastic magically realizes.

One of the few other places in which Barthes resorts to this kind of ontological phrasing is in a discussion of one of his closest contemporaries, Phillipe Sollers, where a (by this point unsurprising) appeal to magical thinking links this avant-garde writer with the purportedly old-fashioned Michelet and allows us to clarify, by way of conclusion, the relationship between a practical approach to language and the more theoretical category of the fantastic itself. Championing the way Sollers's *Drame* seeks "the abolition of separations and, finally, of that separation ... which mistakenly puts things on one side and words on the other" in order to remove the gap between lived experience and narration of that experience—we should hear an echo of Michelet's approach to words here—Barthes describes the result as "giving birth to that chimera, that *verbal being*, neither real nor fictitious, which Spinoza talks about, which is inaccessible to the understanding and to the imagination" (*Sollers* 58, 53). As the suggestion of both hybridity and illusion in the magical image of the chimera combines what can only be brought together in fantasy, it incarnates the incompatibility of language and existence on which the phrase "verbal being" nonetheless insists and presents the impossibility of linguistic presentation. The division that the verbal being of the chimera thus brings out into the open (which is emphatically not to say sutures over) grants some added distinction to the fantastic, which finds its literal articulation in the negative opposition of the "neither . . . nor" that syntactically grants access to inaccessibility as such. The positive opposition of the "real" and the "fictitious" that distinguish this access limns the boundaries between which the fantastic is produced. That is, like the hybrid illusion of the chimera, the fantastic is a "real fiction" on which the separated faculties of "the understanding" and "the imagination" have no purchase. Rather, it is only the language itself, whose magical operation our subsequent chapters will show to involve the labor of both these intellectual modes simultaneously, that can "give birth" to the fantastic.

This labor of the fantastic—which we will amplify in the next chapter by exploring Barthes's conception of the readerly work of notation—is part of what the emphasis on magic and the practical orientation to language that it introduces has been meant to broach. Because, in the end, the sorceress remains the secluded source for the specific metaphors of birth and delivery in his discussion of Sollers; Michelet describes her "sublime faculty of *solitary conception*," a "fecundity of body [that] is no less procreative where conceptions of the spirit are involved."[27] As such, she also stands in for the more general conception of language's own intellectual productivity for which writers like Michelet, Sollers, and, of course, Barthes himself were vilified. Explaining, for example, the readerly resistance to *Drame*'s demand "that the event (the drama) should be in some way transfused from the world which is normally copied (whether real, a dream, or fiction) to the very movement of the words which gaze hard at this world like eyes," Barthes writes of his culture's "very powerful taboo (with the author as witch doctor [*le sorcier*]) against making language into a *subject*, and doing so through language itself" (*Sollers* 52, 66, 5:599). The reference to the witch doctor is here meant to index a common fantasy about writers and intellectuals that denies the consequentiality of language, of verbalization, as itself an industriously imaginative kind of thinking. If his own denunciation in this respect comes most acutely in the famous 1965 controversy with Raymond Picard detailed in chapter 4, the witch doctor imagery runs throughout his writings more generally—from the "accursed and necessary role of a debased witch doctor [*d'un sorcier dégradé*]" that crowns a 1956 analysis of Pierre Poujade's anti-intellectualism to a 1974 column on the "indictment of magic" that is "periodically lodged" against the "witch doctor [*sorcier*]" of cultural criticism (*Eiffel* 135; *Rustle* 343).[28] But what distinguishes the instance of the image in the Sollers essay is the underscored ambiguity in that italicized word "*subject*," meaning both topic and willful consciousness, which comprehends the position that the linguistic constitution of the witch and her powerful magic have played in driving my argument.

In other words, through my readerly attempts to activate Barthes's language of magic in this chapter, I have been trying to engage the very magic of language in a way that would allow me to quite literally inhabit the position of the witch. For displaying the intellectual consequences that come from such a linguistic practice is one of the only ways that this dismissal of language as a subject can be refused and refuted. Doing so has also allowed me to insist on the linguistic mediation of what might otherwise look like the immediacy of my conception of the fantastic, as if I conjured it up out of nothing more than thin air instead of the verbal maneuvers that have helped me to show it at work. And indeed, the very *work* of the fantastic is the next step in our exploration of this linguistic phenomenon. In this, I am naturally following Barthes himself, who ardently assumes the mantle of the sorceress when, in *Roland Barthes by Roland Barthes*, he describes the "great enthusiasm for the *metaphor/metonymy* opposition" that inspired his 1963 essay on La Bruyère. He writes, "Like a magician's wand [*une baguette de sourcier*], the concept, especially if it is coupled, *raises* a possibility of writing: here, he said, lies the power of saying something" (*RB* 110, 4:686).[29] What we see here is not only the way Barthes's interest in those fundamental operations of signification induces the very movement of his thinking but also, and more vitally, how they do so by magically delimiting a space of "possibility" in which writing can take place—where language, that is, can do its work.

With this in mind, we might figure his attempts to move in his later writing "From Science to Literature," as the title of a 1967 essay heralds it, as the simultaneous transformation of a critical science into a criticism of magic. This seems, finally, to be what he is intimating with his comment on Michelet's own language-driven method toward the close of his preface to *La Sorcière*, his assertion that the great historian "has participated in the myth of the witch exactly as the witch herself participated, in his own view, in the myth of magical *praxis*" (*Critical* 114). As he underscores the witch's existential mode of critical practice that his later, more writerly experiments sought to make as perspicuous as possible, he also describes the energy she has imparted to our exploration of the fantastic's practical magic in this chapter. In this, we should also hear the pedagogical part played by the sorceress in this argument and Barthes's career both, which is the lesson that Barthes contends Michelet learned from her. As he puts it, "What he has undertaken once again, in writing *La Sorcière*, is neither a profession (the historian's) nor a priesthood (the poet's), it is, as he has said elsewhere, a *magistracy* [*une magistrature*]" (*Critical* 114, 2:380). Rather than an object of academic inquiry or mystical worship, the sorceress becomes, in these lines, a model or even an authority to be followed, one whose verbal alliance with magic offers the critic (left unnamed here) the power to address the fantastic affordances of language itself.

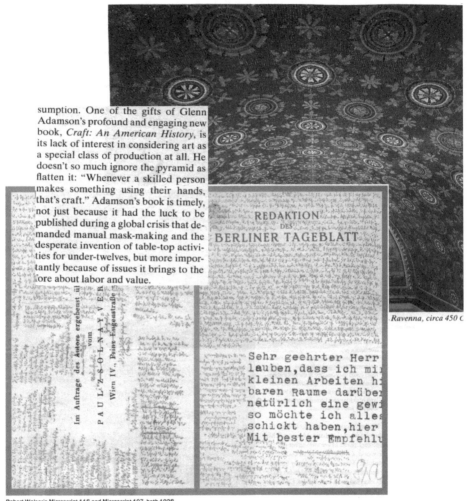

sumption. One of the gifts of Glenn Adamson's profound and engaging new book, *Craft: An American History*, is its lack of interest in considering art as a special class of production at all. He doesn't so much ignore the pyramid as flatten it: "Whenever a skilled person makes something using their hands, that's craft." Adamson's book is timely, not just because it had the luck to be published during a global crisis that demanded manual mask-making and the desperate invention of table-top activities for under-twelves, but more importantly because of issues it brings to the fore about labor and value.

Ravenna, circa 450 C

Robert Walser's Microscript 116 and Microscript 107, both 1928.

As for life, I don't like it. I notice no "interplay of life and art." Life is that which—pressingly, persistently, unfailingly, imperially—interrupts.

6. Untitled (October 2021). Author's handmade collage.

How Notation Works [CHAPTER TWO]

You better work, cover girl.
RUPAUL, "Supermodel"

The magical practice of language to which the previous chapter initiated us finds potential for further elaboration via a brief return to the image of the "debased witch doctor" with which it terminated. Essentially, what characterizes the workings of this witch doctor is that he does no work at all—at least according to Barthes's 1956 discussion of Pierre Poujade's populist screed *J'ai choisi le combat*, where he uses that figure for the first time. Poujade penned his book to defend the "common man" against the elites of government, business, and academia and established the Defense Union of Shopkeepers and Craftsmen in 1953 as part of a short-lived but virulent political movement in France based on anti-parliamentarianism, anti-intellectualism, and xenophobia. Of the various condemnations that contribute to the cursed or "debased" position that the witch doctor-intellectual has in the Poujadist imaginary, Barthes singles out "a theme dear to all strong regimes: the identification of the intellectual with idleness." He clarifies, "Knowledge is discredited insofar as it can no longer be defined as *work*" (*Eiffel* 129). This is a central manifestation of what, in a quotation that is meant to belabor one of my book's main points, he calls "the inevitable basis of all anti-intellectualism: the suspicion of language," the commitment to linguistic production or linguistic practice being the primary form that the intellectual's supposed "idleness" assumes (*Eiffel* 128). What is more, this focus on language also undergirds the curt (and all too familiar) dismissal that "the intellectual is detached from the real" (*Eiffel* 127). But this image of aloof inactivity is exactly what my foregoing focus on the practical magic of language has been trying to counter, an enterprise this chapter extends by focusing on the role that a purposeful embrace of work plays in Barthes's language-based thinking. As we have begun to see, the linguistic magic that Barthes has helped me to concoct has very little in common with the kind of effortless, instantaneous exploits that would align with the indifferent indolence imputed to the witch doctor–intellectual.[1]

In this chapter, I thus investigate how his writing somewhat unexpectedly and no doubt ironically realizes the Poujadist demand that the intellectual "will have to be put to work once and for all, it will be necessary to convert an activity which can be measured only by its harmful excess into a *concrete* labor" (*Eiffel* 129–30). While the "excess" Barthes mentions here refers to the fantasy that a deliberate investment in language as such necessarily and harmfully leads away from "the solid ground of common sense," the alternative emphasis on "*concrete* labor" (achieved through that magical operation of "conversion") names the framework this chapter employs to continue developing language's own fantastic reality (128). As work designates, in other words, the mode in which we experience and engage the more or less pleasurable play of signification, it gives some more elaborate detail to the rhetoric of verbal "operation" and "functioning" entailed in the paradoxical immediacy of mediation we started to explore in the last chapter. This comes out nowhere more clearly than in *The Fashion System*, Barthes's painstaking analysis of the discourse on women's clothing in the 1958–59 issues of *Elle* and *Le Jardin des Modes* that, as we saw in the introduction, describes Fashion as "a reality experienced fantastically . . . the unreal reality of the novel" (*Fashion* 266). An attempt, in the wake of the *Mythologies* collection, "to give a technical, and not just metaphorical, content to what are too loosely called 'languages,'" *The Fashion System* offers a methodical illustration of the otherwise invisible or devalued intellectual work entailed in magically speaking the language of the world (*Grain* 43). And though, in phrasing whose specifics we will return to, Barthes almost immediately disavows the "scientific" terms in which he pursues his project, my argument finds echoes of this work in his later writing on Japan and China as well as in his more deliberate move to the literary in *The Preparation of the Novel* that amplify the fantastically active effects mapped by his semiological thinking.

The essential form taken by Barthes's careful semiological work coincides with the fundamental signifying structure of Fashion as a whole, which he describes most succinctly in an article from 1960 that marks his turn from sociohistorical discussions of clothing to a more semiological account of its modes of meaning. He writes, "The signified fashion is supplied using a single signifier, which, both necessary and sufficient, I will call *notable*: any noted feature, any underlined form, in short any vestimentary fragment points, as soon as it is *cited*, to the signified *fashion*" (*LF* 49–50).[2] The emphasis on a generalized operation of notation asserts its elemental status as the practice by which Fashion establishes itself, while the appeal to a "vestimentary fragment," along with the sentence's own disjointed syntax, reinforces fragmentation itself as the broken bedrock of any kind of meaningful articulation. Barthes develops this idea in more explicitly verbal terms in *The Fashion System*'s own argument: writing "to note that (this year) *skirts are worn short* is to say that *short skirts* signify Fashion this year," he points out how "the true opposition is less between the *fashionable* and the *unfashionable* than it is between the *marked* (by speech) and the *unmarked* (silence)" (*Fashion* 268–69). Picking up on the effect of opposition that I began magically practicing in the last chapter, these lines show Barthes performing his own act of notation, extending his attention beyond the direct attribution of fashion to the operation of speech that underlies it and, more subtly, to what fashion leaves implicit or unspoken. As we explore the cutting distinctions that illustrate how notation works, we will be plotting the very *concrete* and in fact continual intellectual industriousness that activates the fantastic experience of language animating both the Fashion System and *The Fashion System*.

To make such a claim is to somewhat defy the traditional understanding of this point in Barthes's career in terms of a rigid and routinized structuralism, which his own dismissals of *The Fashion System* as "in thrall to scientificity" have authorized (*Contemporary* 22). The faith he puts there into an invariable metalanguage that contrasts with the kind of lively literary sensitivity for which he becomes famous certainly seems like it "exempts its practitioners from writing" (*Contemporary* 22). But he simultaneously gestures to the fantastic resources my argument is trying to cultivate when he looks back on this book in a 1970 interview and asserts that "the whole delight of it lay in elaborating and developing the system, working on that long and passionately" (*Contemporary* 22). Restating this point two years later, he declares, "I didn't think of [*The Fashion System*] as a product—but as a production for myself.... It was a bit different with my other books because there was writing [*il y a de l'écriture*] in them, and hence an erotic game with the reader. But with *The Fashion System*, we're really talking about the presentation of a piece of work [*la présentation d'un travail*]. It isn't a product, it's work being acted out [*un travail qui est mis en scène*] in front of other people" (*Contemporary* 66–67, 4:471–72). The pleasure of this text seems to be less in verbal play than in the intellectual effort necessary to explicitly conceive and approach the world as a fantastic form of materialized linguistic discourse, a project that my collages also take up in their own laborious construction. At the same time, it is time itself that comes to index this effort, the exertion of "work being acted out" that transforms the static "product" into an energetic "production" repeating the "long" temporal extension required for Barthes to develop the system. And it is ultimately with this sense of temporality that *The Fashion*

System functions as something like the prequel to, even the precondition of, the more dynamically textual arguments about the world that he stages in *Empire of Signs*, *The Preparation of the Novel*, and, somewhat more complicatedly, *Travels in China*.

The obscured vitality of Barthes's programmatic structuralism is what his friend and interlocutor Michel Butor draws out in one of the few interpretive readings of this relatively underanalyzed text as he emphasizes the active, procedural valence of the title and almost transforms *The Fashion System* into a kind of manual for working with the text of Fashion that outfits so much of our everyday experience.[3] He addresses the many ways that, "in presenting itself above all as a literary work [*comme oeuvre littéraire*]," Barthes's discussion defies the conventions of the traditional academic thesis for which it was devised.[4] In particular, he highlights "the absence of precise references for the immense majority of the citations," barring later scholars from easily or effortlessly building on his research. Instead, he insists, "the work with notecards [*travail de fiche*] must be entirely redone by those who wish to discuss it in detail."[5] For all its timeless "scientificity," *The Fashion System* also asks for a kind of readerly reenactment or reworking that approaches it less as a trove of knowledge than as a series of techniques, less as an endpoint of semiological thought than as a starting point for semiological thinking. Furthermore, Butor's phrase *"travail de fiche"* concretely verbalizes the connection I've drawn between work and notation and suggests the extent to which we are meant to participate in the kind of conscientious notational practice that Barthes systematizes here. In doing so, we will be working to encounter the fantastic experience of language that, in Barthes's words, Fashion offers us by "constitut[ing] the garment as a signifier of something which is yet nothing other than this very constitution" (*Fashion* 287). And if this triumphant perspective on Fashion as "a kind of machine for maintaining meaning without ever fixing it" by which it "rejoin[s] the very being of literature, which is to offer to read not the meaning of things but their signification" seems at first to underplay the analytical energies aimed at demystifying its presentation of itself as natural, it is only in the name of working out the magical practice by which the textual fabric of the world is woven (*Fashion* 288).

* * *

Barthes begins his practical exploration of the Fashion System's living language by explaining his decision to limit his analysis to what he calls "written clothing" rather than "real" garments or their images. "Only written clothing has no practical or aesthetic function," he writes; "it is entirely constituted with a view to a signification: if the magazine describes a certain article of clothing verbally, it does so solely to convey a message whose content is: *Fashion* [*la Mode*]" (*Fashion* 8, 2:908). Almost immediately, the workings of Barthes's scientific language seem to exceed themselves, the opposition between "practical or aesthetic" and "signification" obfuscating the practical aspects of signification itself that we've just seen animate the book's exultant conclusion. Moreover, as the "content" or signified of the magazine's speech, the word *Fashion* implies as much the cultural phenomenon of stylishness as it does the act of making or fabrication on which that phenomenon relies. And if this way of thinking is less pronounced in the French "*Mode*" (which nonetheless maintains a sense of "method" or "means"), Barthes elaborates this allusion to linguistic fabrication more forcefully a few pages later in his comparison of the slightly divergent roles that "description" plays in Fashion and literature. He points out how literary description "must make the object exist" while the presence of images in fashion magazines takes over this role in a way that "confirms the fact that specific language-functions exist [*qu'il existe des fonctions spécifiques du langage*] which the image, whatever its development in contemporary society may be, could not possibly assume" (*Fashion* 12–13, 2:913). Even more significant than the introduction of the explicitly practical and productive term "language-function" is the way the verb "exist" moves from "the object" (which is to say, the referent) to the much more fantastic "existence" of language's own particular effects and operations.

Though he explores three "specific functions of language," he ultimately positions notation as what links them all together and enacts this linguistic existence most comprehensively. Arguing that the "explicit *note*" in a fashion magazine emphasizes and focuses our attention on a particular feature of a garment, he expands his claim in a footnote (appropriately enough) that reads, "In fact, all Fashion commentary is an implicit *note*" (*Fashion* 15). The clothing descriptions found in magazines thus function as a more detailed performance of the general work of notation, which exhibits the "emphatic function" of language that "single[s] out certain elements in order to stress their value" (*Fashion* 15). More specifically, linguistic notation "endows the garment with a system of functional oppositions (for example, fantasy/classic), which the real or photographed garment is not able to manifest in as clear a manner" (*Fashion* 14). As the magazine's commentary and captions cut our perception into distinct pieces that play off each other in much the same way that distinct words and sounds do when spoken or written, this direction of the reader's awareness "rests upon an intrinsic quality of language: its discontinuity"—what he luridly illustrates by stating that "it is the result of a series of choices, of amputations" (*Fashion* 15). The imagery of dismemberment here not only recalls the introductory discussion of division or segmentation that my collaged divagations structurally materialize but, more significantly, it also works to enliven the plodding and exceedingly technical elaboration of what Barthes comes to call the "vestimentary code" where the almost surgical linguistic operations I'm summarizing are most tangibly demonstrated. In reality, the keen clarity that results from linguistic notation has the overall effect of "reviving the general information conveyed by the photography [in the fashion magazine]," a quickening power he plays up in his claims that "verbalized notation helps to reinvigorate the [photographs'] information" and "to recharge the message they contain" (*Fashion* 15). While his focus here is on the magazine's photography, this ability of language to impart energy and import to what is or has become flat and vague extends to our experience of the world when he turns to a discussion of clothing's reality. And it's at this point where we could be said to be, or at least be in touch with, *living* language.

What I mean comes into sharper focus as Barthes digs more deeply into the way material clothing functions according to the intensely oppositional organization of language's signifying system. The most fundamental aspect of this phenomenon is that its signifying unit, or, more correctly, its "signifying matrix," is a compound one that consists of three elements: the garment itself—say, to use Barthes's example, a cardigan sweater; a particular feature of the garment—say, the cardigan's collar; and a variation or alternative to which the particular feature is subject—say, being buttoned or not buttoned (*Fashion* 62). Immediately, we can see the "amputational" operation of linguistic systematics in the particular focus on the collar rather than any of the cardigan's other features as well as in the differential energy of the button, whose potential for alternation introduces what is effectively a hiccup or a kind of prick in the sweater's otherwise stable and continuous material presentation. The point I'm replicating from Barthes's discussion isn't really that the button makes the collar open or closed; rather, it's the way this very option works as what, in a more deconstructive vocabulary, we would call the cardigan's divergence from itself—the carved-out space where it is able to change its appearance and its significance to become, in the words of the magazine, either "*sporty*" or "*dressy*" (*Fashion* 61). But the real upshot of this rather overworked analysis comes in Barthes's description of the way these elements interact to mobilize that prick and engender a vestimentary signification. He writes, "signification seems to follow an itinerary of sorts: issuing from an alternative (*open/closed*), it next passes through a partial element (*the collar*) and comes, in the end, to touch and, so to speak, impregnate the garment (*the cardigan*) (*Fashion* 61–62).[6] The self-consciously figurative choice of the word "impregnate" alludes as much to a saturation of the garment with meaning as it does to a "penetration" of it by meaning, a thrust that the other verbs "issue" and "pass through" advance further. Moreover, the obvious implications of gestation, labor, and birth activate all the maternal implications of the term "signifying matrix" and link the meaningful rupture of this process with the creation of life and liveliness that would affirm or emphasize the garment's existence as such.

This procreative reading finds additional support, or at least some developmental echoes, in Barthes's account of the abstracting effects that go hand in hand with the piercing operation of linguistic signification, his claim that "the second function of speech is a function of knowledge [*connaissance*]." He continues, "Language makes it possible to deliver [*livrer*] information which photography delivers poorly or not at all . . . in a general way, what language adds to the image is *knowledge* [*savoir*]" (*Fashion* 13-14, 2:914). His particular point has to do with the authority of the writing in fashion magazines to dictate what is fashionable, but this determination is less important for us than the more general suggestion of the way that such dictation supplements material with conceptual experience. Moreover, as the presence of *naissance* or "birth" in the *connaissance* of Barthes's original French indicates the creative nativity that conditions such transformation, it begins to extend the productive labor of signification from language itself to those of us working with it. (And though the French *livrer* doesn't have the same connotation as the English "deliver," Barthes's use of both French words for "knowledge" throws into relief the pregnant verbal resources that the specificity of *connaissance* makes available.) What is born through this knowledge-creating encounter with language is not so much another existence for the garment but another *aspect* of its existence, a fantastically comprehensible body constituted by the "system of abstraction" that, through the operations we've been examining, language allows us to bring to the physical world.

Barthes thus describes how language "helps to grasp [the garment] much more concretely than the photograph . . . because it permits dealing with discrete concepts (*whiteness, suppleness, velvetiness*), and not with physically complete objects" (*Fashion* 12).[7] Significantly, the adverb concretely" migrates from what we might think of as its expected reference to the garment's material makeup to qualify the abstract process of mental comprehension instead, a counterintuitive use that points at the way words systematically sculpt the intellectual outline of what they designate. In this case, as intimated in the rhythmic registration of those parenthetical substantives, it's as if the notation of particular aspects discretely executes the prickly work of amputation and division that we traced in the operation of the cardigan's button. In other words, by affirming one quality rather than another—"Affirmation is nothing other than a suspended choice," Barthes reminds us, opposed to "the anonymous reservoir from which [that choice] is drawn"—it introduces an implicitly oppositional structure that directs our attention and organizes the perceptual space where the garment takes shape (*Fashion* 91). Notation thus "concretely" abstracts its object into a materialized structure of knowledge and lets it live an emphatic, fantastic life that we create by and carry out through language.[8]

Barthes puts this more technically in his account of what he calls "the real vestimentary code" (*Fashion* 34). Not fully identical to the "written vestimentary code," which consists of the words used in the magazine's descriptions, this "real code" refers to the perceptual organization and configuration of garments and sartorial features that result from the processes we've just been noting. But, he insists, this coded, structured reality "is never reached apart from the words which 'translate' it" (*Fashion* 45). As the scare quotes around "translate" suggest, Barthes seems to encounter an intellectual impasse in his attempt to grasp how "the (presumed) real itself constitutes a code" in a way that recalls the alienated position he found himself in at the end of *Mythologies* (*Fashion* 41).[9] Yet, when he admits that "dividing [the real code] into segments, necessary as that is, demands a certain amount of 'preparation' and, so to speak, 'compromise,'" he gestures further at his own practical participation in that work insofar as he quietly, even unknowingly, assumes some of language's notational agency for himself (*Fashion* 43). That is, in those impersonal, anonymous processes of "preparation" and "compromise" on which the divisionary organization executed by the fashion magazine's speech depends—which, indeed, it "demands"—Barthes stakes out an arena of articulating activity where he might join in the invigorating speech of the world. And if these particular words suggest that his entry into this arena remains preliminary and somewhat irresolute, this diffidence disappears by his 1978-79 course on *The Preparation of the Novel*. Here, as Barthes focuses on "the life of the present, structurally mixed (there's *my* basic idea) with the desire to write it," he seems to have internalized the coded textuality of the real so that "the 'Preparation' of the Novel therefore refers to the capturing of this parallel text, the text of 'contemporary,' concomitant life" (*PN* 17).

As these lines makes clear, Barthes has jettisoned any sense of a preestablished, homogeneous real on which verbal segmentation would come to work and imagines it instead as already textually "prepared," a condition he can link to by "preparing" his own text.[10] In this case, writing and language are more explicit versions of—not additions to—his phenomenal experience, a transformation in his thinking that is signaled by the move from a more static, externalizing vocabulary of the "real" or "reality" to the dynamic flux and verve suggested by "life of the present."

Rachel Sagner Buurma and Laura Heffernan help to explain this shift by reading *The Preparation of the Novel* as Barthes "circularly returning to notation armed with an account of the subject that structuralism so signally lacked in order to replace structuralism's vision of a world made of *langue* with an account of the subject's meaning-making capacities and embodied practices."[11] As part of an argument against "the opposition between the living and the meaningful" so that we can "experience representation as a part of life," their focus on practical action speaks to the notational effort of meaning-making I've been anatomizing, which takes on a more active and intentional pulse in Barthes's last lecture course.[12] While notation might seem a more theoretical, detached process in *The Fashion System*, it later becomes something he methodically does *with* language in order to produce the present: as he puts it, "it would be wrong to say that you can't make writing out of the Present. You can write the Present *by noting* it—as it 'happens' to you or under you (under your eyes, your ears)" (*PN* 17). To this extent, then, we might patch Barthes's more deliberate account of notation in *The Preparation of the Novel* into the seam *The Fashion System* has sewn in between the real and the written.

What is particularly significant about this last comment of his is the way that "*noting*" refers to both the seizure of attention by what "happens" and the more literal inscription that records it in words. While Barthes is gesturing toward a genre of writing that attends to the fine details of our everyday experience (he spends the next eight weeks discussing the haiku), his statement also includes the very process by which we perceive and recognize the world as itself a form of "writing," as itself a divisionary, differential operation that we effectively read.[13] Accordingly, when Barthes expands on his initial idea of noting the Present, he zealously performs the invigorating incisions we've been tracing in the work of words. Explaining what he calls "the double problem, the key to which organizes the Preparation of the Novel," he writes, "On the one hand, *Notation*, the practice of 'noting': *notatio*," and "On the other hand, how to pass from Notation, and so from the *Note*, to the Novel, from the discontinuous to the flowing (to the continuous, the smooth)?" (*PN* 17–18). The staccato repetition of minimally different words for the linguistic operation that concerns us offers a stop-and-start tempo that not only recalls the birth of the garment in the magazine but also emphasizes the persistent effort, the multiple stabs by which notation as such occurs.[14] The disjointed rhythms of both statements should give us pause in that they insist not only on the paralyzing discontinuity introduced by notation but also on the lively flow that the syntagmatic progress of the sentences makes out of those discontinuities. As what "organizes the Preparation of the Novel," these sentences describe the mostly disregarded, routinized exertion that goes into the perceptual "preparation" of the real, the readerly blocking and basting entailed in attending to it at all.

This effort is also the condition for excavating the verbal language of the present—for "writing" it in the narrower sense—the description of which is where we get perhaps the most concise illustration of how this active notation works. He writes, "*Notatio* instantly appears as the *problematic* intersection between a river of language, of uninterrupted language—*life*, both a continuous, ongoing, sequenced text and a layered text, a histology of cut-up texts, a palimpsest—and a sacred gesture: to *mark* life (to isolate: sacrifice, scapegoat, etc.)" (*PN* 18). The density of this sentence in the lecture notes is itself notable, as it splices a lengthy appositive defining "*life*" into a penetrating description of verbal notation itself. Significantly, this appositive asserts the correlation of language and "*life*" by explicitly framing the latter as a textual construction understood according to its syntagmatic ("sequenced") and paradigmatic ("layered") aspects, themselves figured in throbbing phrases that fantastically index living vitality through linguistic structures.[15] In assembling or constructing the sense of life as an "uninterrupted" river of language by means of a grammatical element that is actually interrupting the sentence, we effectively practice the paradoxical condensation of connection and disconnection—of, indeed, cutting and pasting—by which the work of notation fashions a perceptual and conceptual experience. The constructive creation of this cutting finds further characterization in the sentence's strange closing appeal to a "sacred gesture" that "*mark*[s] life" and the equally puzzling parenthetical "(to isolate: sacrifice, scapegoat, etc.)." As the explanatory examples of sacrifice and isolation recall Abraham's aborted slaughter of Isaac and the substitute slice of circumcision that sets the Jews apart as God's chosen race, they offer something like an inaugural image of notation's emphatic, oppositional incision that binds the Jewish world to the word of God. Accentuating even as it assuages the more acute imagery of amputation which we've been working with, the less harsh figure of the "*mark*" comes to stand in for the slashes by which the world is endowed with legible form. The mark of words becomes something like a nonviolent cut, a literally metaphorical contact between life and language that notation opens up.

* * *

Up to this point, I have been working to synthesize the divisionary labor that animates notation as a living linguistic practice, but it is now time that notation becomes its own object of discrete dissection, which will take us more deeply, if somewhat less concretely, into the fantastic notational effort with language we've begun to broach in *The Preparation of the Novel*.

Because, of course, notation is by no means monolithic; rather, it ramifies into several different signifying systems that are articulated with—joined to—one another. In this chapter, our exploration of the discontinuous link between the "real vestimentary code" and the "written vestimentary code" has displayed what Barthes and his predecessors call the system of "denotation," the privative, negating prefix "de-" offering an etymological index of the constitutive discontinuities we've been examining. But the system of "connotation" takes denotation as its support or content, its additive prefix "con-" indicating the way it introduces additional significations to go along "with" the original denotation—even as the false etymological echo of deceit and fraud (e.g., "con artist") suggests its meaningful trickery if not its outright deception. Part of this deception is, in fact, the very appearance of language's effortlessness, the easy, frictionless use of well-worn significations that comes from taking the discontinuities by which denotation works as already accomplished, an established condition rather than an assertive action. This omission of effort is what leads someone like Poujade to discount the intellectual industry entailed in speech as such, and Barthes certainly acknowledges the way such misleading secondary meaning "opens the message to the social, affective, ideological world," which has made connotation central to all manner of important critical demystifications (*Fashion* 33).

But in Barthes's discussions of this particular linguistic confidence trick, he places as much focus on the operative "opening" of the message as on its ideological formation. Doing so, he further excavates the excisions that styled our perceptual experience in the previous section and essentially enlarges our sense of how we actively work with language. Quoting the full comment I just excerpted frames connotation (what Barthes here calls "the rhetorical system") as an especially expansive though not necessarily unimpeachable instance of the fantastic: "The communication set in motion by the rhetorical system is in a sense larger, because it opens the message to the social, affective, ideological world: if we define the real by the social, it is the rhetorical system that is more real, while the terminological system [i.e., "denotation"], since it is more formal, akin to a logic, would be less real" (*Fashion* 33).[16] The contortions Barthes is obligating the word "real" to undergo here stretch it to the very limit of its logic, or, put otherwise, to the fantastic apex of its intelligibility as it comes to describe the more or less substantial encounter with linguistic signification itself. The ideological form that this fantastic encounter most often takes comes, not coincidentally, from the domain of work whose outline I have been trying to trace: as he puts it, "the notion which best explains the coherence of the Fashion universe, or rather, which does not contradict any of its features, is the notion of work [*la notion de travail*]"

(*Fashion* 248, 2:1146). His point is that Fashion often relies on an appeal to activities, occupations, or events that grant an imaginary context or setting in which the meaning of a particular garment or outfit becomes legible ("*If you want to signify what you are doing here, dress like this*," he ventriloquizes [*Fashion* 249]). He immediately qualifies his focus on work by acknowledging "leisure" as the sphere most frequently associated with Fashion: "But," he specifies, "it is precisely a matter of a complementary pair: the world of Fashion is work in reverse [*travail en creux*]" (*Fashion* 248, 2:1146). It seems obvious that this analysis is leaching all force from the suggestion of activity we've identified in the English word *fashion*, the phrase "*travail en creux*"—literally "work hollowed out"—underscoring the empty, abstract shell that his presentation of work as only a "notion" would also emphasize.

Yet, the "complementary pair" of work and leisure locates the persistence of the oppositional friction by which meaning itself is generated while the image of "hollowing out" echoes the linguistic lacerations that effect such opposition in the first place. What we have here is, in a sense, the denotative aspects *of connotation*—not just the words that define this second signifying system but also the operations that elicit the incisive effort cutting across and animating both levels. This is what he is referring to in his concluding account of the naturalization of signs, where he emphasizes the purposeful effort entailed in the "tireless activity . . . to constitute strongly and subtly organized semiological systems" that are accompanied by the "equal activity in masking their systematic nature, reconverting the semantic relation into a natural or rational one" (*Fashion* 285). The complex status that "activity" has here finds more nuanced expression in Barthes's further comments on the modish interpenetration of work and leisure, the fact that "in Fashion, all work is empty, all pleasure is dynamic, voluntary, and we could almost say, laborious: by exercising her right to Fashion, even through fantasies of the most improbable luxury, the woman always seems *to be doing something*" (*Fashion* 253-54). The inescapability of work is striking: exertion transfers from the sphere of professional occupation to the rhetorical speech of Fashion as such, the piling on of adjectives and examples underscoring the explicit reference to the effort of even his own saying in this moment. Furthermore, the insistence on action—especially in the inverted, oblique form that it is taking here—suggests the extent to which the connotations of Fashion ask us to notice *more*, to *continue* to notice, to *prolong* what and how we notice at all.[17]

This is not to deny the ideological presentation of modern careers that Barthes refers to in his claim that "'doing' in Fashion (and therein lies its unreality) is ultimately never anything but the decorative attributes of being, since work is never presented apart from a population of psychological essences and human models" (248). Rather, it is to accentuate that this evacuation of traditional conceptions of employment allows for nothing other than the work of words to emerge—and to emerge, we will continue to see, as an ongoing extension of our attention. Accordingly, when Barthes insists that the "human activity" Fashion tries to signify "is tinged with a *certain* unreality [*d'une certaine irréalité*]," he speaks as much to a "particular" unreality as to a "definite" one in a way that affirms or paradoxically concretizes the very hollowness, the very emptiness I've been engaging the cut of notation to substantiate (*Fashion* 248, 2:1146; emphasis added). As this phrase intersects with "the unreal reality of the novel" we have seen him use to exemplify a reality "experienced fantastically" (*Fashion* 266), it again gestures beyond the realm of Fashion's luxurious "fantasies" to an alternative and specifically fantastic framework for approaching and attending to such unreal, rhetorical "doing." Within such a framework, Barthes's claim that "to dress *in order* to act is, in a certain way, not to act, it is to display the being of doing, without assuming its reality" reads not just as a condemnation of nonaction but also as an *expansion* of action to include the "display" effected by signification itself (*Fashion* 249).[18]

Barthes comes to embrace a version of this perspective as he moves to a more performative kind of writing over the course of his career, but here it remains in embryonic form, articulated in stridently negative terms that dismiss or implicitly devalue the opaque working of the signifier. A few pages later he thus writes, "the activity assumed by Fashion neither initiates nor exhausts itself; it no doubt constitutes a dreamed pleasure, but this pleasure is 'cut short' fantastically [*est fantastiquement 'raccourci*'], in an absolute instant, divested of all transitivity, since no sooner are they spoken than the weekend and the shopping no longer need 'doing'" (*Fashion* 252, 2:1150). His recourse to diction linking the fantastic with the very cut of speech hints, in spite of himself, at the very work of vestimentary signification standing in for the undertakings and errands of daily life, the difference that a particular garment makes in our sense of a situation. I am not claiming that the shopping he is referring to is accomplished by simply wearing the right clothes—which is the main fantasy Barthes is critiquing—rather, I am noticing the way Fashion intervenes in and constitutes, in all its intransitivity, a *literally significant* part of our practical experience. More specifically, the obscured functioning of time here becomes the means for disregarding the work of signification, the imputation of instantaneity extending from the unnoticed (because "intransitive") activity of Fashion to unperformed activity more broadly. Yet, in asserting that "the activity assumed by Fashion neither initiates nor exhausts itself," Barthes also ambiguously conjoins the sense of Fashion's timeless simulation with the simultaneous suggestion of a committed undertaking without beginning or end, suggesting the relentlessness and temporal extension with which Fashion asks us to attend to the never-not-operational cuts of signification.

This is how we might understand his subsequent claim that "thus, we realize the double quality of the Fashion action: it is simultaneously voluptuous and intelligible," a titillating assertion that describes the condition in which we find signification thickly embodied and sensuously, even sensually, perceptible (*Fashion* 252).[19] Rather than taking up the obvious critical resistance he is advancing against Fashion's presumed immediacy, this point looks ahead to the vivacious, hedonistic arguments Barthes makes in *The Pleasure of the Text* at the same time as it looks back to the invigorating effects of notation as we discussed it in the previous section—the fact that noting the emptiness of Fashion's significations is paradoxically a way to activate their fantastic substance. Accordingly, Barthes's explicit appeal a few lines earlier to the discontinuous incisions shared between connotation and denotation involves its own lively linguistic implications. He writes, "through the connotation of its second system, Fashion divides human activity not into structural units available to a combinatory (such as the analysis of a *series of technical actions* might generate) but rather into gestures which carry their own transcendence within themselves; it can be said that the function of rhetoric here is to transform uses into rituals" (*Fashion* 252; emphasis added). Their censorious tone notwithstanding, these lines paint a picture of "human activity" that is far from the instantaneous availability or unconscious naturalness usually associated with ideology or mythology. Instead, in the conversion of simple "use" to formalized "ritual," they offer a potentially *knowing* sense of performance that echoes the previous chapter's focus on language as a kind of magical practice, in which case the "gestures which carry their own transcendence within themselves" consolidate the signifier-signified relationship to function as a condensed form of acted and active signification. In other words, these gestures become potted dramas of connoted meaning that take place in the temporal world rather than in some abstract, "transcendent" conceptual ambit. (His other explanatory images are the "liturgy, or, better still, a theory of fantasy" that the introduction's exploration of the word *fantastic* also worked to bring out of the heavens and down to the practical space of earth.)

It should be obvious that I am reading this argument "against the grain" as we say, the purpose of which is to continue to enrich our sense of the value that comes from working with sign systems. And while the dense space of value itself will complicate this point when it takes center stage in our next chapter, the way the rigorous semiological orienta-

How Notation Works 67

tion of Barthes's inquiry in *The Fashion System* treats signification as "a series of technical actions" is what allows me to locate at least the promise of an intentional or deliberate relationship to the operation of denotation and connotation in his otherwise denunciatory assertions (*Fashion* 252). If this intentionality is what I began trying to exhibit in my discussion of his project in *The Preparation of the Novel* (as well as what my collages take up in their own way), the reappearance of the wording that let me cut a conduit between his early and late analytical efforts here distills a more traditional but, we will see, no less fantastic sense of the workaday issues at play in this linguistic labor: "Applied to 'doing,'" he writes, "the rhetoric of Fashion appears as a 'preparation' (in the chemical sense) destined to rid human activity of its major scoria (alienation, boredom, uncertainty, or more fundamentally: impossibility), while retaining its essential quality of a pleasure and the reassuring clarity of a sign" (*Fashion* 252). Even as the word "preparation" invokes a ready-made solution that shunts the magical, alchemical effort of articulation into an unspoken preaccomplishment, this dressing-down of Fashion's ideological representation of the world also provides a more finely formulated inventory of what that effort involves. This is to admit the more negative aspects of the fantastic experience of language, the way it also involves the open-ended drudgery of paying attention to well-worn words that are, simultaneously, never really one's own.[20]

These boring and alienating complements to the "uncertainty" and emphatic "impossibility" by which I inaugurated the fantastic find verification as much in the plodding and ponderous connotations of *The Fashion System*'s argumentation (that led Barthes and his readers to minimize the work of this work in his oeuvre) as in the forthright disaffection and unromantic ennui that Barthes expresses in the often-tortured notations he penned during his 1974 trip to China. Less ecstatic than the justly famous *Empire of Signs* that we will detour through in our conclusion, the notebooks posthumously published as *Travels in China* offer an opportunity to temper what might otherwise be read as the overly cheerful and seemingly apolitical celebration of the fantastic work of and with language while also displaying that work in the very place where its effects seem not to exist. Noticing the "total uniformity of Clothes" almost immediately on his arrival in Beijing, for instance, Barthes remarks, "What an impression! The complete absence of fashion. Clothing degree zero. No elegance, or choice" (*China* 9). The lack of significant sartorial expression that strikes him here and that blunts his interpretive attempts throughout the notebooks leaves him nothing really to note except nothingness as such. Though Barthes does not recognize it, these initial impressions suggest the possibility that *everything* is something to notice—including what seems like and what may very well be nothing at all (a statement that could function as one of the fundamental credos of literary and linguistic study). When he comments again a few days later on "the absolute uniformity of clothes," he admits, "All these notes will probably attest to the failure, in this country, of my writing (in comparison with Japan). In fact, I can't find anything to note down, to enumerate, to classify" (*China* 57). As the concluding string of infinitives here stands in for the cultural phenomena he's unable to single out, it replaces the nonexistent fashion features with different words breaking down notation itself, creating a kind of closed hermeneutic circle that materializes the work of making meaning to the same extent that it eviscerates it. This isn't so much to pinpoint meaning's absence as it is to emphasize the effort, however unproductive, that Barthes's boredom and alienation are making particularly, exasperatingly, even voluptuously perceptible.

He expresses a more general experience of exasperation in an aside during a discussion the day before: "[What did you do on this trip?—We worked!]" (*China* 48). As Andy Stafford explains, the brackets here signal where Barthes "breaks off from the speedy note-taking in which he is involved to record a seemingly insignificant common and daily phenomenon," moves that both Stafford and Neil Badmington mine as sites of shimmering significance in the trip's otherwise monologic tedium of stereotypes.[21] But this break doesn't so much reduce as redouble the alienated exertion that the monotony of Chinese dress incites in him, suggesting that the asymbolia of apparel is only an especially concrete example of the unceasing demands that this general cultural uniformity makes on our interpretive intelligence. Moreover, his futile attempts to penetrate the fabrics worn by the people of this society lead to an image of this society's own impenetrable ideological *fabric*: "the rational tablecloth has been draped over us, so incidents, folds, the absurd are rare" (*China* 64). While this metaphorical elaboration of clothing into cloth indicates a blanketing of semiotic operation, it also implies the expanded vigilance necessary to note the rare instances of signification, which is to say, the sharpening but also the *spreading out* of Barthes's notational attention. Barthes must both intensify and extend his attention, to note more carefully and also more persistently. We thus see him, ten days into his trip, revising his comments about the people's dress: "Bring out clearly the uniformity of clothing," he writes, "but also its implacable subtle differentiation (cadres/workers/functionaries). In fact, unlike what I had noted down, it's the structure of the uniform (homogenous but with marks)" (*China* 117). The increased sensitivity to detail is obvious, but what is also at play is that he *has not stopped* trying to notice, has prolonged his notational work beyond the instant of its first instantiations. (As he puts it in *The Preparation of the*

How Notation Works 69

Novel, "In order to practice *Notatio* in its most *consummate* form, in order for it to give a feeling of plenitude, of enjoyment, of being worthwhile, there's a condition: you need time, lots of time" [*PN* 91]). China's opacity means not that he must pay less attention but that he must pay *more*—even, or especially, to what resists his notice.

This observation allows me to build on what, in her Orientalist diagnosis of the short, noncommittal article "*Alors la Chine?*" that Barthes published based on his notes, Lisa Lowe identifies as a fantasy "refutation of European hermeneutic and political traditions" (160).[22] As much as China functions as a dehistoricized and presymbolic space in the French intellectual imagination at this 1960s/1970s moment and allows Barthes to envision an escape from ideologies bound up with Western modes of meaning and signification, it simultaneously *reveals* the inescapability of those modes to the extent that Barthes repeats—in more protracted form—the very notational efforts of semiological analysis whose inefficacy he bemoans. The fabrication of an irreducible and idealized Eastern Otherness that, according to Lowe's trenchant analysis, enables him to formulate this fantasy escape from Western sociosymbolics enacts exactly the distinguishing operation of differentiation and opposition by which meaning takes place and reinscribes or, more sharply, reengraves those very symbolics in an outspokenly frustrated and palpably boring form. In this sense, *Travels in China* is a replay of *The Fashion System*, not just because of the focus on clothing that they share or even because of their forthright confrontation with ideological systems but because both display Barthes persisting in the protracted rituals of notation. What the later notebooks add, however, is an illustration of analytical gestures whose significance inheres less in what they unearth and more in their own performance, their own execution as a fantastic if also detached mode of being in the world.

* * *

Having sliced and diced the fantastic workings of denotation and connotation, we have come to the moment in which we might put some more discriminating analytic pressure on the tentative claims I've been making for the active intentionality or the intentional activity at play in the work of notation. For I do not mean to posit anything like a wholly sovereign or self-sufficient semiological capacity, even as the snippets we have taken from *The Preparation of the Novel* and *Travels in China* have previewed, in their particular ways, the power percolating through the practice of language. What I want to clarify in the final section of this chapter is how the emphatic agency of this power is predicated on a form of inescapable impotence that makes the most significant part of how notation works a kind of purposeful patience on which all the linguistic efforts I have been performing rely. We get something like a glimpse of this active impotence and the patience with which it is woven when Barthes underscores the indeterminate border between the figurative and the literal on which his research subject fantastically situates his discourse—cutting being, of course, an important part of the expressive work that a clothing designer, a tailor, and even a fashion magazine editor assume in their day-to-day doings. Quickly unraveling any clear distinction between the real and the rhetorical at the end of *The Fashion System*'s methodological introduction, he directs us to "Imagine (if possible) a woman dressed in an endless garment, one that is woven of everything the magazine of Fashion says, for this garment without end is proffered through a text which is itself unending. This total garment must be organized, i.e., cut up and divided into significant units, so that they can be compared with one another and in this way reconstitute the general signification of Fashion" (*Fashion* 42). While the connection to the cuts and divisions by which we've looked into denotation and connotation should be clear enough, the imperative "Imagine" that precedes them asks us to visualize what, in effect, can't actually be seen. I'm not talking just about the "endless garment" on which we will comment in a second. Rather, the more extreme visual impossibility here regards that garment's signifying "organization": we might be able to picture the edges of a garment that have been split from each other, but the split itself, the slice that structures our perception, is precisely what is *not* there. In a sense, however, this visualization of absence follows the sentence's directive to the letter, as "Imagine" invokes a nonexistence or unreality that, as we have seen, is what the fantastic is designed to name.

As a kind of fantasy of the fantastic itself, these lines also figure the temporal extension of signification that we've been exploring in the "endlessness" shared between couture and its communication. Imaginatively spatializing the temporality to which Barthes alludes in a footnote to this comment—he specifies that "We understand *signification*, not in the current sense of signified, but in the active sense of process"—the "endless garment" returns us to time itself as the thread stitching together the abstract process of meaning's fashioning and our experience of the physical world's concrete materiality (*Fashion* 42). In this, Fashion embodies Todorov's account of the fantastic as a literary genre, in which narrative time prolongs the experience of uncertainty and ambiguity about the reality of a world that essentially exists only as a construction of words. If this sense of extended process and passing time is precisely *not* how Barthes describes Fashion and its "euphoria," which derives "from the fact that it produces a rudimentary, formless novel without temporality," it shows us what is at stake in this insistence on the timely work of notation—namely, the rejuvenation of the practice of language to attend to the moment-by-moment fabrication of the material world's fantastic significance (*Fashion* 262). To say this attention is as unending as the garment itself is not only to maintain its relentless extension and the continual reiteration of the cuts that distinguish the patterns of its shape. It is also to recognize that these cuts don't really end anything but rather paradoxically constitute the continuous persistence if not quite the persistent continuity of its appearance—what we have seen Barthes call the "real vestimentary code."

Barthes's more general comments on the very idea of a "real code" in an earlier chapter (tellingly entitled "Between Things and Words") develop this sense of temporality in a way that affirms my opening gesture toward *The Fashion System* as a kind of manual for the practice of language we are working to learn. Using the highway code or the stoplight as an example, he compares the experience of "learn[ing] the highway code in an empirical (extra-linguistic) manner" that would entail "repeatedly associating the green with going and the red with stopping," on the one hand, and "learn[ing] the meaning of these signals from an instructor [whose] speech relays the real code," on the other (*Fashion* 29-30). One of the main differences in these signifying activities involves the fact that "the real code presupposes a practical communication based on apprenticeship and thus on a certain duration" while the "terminological system implies an immediate communication (it does not need time to develop, the word economizes the duration of apprenticeship) but one that is conceptual" (*Fashion* 32-33).[23] The differing emphasis on duration indexes the tendency of speech and language to disconnect us from the practical, time-bound character of our communicative experiences by sheltering us in the "immediacy" of the "conceptual." However, the common appeal to an "apprenticeship" in both these situations echoes the implicit association with the practical, material work of tailoring we just examined—as well as the more fanciful training in the magic of language we discussed in the last chapter—in a way that resists the link between words and instantaneous, "economized" comprehension.

We might even go so far as to say that the analysis in *The Fashion System* as a whole works to weave a sense of time and practical action back into our relationship to speech and language, a project that Barthes's comments in the book's foreword rather explicitly if also inadvertently support. Addressing the somewhat "belated" position of his "venture"—begun in 1957 but not published until 1967 after several "important works" in semiology had already appeared—Barthes characterizes *The Fashion System* as "a kind of slightly naïve window through which may be discerned, I hope, not the certainties of a doctrine, nor even the unvarying conclusions of an investigation, but rather the beliefs, the temptations, and the trials of an apprenticeship: wherein its meaning; hence, perhaps, its use" (*Fashion* ix–x). My initial, lazy impulse is to leave the clear resonances between his diction and the practical emphasis of my argument to speak for themselves, but the whole point is to underscore the extended linguistic labor that *The Fashion System* both displays and enables, the way that the image of "apprenticeship" denies any sense of accomplished linguistic or semiological mastery and instead implies an ongoing effort tracked by the punctuated rhythms moving us through "the beliefs, the temptations, and the trials" of using language. If Barthes's appeal to the book's "use" is as "a certain history of semiology," this history is as much the broader intellectual development of the field as it is the temporally extended and never finished employment of words to make the world mean.

Barthes gives us one concrete though admittedly "modest" sartorial example of a Fashion signification that preserves rather than abolishes this sense of time in "what Fashion calls the *transformation* (*the summer dustcoat which will become the autumn raincoat*)" (*Fashion* 291). Framing this phenomenon as "a certain solution to the conflict which constantly sets the order of transitive behavior in opposition to that of signs" (which is what my determination in bringing out the *work* of notation and signification has been aiming at), he describes how "through transformation, diachrony is introduced into the system" (*Fashion* 291). In this case, Fashion no longer ruthlessly denies the temporality of its significations by substituting a new look that completely obliterates that of the previous year. What we get instead is "a new 'doing'" in which "the language of fashion becomes a true fabricator" according to the sense I am trying to unearth and effect through my practical readings of Barthes's texts (*Fashion* 291). If the practical performance of this "doing" has been arguably most apparent in the intertexts that have made *The Fashion System* look something like a preparatory study for what he himself saw as his later, more "writerly" period, it is once again to preparation that I turn in order to cut this chapter off at what will nonetheless also be a point of continuity with the arguments that follow. In the rapturous meditations that comprise *Empire of Signs*, we thus find a closing but not conclusive collocation of the operative terms we have been using to disclose notation—work, time, division—mobilized in a sphere more obviously expressive of the ongoing, interminable practice that is ultimately at stake here.

For not only do these terms contribute centrally to what Barthes fantastically calls "a graphic mode of existing"; they do so most cogently in his discussion of Japanese meals, where "eating remains stamped with a kind of work or play which bears less on the transformation of the primary substance . . . than on the shifting and somehow inspired assemblage of elements whose order of selection is fixed by no protocol" (*Empire* 80, 12). One major implication of the echo between the emphasis on activity in this sentence and the notational work I have been exploring is the way that, however much we eat, we know that there will soon come a time when we must eat again, the continual maintenance demanded by our physical metabolism serving up an inexact metaphor for consciously supporting the persistent practice of language. And though the recurrent regeneration of our hunger isn't exactly what Barthes is talking about in this assertion of the playful work entailed by Japanese eating, the turn to the alimentary in these final moves is meant to keenly nourish my argument by converting the amnesiac cycles of Fashion into a rhythmic set of reminders to repeatedly renew our relationship to signification. That this transformative conclusion also involves the ramification of the probing work I have been tracking is, as we say in the West, just gravy. And Barthes might repeat his focus on "assemblage" a few lines later—"the entire *praxis* of alimentation being in the composition," he writes—but such fabrication is inseparable from separation itself (*Empire* 12).

The "order" presented by the "dinner tray" of the Japanese meal, for instance, "is destined to be undone, recomposed according to the rhythm of eating"—the caesura of the comma in that citation embodying the divide that links de- and reconstruction (*Empire* 11). More elaborately, the playful activity of "taking up here a pinch of vegetable, there of rice, and over there of condiment, here a sip of soup" also proceeds according to a cadenced chopping that extends the preparatory cuts constitutive of both "the only operation [the foodstuffs] have actually undergone" (rather than being cooked) and the visual presentation of the dinner tray itself with its "bowls, boxes, saucers, chopsticks, tiny piles of food, a little gray ginger, a few shreds of orange vegetable, a background of brown sauce" (*Empire* 12, 11). As these performative sequences offer a verbal version of Japanese food's punctuated pacing, they collect the disaggregation of ingredients whose erratic and shifting combination make each moment of the meal, in Barthes's fantastic language at least, a vibrant sensory experience of differential significance.[24] When he thus locates "the *living* (which does not mean *natural*) character of this food" in the fact that "by composing your choices, you yourself make what it is you eat," the vitality made available by the activity of "composing" has as much to do with the work of bringing these ingredients together as it does with that of taking them apart (*Empire* 12).

Whatever perversity attends my emphasis on splitting and separation in an analytical account so overtly committed to composition, it is only in order to draw out how the notational work I've been developing inheres in the very convergence (or is it divergence?) of those two activities. Barthes offers imagery that seems to address or at least substantiate my parenthetical question while also expanding the sense of temporality that sustains this mode of comestible consumption in his discussion of "cooked rice," which is "at once cohesive and detachable." He elaborates, "what comes to the table, dense and stuck together, comes undone at a touch of the chopsticks, as if division occurred only to produce still another [*encore*] irreducible cohesion" (*Empire* 12–14, 3:359). Locating the vital dialectic of composition in the realm of the inanimate and raising it beyond the particular domain of human subjectivity, the "contradiction of substance" Barthes parses here manifests itself according to the impersonal progress of time as the French adverb *encore* expressive of both persistence and recurrence succinctly indexes the force that links one moment to the next by distinguishing them from each other. This temporal impersonality has the effect of disarticulating the work of notation from any essential dependence on a perceiving, speaking agent, establishing it instead as a more generalized condition to which our arduously discriminating practice of language gives us explicit, fantastic access. We thus find time working without an obvious human subject in Barthes's subsequent commentaries on the stew the Japanese call *sukiyaki*, "this food—and this is its originality—unites in a single time that of its fabrication and that of its consumption," and on tempura, the fried food that "has for its envelope nothing but time, the time (itself extremely tenuous, moreover) which has solidified it" (*Empire* 22, 25). As a result, the "dinner tray" we just discussed, which "was a motionless tableau at the start," transforms into "a workbench or chessboard, the space not of seeing but of doing—of *praxis* or play" (*Empire* 11). The doing of this practice that I have been at pains to figure as the determinate work of noting finds a final illustration in "the manner of a (specifically Japanese) graphic artist set down in front of a series of pots who, at one and the same time, knows and hesitates" (*Empire* 11). Protractedly performing time's operative negativity, hesitation cuts into our attention to cut out a momentary notation. Indeed, it is perhaps *hesitation* that is the most elementary action out of which notation constitutes itself, the delay that holds off or holds up the occurrence of meaning long enough for us to work with or on it.

Accordingly, there is perhaps no "final illustration" of how notation works, which suggests a synthesizing, totalizing accomplishment that would lay all this incisive effort to rest. And I don't think it's by chance that the very next book Barthes publishes after *The Fashion System*, in the same year as *Empire of Signs*, is that deliberately cut-up text *S/Z*, which is about barely more than cutting itself—as we will see in the next chapter. If this initiates Barthes's increasing use of the fragment as a rhetorical form as opposed to the attempts at discursive unity in his works of the 1960s, it simultaneously extends the theoretical content of those works as we've been working through it here. In the resonant argument that, as one of the key contemporary commentators on Barthes, Claude Coste makes about the place of the word *travail* in the closing lines of *Roland Barthes by Roland Barthes*, he allows me to splice a distinguished and distinguishing voice at and as the integrating ending of this chapter's wide-ranging attempts at critical coherence and also projects my points into their own writerly future: "as long as he works, the writer [*l'écrivain*] coincides with himself, apprehends himself as a happy totality (I am he who writes) and holds off the moment of turning around as long as possible—this moment of bad distance that constitutes the work into an oeuvre and the subject into an author [*qui constitue l'oeuvre en oeuvre et le sujet en auteur*]" (44-45).[25]

7. Untitled (October 2021 to May 2023). Author's handmade collage.

The Value of Literary Reflexion

[CHAPTER THREE]

Up to this point, readers could be forgiven if they have found themselves thinking that literature occupies only an abstract place in my account of Barthes's work, an ancillary ideal to be mined for writerly magic or metaphorical description of more obviously material cultural texts. As we have seen, literature certainly offers him intellectual resources for his varied critical endeavors, but it also receives its own trenchant analyses in forms both general and particular. The first pages of Barthes's very first book center themselves, in fact, on the distinctive category of literature as such in terms that will help launch the more focused engagement of the literary as a practical engine of the fantastic in the next two chapters. In *Writing Degree Zero* from 1953, that is, he announces his interest in "something other than [literature's] content and its individual form, something which defines its limits and imposes it as Literature" (*WDZ* 2). The work of the book consists of elaborating both the conceptual and historical silhouettes of this "something," which he describes further as "a set of signs unrelated to the ideas, the language [*la langue*] or the style, and setting out to give definition, within the body of every possible mode of expression, to the utter separateness of a ritual language [*un langage rituel*]" (*WDZ* 2, 1:171). Such a "set of signs" is what he uses the word *writing* to index, a helpful term that institutes and formalizes the delicate difference between the two French words for "language" on which Barthes founds Literature's distinctive identity. Where *la langue* refers to the system of verbal communication shared by a cultural and/or geographic community, *le langage* names the more general ability to use symbols in an organized and meaningful way. Endowing the latter with a "ritual" quality (which faintly recalls the magically performative speech of the witch), Barthes frames Literature as a practical and self-aware project of verbal manipulation whose purposeful performance is further emphasized by the suggestion of activity in the term *writing*. Literature thus comes to be defined as a category of language use that reflects on itself and its own symbolic and systematic properties, a practice of verbal reflexion that it imparts to its readers and that builds on and through the cutting work of notation we explored in the last chapter.[1]

Though the framing of Literature in these reflexive terms might at first seem to sequester it in its own self-referential sphere of linguistic autonomy, the entire project of *Writing Degree Zero* is aimed at tracing the history of "writing"—the history of the "Signs of Literature"—in a way that makes its argument particularly valuable for our discussion of the fantastic coincidence of the literary and the lived. By locating Literature's historicity, its worldliness, in the different stances it takes toward its own status as a special, "ritual" form of language, Barthes suggests that the determinative distinction is less one between Literature and History than one between mindful and mindless language use. Playing once again on the *langue/langage* differentiation, he writes, "A language [*langue*] and a style are data prior to all problematics of language [*langage*], they are the natural product of Time and of the person as a biological entity," what he calls "blind forces" on the next page (*WDZ* 13–14, 1:179). In contrast, "a mode of writing is an act of historical solidarity . . . it is the relationship between creation and society, the literary language [*le langage littéraire*] transformed by its social purpose [*destination sociale*], form considered as a human intention and thus linked to the great crises of History" (*WDZ* 14, 1:179–80). Here, the more abstract conception of language as a general system of signification provides entrée into concrete historical experience; indeed, *le langage littéraire* becomes the site of historical commitment to the extent that it allows for "human intention."[2] As an echo of the previous chapter's argument, I want to insist on reading this last phrase to indicate the very real effort entailed in consciously or reflectively *working with* the lexical, grammatical, and generic structures offered by the writer's *langue* and culture to hone the existential configuration of history's lived experience.

We will see Barthes execute this work of reflective literary articulation with greatest acuity when he maps the readerly actualization of this writerly practice in what is undoubtedly his most extensively developed account of the life-literature nexus—namely, the concertedly cut-up Balzac commentary he gathers under the split siglum *S/Z*. But his earlier arguments anticipate the indeterminate relationship between art and reality that zigzags through the later work in a way that splices the two books together and allows them to reverberate with each other across the very slash of the *Z* connecting their titles. In what we could read as an inaugural formulation of literary language's reflexive significance, he thus posits writing as "an ambiguous reality: on the one hand, it unquestionably arises from a confrontation of the writer with the society of his time; on the other, from this social aim [*finalité sociale*], it refers the writer back, by a sort of tragic reversal, to the sources, that is to say, the instruments of his creation" (*WDZ* 16, 1:180-81). Functioning as an encounter with both "the society of his time" and "the instruments of his creation," writing here names a chiasmic dynamic in which it is impossible to distinguish social life from its linguistic formulation, an intertwining in which to engage with language is also to engage with the historical world (and vice versa). This chiasmic intertwining is what the word *reflexion*, with the crisscrossing *X* of its variant spelling, is meant to comprehend: not the unilateral mirroring of a preconstituted world in words but the ruminative, revelatory process wherein language and life institute and organize each other. And if, at this point, the impossibility of direct intervention into society frames the inescapable mediation of language as a "tragic" condition, we should recall that this is also very much the conflicted position in which Barthes finds himself in *Mythologies* (whose individual essays he was just beginning to produce at the time of *Writing Degree Zero*'s publication). His portrayal of writing as "an ambiguous reality" thus seems to prefigure the reconciliation of language and life that chapter 1 developed in his extended and varied recourse to a specific vocabulary of efficacious verbal magic at the same time as it also speaks to the more general experiential ambiguity that we are exploring under the banner of the fantastic.

Making these textual connections is meant to shore up the intellectual formation I have been fashioning, which understands our experience of the world as a function of—not separate from—the operations of signification, which perceives linguistic construction as what allows us to have a world in the first place, and which approaches literature as the thoughtful attempt to give that world significance by making it overtly though by no means instantly or conclusively legible. This is the basic frame that I am drawing from *Writing Degree Zero*, though the Sartrean-Marxist context of Barthes's relatively youthful intellectual intervention keeps him from fully unfolding the worldly linguistic reflexion that literature affords. The conceptual space from which Barthes initiates his early account of writing roots the language of social commitment in the more exploratory and emergent terminology of "Literary Semiology" (to use the title of his eventual chair at the Collège de France) that *S/Z* pursues with particular perspicacity.[3] In the first lines, to begin answering the question that titles the book's initial chapter ("What Is Writing?"), he thus asserts, "Now every Form is also a Value [*Valeur*], which is why there is room, between a language [*langue*] and a style, for another formal reality: writing. Within any literary form, there is a general choice of tone, of ethos, if you like, and this is precisely where the writer shows himself clearly as an individual because this is where he commits himself" (*WDZ* 13, 1:179). Here, I am as interested in the complex and counterintuitive interaction between the sociality of writing and the *engagée* individuality of the writer as I am in the word that evidently enables it: "Value." Significantly, value opens up writing's empirically ambiguous "formal reality" (which is to say, the schematized form by which historical reality comes to be recognizable as such) to the extent that it involves a differential operation or a reflective process of comparison. And this comparison is not just, indeed not even principally, with the phenomena of language and style; the conscious "ethos" by which Barthes characterizes writing is able to supplement the other components of the literary and give shape to the world because the paradoxically individualizing "general choice of tone" is necessarily defined by its relationship with all the other choices the writer could have made. As he puts it on the next page, "the choice of a human attitude . . . links the form of his utterance, which is at once normal and singular, to the vast History of the Others [*la vaste Histoire d'autrui*]" (*WDZ* 14, 1:179). The suggestion of historical distance makes the link being asserted here subtly contradictory, especially since it is not clear whether that final, magisterial phrase refers to those with similar or those with different "human attitudes." The answer is both, I think: a position that underscores writerly value as what lets us encounter and even commit to the world as a meaningful, intelligible phenomenon by forestalling our immediate identification of it—by putting us in touch, rather, with the differentiating otherness on which signification as such depends.

Barthes's early translator and interpreter Annette Lavers brings this meaning-making process into sharper focus when she reads his statement in protosemiological terms. Noting the distinctions operative in his discussion (though she limits herself to writing's difference from language and style), she writes, "Barthes' structural presentation shows that the notion of value, despite its dominant ethical connotation here, is also used in the Saussurean sense" (as it is, she points out, in *Mythologies* as well).[4] The sense she is referring to is one of the most powerful and perplexing ideas in Saussure's linguistics and has to do with the fact that the meaning of any sign is determined by its implicit interaction with other, similar signs in a particular language or specific semiotic system. As Barthes explains in *Elements of Semiology*, which was published together with *Writing Degree Zero* in the latter's 1965 paperback reissue, this determination is distinct from the signifier-signified relationship on which we focused in the last chapter: value "tackle[s] the sign, no longer by way of its 'composition,' but of its 'setting' [*ses 'entours'*]"—speaks not to the internal components of the signifier and the signified but to the place that their connection has among comparable signs in a larger linguistic landscape (*Semiology* 54, 2:669). It refers, that is, to a sign's position in a shifting network of related terms that complement and contextualize any particular signification, any particular signifier-signified relationship, to establish a meaning through a fundamentally comparative process. Another way to put this is to say that value accompanies the signifier-signified relationship that associates a sound with a concept and situates this signification within a larger system or network where it receives a particular meaning.[5] Something like the abstract "form" of meaning as such or what linguist Paul J. Thibault describes as "a meaning-making potential," value "in the Saussurean sense" thus names the general structure of differential relation by which significance is produced.[6] And while we will return to the baldly financial facet of this word—the economic exchange of a narrative in Balzac's *Sarrasine* being a central part of the reading in *S/Z*—the speculative payoff of its introduction here inheres for now in the implicit link between this explicitly relational articulation of meaning and the "ethical connotations" to which Lavers alludes. What I mean is that the self-consciously comparative, differential manner of making meaning that Barthes is describing comprises its own kind of linguistic, literary "ethos," its own kind of practical approach to the world, which this chapter finds in what I have been calling reflexion.

My choice to spell the linguistic practice animating the central stretch of the book in this specific way is intended to keep the comparative operation of value at the forefront of my discussion. My desire is not only that the less standard "reflexion" will be constantly shadowed by its more customary counterpart, allowing this word to actively, if perhaps a little affectedly, practice what it preaches. But I also want to be able to capitalize on the expanded network of associations made available by what the dictionary tells me is this chiefly British spelling (borrowed, appropriately enough, from French and its Latin roots). That is, in a way that "reflection" doesn't, "reflexion" branches into *reflex/reflexive*, with suggestions of both the self-referential and the automatic, as well as *reflect/reflective* and their senses of contemplation, exhibition, and even exchange—as if it names and exhibits in a word the kind of habitually pensive practice that literature helps us make more broadly manifest in the world. As perhaps the most explicit illustration of the reflexion I am exploring and exploiting, these comments describe that practice as the necessarily partial invocation of the infinite virtual network in which any term is enmeshed and from which it receives its meaning. (Thibault puts it in other, resonant phrasing when he describes how value "is produced in and through the *work* whereby a term is positioned in a given field of relations—systemic, textual, contextual, intertextual.")[7]

This profligate activation of verbal value as such also plots the intellectual grafting by which language finds itself linked up with life—but not in any facile analogy that would imply a direct correlation with the aspects of the world words are meant to represent. Rather, the emphasis that Barthes's explanation of value places on the sign's "surroundings," to translate his French more literally, opens up a particularly expansive understanding of signification that conceives the sign's worldly situation as included in the network that reciprocally determines its sense: as Thibault states, "the value-producing relations which are internal to the organization of language are themselves the means through which meanings are constructed in relation to what lies 'outside' language."[8] This is to think the word-world relationship not by way of a signifier-signified paradigm but via the complementary and mutually determinative relationships among different signs. In other words, the world takes on value and significance to the extent that it is quite literally implicated in the differential dynamic on which meaning depends, to the extent that we "use the categories of the language system to construe order, pattern, and meaning in the phenomena of experience."[9] As the common comparative structure by which the intelligibility of both verbal signification and lived experience is constituted, value thus indexes the homological relation between word and world that literature ritually animates, which is also to say the gap through which they reflect each other. Turning to *S/Z* (as well as, in the end, to an early discussion of Proust) will make this claim both more concrete and more explicitly literary as Barthes's captivating reading explores the literal value of studying literature as the existential extension of the reflexive network by which an aesthetic text fantastically formulates the world.

* * *

S/Z begins the ritual of its own literary reflexions with the incisive title of its opening "divagation," to use the aptly knife-life term of Richard Howard's that I've also borrowed for my collages (which begs the question, *Divagation from what?*): "EVALUATION" (3). Preceding more obviously Barthesian labels like INTERPRETATION and CONNOTATION that head up the next few divagations, EVALUATION asserts the foundational place of value in his discourse in a way that immediately introduces the comparative space in and through which our own reflexive linguistic practice takes place. He thus commences his discussion not from the well-known paradigm of the readerly and writerly texts but with the deviation (the "divagation") of his project from the great structuralist dream of finding a key to all narrative mythologies: "to see all the world's stories (and there have been ever so many) within a single structure" (*S/Z* 3). In contrast, his strategy will be "to restore each text, not to its individuality, but to its function, making it cohere [*le faire recueillir*], even before we talk about it, by the infinite paradigm of difference, subjecting it from the outset to a basic typology, to an evaluation" (*S/Z* 3, 3:121). If we are about to follow him to the "basic typology" of the readerly and writerly, it is only on the basis of another, even more primary evaluation composed of the relational, differential operation that underwrites the operation of reflexion as such. To observe this is not only to place *S/Z* on the bleeding edge of poststructuralism; it is also to expand—and expand on—the apparent contradiction between the sense of integration or unity evoked by the task of "making [a text] cohere" and "the infinite paradigm of difference" by which that task is supposed to be achieved. That is, Barthes imagines the structured coalescence suggested by "coherence" as a function of (or at least dependent on) coming apart, an operation that the French verb *recueillir*—to reap or gather—signifies in its implicit combination of both hacking and harvesting, both cutting and collecting. In terms that speak almost too clearly to my collage work, we could say that what Barthes wants to collect in *S/Z* is nothing other than the comparative cuts that create or instigate a meaningful network of significations.

Indeed, this is the momentum driving the statements he goes on to make: "Our evaluation can be linked only to a practice, and this practice is that of writing. On the one hand, there is what it is possible to write, and on the other, what it is no longer possible to write: what is within the practice of the writer and what has left it: which texts would I consent to write (to re-write), to desire, to put forth as a force in this world of mine? What evaluation finds is precisely this value: what can be written (rewritten) today: the *writerly*" (*S/Z* 4). If the writerly has come to be a familiar term for the infinite play of the signifier, the length of the quotation here is meant to help us locate the potential for that play in the value staked out by Barthes's insistently reflective syntax. Codified most clearly in the "on the one hand . . . and on the other" construction, this comparative composition characterizes almost every clause and positions the writerly in—or as—the collective space between his articulations. More than this, in the question that brazenly links the writerly to the fantastic continuity of literature and life—"which texts would I consent to write (to re-write), to desire, to put forth as a force in this world of mine?"—he doubles down on this dynamic and underscores, in the list of comparable, synonymous infinitives, the power and energy produced by the way words reflect on each other. As he thus gestures toward the role played by linguistic value in wielding the worldly textual "force" that the cadenced beat of the line's phrasing rhythmically exhibits, he amplifies the early argument about literary language in *Writing Degree Zero* and locates verbal reflexion as the writerly activity that life and literature share. In this context, his subsequent claim that "the goal of literary work (of literature as work) [*l'enjeu du travail littéraire (de la littérature comme travail)*] is to make the reader no longer a consumer, but a producer of the text" extends beyond the words on the page and effectively conditions the fantastic elaboration of what can no longer really be called our "extra-literary" experience (*S/Z* 4, 3:122).

As a quite literal reflexion of the narrative that Balzac plots, this cutting literary conditioning is what the notations in *S/Z* work out. Accordingly, when Barthes explains the idiosyncratic, "step-by-step" reading method he pursues in his commentary on "Sarrasine," he figures it as "a renewal of the entrances to the text" that is motivated by a desire "to remain attentive to the plural of a text" (12–13). We have remained assiduously attentive to conceptions of textual instability and the plurality of meanings since *S/Z* appeared in 1970, but I find an untapped surplus of significance in the dual images of "entrance" and "renewal," particularly their suggestion of both penetration and restoration that casts his notations as a fortifying formalization of the text's own constitutive, comparative hollows. (Later figuring the text as "a piece of Valenciennes lace," he emphasizes its fabrication out of an interwoven series of holes: "the progress of each thread is marked with a pin which holds it and is gradually moved forward" [*S/Z* 160]). Implied here is the way each "entrance" has the effect of desubstantializing the text, of excavating echo chambers in which the various significations and interrelationships of its words can resound and in which we as readers might be able, in more ways than one, to reflect. In other words, this reading strategy aims not at a meaning but at its possibility—at verbal value. Furthermore, the original French phrases this vacuous reinforcement as "*renouveler les entrées*," in which the echo between that verb and *nouvelle*—the specific generic form of *Sarrasine* itself—stages the readerly engagement of value as its own short novel (3:128). We will see this novel semiotics most obviously when *S/Z* leads us to one of Barthes's early essays on Proust, but in this case, it simply grants each lexia a meaningful linguistic life of its own, carves out its place in a network of significations mobilized by but not completely coextensive with that of the larger text.

Such *nouvelle*-istic fortification is further disclosed by what we should call the opening lexia, a phrase that indicates both their position toward the beginning of Barthes's sequential analysis and their reflective expansion of our worldly experience. The multiple registers of this expansive reflexion come out with quiet force to encompass both the constitution of subjectivity and the social configuration with which that subjectivity is entangled as soon as Barthes introduces the title of Balzac's tale. In its distinctive morphology, which plays such a pivotal role in his argument, the name "Sarrasine" folds back on itself in the mirror image between the *sar*

The Value of Literary Reflexion 85

and the *ras*, leaving the tail of the "-ine" as a "specifically feminine" form of a linguistically instituted interiority that the "in" intimates (*S/Z* 17). The purpose of this excessive, improper onomastic segmentation is not only to highlight the entrance into the network of gendered oppositions that we will touch on momentarily. By subverting the literal integrity of the story's principal name and its indication of a similarly integrated person or character, it is also an incipient incision into the more individual or subjective implications of the value of reflexion. Though the full sense of this move will only come out as our discussion progresses, Barthes offers a preliminary illustration of its drift in the arguably fatuous explanation for choosing this particular text, which immediately precedes his commentary on the title: "All I know," he writes in a long parenthesis, "is that for some time I have wanted to make a complete analysis of a short text and that the Balzac story was brought to my attention by an article by Jean Reboul, who in turn is supposed to have been inspired by George Bataille's reference; and thus I was caught up in this 'series' whose scope I was to discover by means of the text itself [*par le texte lui-même*]" (*S/Z* 16, 3:131). While Barthes's critical desire locates him in a circuit of readerly exchanges (the nodes, we should note, are all verbal entities), he also finds this circuit articulated by *Sarrasine lui-même*, the social network of his intellectual life fantastically conjoining with the thematic and semiotic network of this text. Moreover, the importantly inescapable masculine gender of the French reflexive pronoun opens up space for the possibility that it is Sarrasine the character, in his constitution out of nothing but signifiers, with which Barthes is also fantastically identifying. The forceful interpretive torsion I'm applying to his words here is meant to hyperbolically highlight the extent to which his reflexions on his reading are themselves a reflexion of that reading, the linguistic machinations of Balzac's literary text allowing Barthes to verbalize the very codes by which he also realizes the *nouvelles* of his life and self.

We can illustrate this more specifically by looking at the way the codes Barthes uses to schematize "Sarrasine's" infinite textual complex display a fundamental and fantastic ambiguity according to which it is impossible for us to tell whether they originate in the language of Balzac's text or the experiences of Barthes's life. Take, for example, his comment on Sarrasine's name regarding the "additional connotation, that of femininity, which will be obvious to any French-speaking person, since that language automatically takes the final 'e' as a specifically feminine linguistic property" (*S/Z* 17). This observation leads him to designate the "semic code" that will collect and classify the various connotations evoked by the text's diverse signifiers, which is what makes the insistence on the "obvious" and the "automatic" in these lines so curious. As it is language itself that is operating automatically and obviously here, these terms reflect an otherwise unreflective signifying situation from the life of "any French-speaking person" that seems to be what allows them to grasp the significance of this word or this name within Balzac's story. (Indeed, it is partly in this sense that the code "has always been *already* read, seen, done, experienced" [*S/Z* 20].) On the other hand, Barthes almost immediately goes on to claim that "Femininity (connoted) is a signifier which will occur in several places in the text; it is a shifting element which can combine with other similar elements to create characters, ambiances, shapes, and symbols"—suggesting that the "automatic" legibility of the "final 'e'" as an indication of the feminine also comes from its place within the more explicitly elaborated signifying network established by written texts like the one we are reading (*S/Z* 17). But the "combining" he is referring to here need not—and does not—stop at the border of the story world, making connoted femininity another place where the signifying network of Balzac's text links up with that of Barthes's life.[10] If this is, in the end, an illustration of one of Barthes's most important claims in *S/Z*—"the basis for all reality, which is art, whence flow truth and facts alike," as he puts it later—allowing these two assertions to reflect on each other suggests a more complicated dynamic than the unidirectional determination implied in the word "flow" (*S/Z* 167). Recalling the "ambiguous reality" of writing in *Writing Degree Zero*, the flow seems to go both ways, in a mutually reinforcing network that doesn't so much cross the putative boundary separating art and life as compose their interconnected, chiasmic constitution.

The homology that organizes this complex relationship is what a chance but fitting reference to the very network of the fantastic we will soon be exploring in Barthes's discussion reflects. ("But what is chance?" he asks regarding the five codes' appearance in the first lines of the story [*S/Z* 18].) "The old man's *fantastic* quality," he writes with italic emphasis, "has no semantic value unless the exceeding of human limits, which is one of the primitive 'components' of the word (one of its other 'names'), can recur elsewhere [*peut réessaimer ailleurs*]" (*S/Z* 93, 3:196). Though the focus here remains on intratextual references, the way these lines emphasize the piecemeal, fragmentary construction of a literary character in particular and literary meaning in general underscores the comparative or reflective dynamic that Barthes's reading brings to light. More specifically, the original French "*réessaimer*," which means "to spread" or "to swarm" and usually applies to bees, figures significance in terms of a collection made from numerous individual entities that assemble in expansive and fluid ways—that work together *to the extent that* they are dispersed. Moreover, in a comment seventy pages earlier on the practice of citation (which we will take up more bullishly in the next chapter), he describes "the distri-

The Value of Literary Reflexion 87

bution of a discontinuity ... the greater the syntagmatic distance between two data, the more skillful the narrative" (*S/Z* 22). The apian implication in this moment, however, echoes the "exceeding of human limits" by which Barthes is characterizing the fantastic here and hints that the proliferating "recurrences" by which potentially meaningful minutiae coalesce in a text is not necessarily cut off by the divide our human culture imposes, at least in the West, between signification and experience. But what fantastically extends from the signifying weave of a literary text to the significant texture of the world is not so much the content of this—or any—particular network as it is the network as such, the general operation of its diffuse and discontinuous construction. The ultimate reflexion between art and life, in other words, emerges in the scattered structure of recurrence itself, the differential systematics by which semantic value comes together.

Barthes brings these heady theoretical points back down to earth in the more material, or at least materialist, articulations he provides when he begins to leverage the economic valence of the idea of value in his larger account of "the reader's activity" (*S/Z* 92). Approaching this activity as a "struggle to name, to subject the sentences of the text to a semantic transformation," he describes the tension between the impulse "to yield to an expanding nomination" (to explore the various possible or implied connotations of a phrase) and the need "to return to these various substantive stations in order to create some constant form" (to settle on a stable, coherent meaning) (*S/Z* 92–93). What institutes and even animates this tension is the fact that "the exchange value of a seme, its ability to participate in a thematic economy, depends on its repetition" (*S/Z* 93). While the key role played by "repetition" here echoes the emphasis on "recurrence," the added imagery of "exchange value" brings out (metaphoric) substitution or replacement as the mediating function in the readerly struggle between the multiplication and consolidation of meaning. The result is literary meaning as a process of unstable and ongoing semantic trading, a "constant form" of verbal exchange that finds its paradigm in the monetary transactions characteristic of modern capitalism. Indeed, such a commercial perspective is one of the places from which his specific understanding of linguistic value derives: for instance, he paraphrases Saussure in appealing to the functioning of a "five-franc note" in the programmatic discussion he gives of value in *Elements of Semiology* (*Semiology* 55). *Sarrasine* enacts this economic thinking of value most overtly in the contract between the story's narrator and the Countess de Rochefide who wants to learn the fantastic secret behind the Lanty family fortune and the strange old man at the party—"tit for tat: a moment of love in exchange for a good story," to quote the translation and its fortuitous, mammary pun (*S/Z* 86). The contract is an explicit if not an entirely real-world example of a kind of open-ended literary form having extraliterary purchase, a model for the fantastic reflexion between art and life based on shared value structures that we are working out.

Barthes thus describes what he calls "the theory that *Sarrasine* offers as a fable," which he elevates beyond this singular text by positing it as "the question raised, perhaps, by every narrative," asking, "*What should the narrative be exchanged for? What is the narrative 'worth'?*" (*S/Z* 89). In their slight difference from each other, the two questions allow us to refresh our understanding of value as a concept: whereas the first focuses on the particular item to trade for the narrative, the second raises the level of abstraction and asks more generally about equivalence as such, about the very principle of exchange. But what makes *Sarrasine* so useful or so *valuable* for Barthes is the way that, in the story, the two questions come to reflect or be equivalent to each other. Since "the young woman, upset by the *narrated* castration, will withdraw from the transaction without honoring her pledge," the exchange is never completed, a situation in which the worth or value of the tale becomes nothing more than the exchange of its own telling—the exchange of its own . . . exchange (*S/Z* 89). What strikes me first about this situation is the extent to which the literary performance not only retains its abstract value but, without the sexual act to complement and eclipse the narrative one, is also revealed to involve its own particular form of concrete experience. And what strikes me second is how the involution of the narrative exchange onto itself realizes the monetary model of value, imitates the way money functions in our world as value's most manifest materialization.

Barthes draws out the implications of this observation when he stresses that "narrative is determined not by a desire to narrate but by a desire to exchange: it is a *medium of exchange* [*un valant-pour*], an agent, a currency, a gold standard" (*S/Z* 90, 3:193). As part of his attempt to counter the understanding of *Sarrasine* as a set of "nested narratives," which would distinguish the evening at the Lanty mansion as the constraining frame for Sarrasine's adventure in Rome, the emphasis on exchange sees them as two homologous sides of the same narrative coin, two interpenetrating instances of a common "medium," of a generalized "value-for" open to, actually constituted by, continuous conversion or translation. This line of analysis is thematized in Balzac's story as the indeterminate origin of the Lanty fortune, which Barthes discusses in terms of the transition from a feudal economy where land secures wealth in a stable, materialized form to an industrialized bourgeois economy where the value of assets has no basis other than the "limitless process of equivalences" that money, so to speak, represents (*S/Z* 40). The apotheosis of value as such, money fantastically forecloses any possibility of a stark distinction between signification and material reality, indexing instead the empty space through which they are constantly exchanged. Though it might be castration that embodies this emptiness most flagrantly, money is what helps us see it also in the more commonplace commerce of everyday life. (It is not for nothing that Barthes points to the way "this money is as empty as being-castrated" (S/Z 40).) In other words, as a very real kind of signification, money practically reveals the quotidian coincidence of linguistic operation and lived experience.

* * *

These monetary metaphors also secure our entry into the more general dynamic that animates the whole of Barthes's argument—namely, the transgression of antithesis that figures this intertwining of life and literature more abstractly. In his reading of S/Z, Fredric Jameson frames this transgression in terms of "Sarrasine's" genre and tellingly characterizes it as "only one of a cycle of what we could call 'fantastic tales,'" its appearance just a few weeks before the more obviously supernatural *La Peau de chagrin* with which it came for a moment to be collected as a "*conte philosophique*" adding historical, generic support to the more practical, worldly claims of my argument.[11] Jameson contrasts this classification with the more assertively realist collection of "*scènes de la vie parisienne*" under which Balzac later integrated *Sarrasine* into the larger organization of *La Comédie humaine*. At stake in these taxonomic subtleties is whether to read the tale in terms of the opposition it sets up between the modern, rationalized capitalism of Parisian money and gossip and Rome's *ancien régime* of popish patronage and castrating passion or by way of the more "philosophical, metaphysical, or mystical pretensions" taken up by the convergence of life and art in Sarrasine's hermeneutic quest.[12] What the shifts in Balzac's sorting suggest, however, is the potential fungibility of these categories, the way that, as we have just seen, the tale's social realism and its artistic mysticism function as reflexive ciphers for each other. Within this context, we will be able to appreciate how Barthes's critique of literary realism also mirrors a kind of real literariness that, like the crisscrossing of *langage* and social life in *Writing Degree Zero*, refuses any sense of antithesis between the terms at play here.[13]

For this is the very place from which *Sarrasine* begins when its first line announces a coincidence of reality and fantasy: "*I was deep in one of those daydreams* [*J'étais plongé dans une de ces rêveries profondes*]," as Barthes quotes it (S/Z 17, 3:132). In a fashion we will see again, the speaking *I* installs itself in a rather unreal space that the intersection between waking life implied in "day" and the imaginary world of the "dream" parses with penetrating precision. Barthes initially overlooks the fantastic implications of this narrative mise-en-scène, focusing instead on the "vast symbolic structure" that this combination grounds and the "series of antitheses" that, as the content of both the narrator's reverie and the story itself, it launches. It is only when he offers further explanation of antithesis as "the battle between two plenitudes set ritually face to face like two fully armed warriors" (rather than the "complementary, dialectical movement" of ordinary "paradigmatic opposites") that he emphasizes the narrator's transgressively liminal position between these fixed poles, a position he links to a set of explicitly fantastic references (S/Z 28). Concentrating on the role that the body plays to contravene the division of antithesis (which La Zambinella climactically amplifies), Barthes writes how "it is at the level of the body that two *inconciliabilia* . . . are brought together, are made to touch, to mingle in the most amazing of figures in a composite substance (without *holding together*), here whimsical (the macédoine) and later chimerical (the arabesque created by the old man and the girl when seated side by side)" (S/Z 28). He expands on this strange coincidence of distinction and connection when he comments on the latter image in his analysis, borrowing vocabulary from the story itself to describe "the old man and the young woman, pressed close together into a single fantastic creature [*l'être fantastique*]" (S/Z 63, 3:171). His point is that the vitality of Mme de Rochefide's youth combines with the enervation of the castrato's old age to violate the traditional antithesis of life and death.[14]

But just a few pages earlier, when this violation is embodied in the animated decrepitude of the old man himself, Barthes repeats his appeal to the fantastic as a linguistic category in his discussion of the supplementary rhetoric of painting or portraiture that figures the transgression of the life-death antithesis as also that of life-art. Specifically referring to the lexia "*on his bluish lips a fixed and frozen smile, implacable and mocking, like a skull*," he writes, "The fixed, frozen smile leads to the image of stretched skin (as in plastic surgery), of life lacking that minimum skin which is the very stuff of life. In the old man, life is endlessly copied, but the copy always offers the *less* of castration . . . (SEM. Fantastic [*Fantastique*]. Out of the world)" (S/Z 60, 3:168).[15] The explanatory imagery of "plastic surgery" and the emphasis on the "copying" of life refigure the deathliness suggested by the "fixed, frozen smile" and point to an aesthetic or mimetic version of this vibrant morbidity, a kind of living form of representation marked out by the fantastic. Thus, in the early version of S/Z's argument that Barthes wrote in 1967 and published as the essay "Masculine, Feminine, Neuter," he asserts that "the work of art and la Zambinella coincide exhaustively: . . . it is very precisely because la Zambinella is a fake woman—or, more exactly, an imitation woman—that she is fully a work of art"

(*MFN* 154). This idea receives a more rigorous, which is to say, more semiotic, schematization when he reformulates it three years later in regard to the story's painterly presentation of the old man's appearance: the descriptive portrait, he writes, "is a scene made up of blocks of meaning, at once varied, repeated, and discontinuous (outlined); out of the arrangement of these blocks comes a diagram of the body, not its copy (in which the portrait remains totally subject to a linguistic structure, language recognizing only diagrammatical analogies: analogies in the etymological sense: proportions)" (*S/Z* 61). His point, of course, is to resist any sense of a straightforwardly analogical realism, which he replaces with a kind of homological thinking whose correspondences are structural, not substantial. The punctuated emphasis on "the diagram" with its "blocks of meaning" excavates the fantastic signifying network that coordinates the reflexion between representation and reality by imparting a shared system of value to them.

Barthes provides a further, even more thorough-going demonstration of this reflective phenomenon, one he extends all the way into his own historical world, in his wide-ranging analysis of Vien's portrait of Adonis to which the story turns at this moment as a literalization of the painterly rhetoric we've been examining. Analyzing the alabaster globe lamp that lights the painting, he makes an altogether peculiar claim: "The light diffused by the lamp is outside the picture; however, metonymically, it becomes the interior light of the painted scene: alabaster (soft, white)—a conducting rather than an emitting substance, a luminous, cold reflection—this boudoir alabaster is in fact the moon which illuminates the young shepherd" (*S/Z* 69–70). Prefiguring the metonymical magic by which this fictional Adonis becomes the inspiration for Anne-Louis Girodet's painting of Endymion—more on which anon—Barthes here imagines the transgression of the interior/exterior boundary created by the painting's frame through what at first seems like a direct reflexion between the moon in the painting and the lamp in the story world. But this transgressive metonymy actually takes place through a mirroring of the "conducting rather than emitting" quality of their luminosity. The art-life reflection here is, in reality, double: a reflection of the "luminous, cold reflection" shared by the moon and the lamp. What is being reflected is their similar divergence from other, more immediate light sources (like the sun or a candle), a shared distinction that endows them with a similar value within a larger structure of significance that comprehends both the painting and the world within which that painting exists.

If we have just fleetingly seen the intercalation of these two registers go by the name of the fantastic in reference to the old man in the story, this is no less the case here, for the early lexia that lays the groundwork for the metaphorical equivalence of lamp and moon is governed by a semic code he explicitly characterizes as "Fantastic" and explains once again as "what is outside the limits of the human: supernatural, extra-terrestrial" (S/Z 24). Significantly, his elaboration of this supernature once again embodies the very operation of representation: "The moon is the *nothingness* of light, warmth reduced to its deficiency: it illuminates by mere reflection without itself being an origin; thus, it becomes the luminous emblem of the castrato" (S/Z 24). The emphasis on nothingness that allows the moon to stand in for—if not, in its way, to reflect—the castrato is also what makes it almost a materialization of metaphor as such, a shining emblem of the emblematic. It is not just a relay of or an empty reference to an original reality but also the empty reality or, better, the real emptiness of relay itself. Such fantastically real emptiness is ultimately what is at stake in the emphasis I am placing on the linguistic practice of reflexion, which, as this chapter concludes, I will exfoliate in terms that speak more directly to the literary construction of subjectivity. In "Masculine, Feminine, Neuter," Barthes forecasts this point in more broadly artistic terms, writing that "the whole novella brings out what we might call the dialectic of Pygmalion (a theme expressly cited by the sculptor) which, for the artist, consists in loving the illusion itself, not its content, and defining his creation not so much by the fullness of its reference as by the divergence of its reflection" (MFN 154–55). In that concluding phrase "the divergence of its reflection," an ambiguously subjective and objective genitive that also diverges from itself, we find the empty, illusory space carved out by the interplay of similar signs that we have also called their value.

This space is also, of course, at the heart of *S/Z*, which revolves around "Sarrasine's" fantastic ability "to make *being-castrated*, an anecdotal condition, coincide with *castration*, a symbolic structure"—another example of a real ambiguity between language and lived experience that, by no means coincidentally, Barthes claims "accounts for this story's perhaps unique value" (S/Z 163, 164). But enough words have been rung around the direct operation of this absence's presence for me to take a step back and continue to approach the cut of castration reflectively, this time through the operative absence of the moon as the emblem of the castrato.[16] A further comparison between the two lexia through which Barthes sets up the link between the moon and the Vien painting in the story shows this connection to be emphatically, almost methodically *unsubstantiated*. In lexia 8, where Barthes gives his first comments on the moon, he thus writes, "we will come upon [the moon] again endowed with ambiguous softness when in the form of an alabaster lamp, it will illumine and feminize Vien's Adonis (No. 111), a portrait which is the (explicit) reflection of Girodet's Endymion (No. 547)" (S/Z 23–24). Turning to lexia 111, we find, in the English translation at least, only the italicized quotation from Balzac but none of the careful interpretive coding that usually follows. Instead, we enter sharply into divagation XXIX, entitled "THE ALABASTER LAMP," from which I have already quoted the line declaring its association with the moon on the basis of their shared qualities of coldness and reflection: "This boudoir alabaster is in fact the moon which illumines the young shepherd" (S/Z 70).[17] There is much to note here, not least of which is how the metaphorical connection between the two images hinges on a mere echo of referential assertions. The only reason that Barthes's initial claim about reencountering the moon in the form of the lamp holds up is because, when we get to the lamp, he points us back to the moon, creating a purely formal, self-supporting relationship between them. And if the shared association of "coldness and reflection" on which he bases this correspondence provides some motivation for their connection in a way that destabilizes the full homological force of my claim, we should also note that those associations are themselves barren, even hollow—reflexion here being nothing more than the unending transit between two images. As he puts it in the seminar where he begins developing S/Z's argument, the moon is "the agent of the category of the Sketched, of the Incomplete, of the Incompletely readable, of the *Fantastic*," a sally of phrases that approach this empty structure in terms of an ongoing, unfinishable interpretive undertaking explicitly synonymous with the fantastic itself (*Sarrasine* 136).

But there is more—or rather, there is even *less*: the commentary on the reference to Girodet's Endymion that Barthes pursues at this point is in the service of spotlighting the castrating absence that my own readings have been insistently reflecting. Tracing the associations of femininity and the sexual inversions that the painting introduces, he sums up by outlining, in illuminating terms, "the exchange which controls the symbolic interplay: a terrifying essence of passivity, castration is paradoxically superactive: its nothingness contaminates everything it encounters: deficiency makes everything radiant [*le manque est irradiant*]" (S/Z 70-71, 3:177). As the concatenation of colons here aerates the sentence into a succession of floating assents, it syntactically articulates the mobility that the appeal to radiation claims for castration's connotations. And it's with this mobility that the reference to Endymion breaches what we could decisively call the tale's fictional boundaries, radiating the transit of empty images into "our" world: as he puts it, "the Endymion in our text is the same Endymion which is in a museum (our museum, the Louvre)" (S/Z 71).[18] Yet, for all the careful analysis he devotes to the picture, it is not the painting itself that he ultimately emphasizes but rather its photograph—reproduced as a frontispiece to S/Z—that allows him to realize a dizzying, dazzling series of exchanges that vividly plots the textual structure of lived experience *as well as* the lived experience of textual structure. The ambiguity in the phrase "our text" begins to hint at this exchange since it is not and could never be clear whether that "our" refers to Balzac's novella or Barthes's commentary. Furthermore, his subsequent claim that "the photograph of the fictitious castrato is part of the text" shifts the ambiguity between Barthes and Balzac to one between Barthes's writing and the world according to whose codes this real image also takes its place.

When he thus goes on to assert that "retracing the line of the codes, we are entitled to go to the Bulloz establishment in the rue Bonaparte [*chez Bulloz, rue Bonaparte*] and ask to be shown the box (most likely filed under 'mythological subjects') in which we will discover the castrato's photograph," we are able to see how the effect of these confusions is not to undercut but to fantastically cut open our sense of reality itself as, in a way, *living literature* (*S/Z* 71, 3:177). Notice, that is, how La Zambinella's Z radiates and "retrac[es] the line" directly through that real-life (if, since 1999, defunct) collection of museum photographs where we would have encountered what Barthes punningly calls "the most literal image of La Zambinella" (*S/Z* 71). As these lines picture us within an explicitly commercial framework of exchange that reflects "Sarrasine's" own economically inflected narrative structure, they also stage Chez Bulloz as an extension or a literal materialization of its tale. But the result is not just that the codes constitutive of Balzac's story come to play out in the world beyond its pages, as we discussed in the previous section. It's also that Chez Bulloz takes on new, radiant value from its imbrication into "Sarrasine's" signifying network. Suddenly, Chez Bulloz *means more* than it did before, is fantastically enriched or, we might also say, enchanted by the entire force of the story's reflective significations. Moreover, the imagined discovery of La Zambinella's photograph also implies an encounter with the visible manifestation of the hole or the emptiness that we've been carving out and offers us a mirror image of our own "mythological subjectivity," which the rest of this argument will develop in its examination of the symbolic network through which literary character is given verbal value. In doing so, we will be thinking through what Barthes calls "the economic nature of the Name," its status as "an instrument of exchange [that] allows the substitution for a collection of characteristics by establishing an equivalent relationship between sign and sum" (*S/Z* 94–95). Exploring the symbolic network that composes a sense of character under the figure of the proper name will thus let us approach the more subjective, if not necessarily more personal, implications that the Name locates in the value of literary reflexion.

* * *

Barthes opens divagation XLI, entitled "THE PROPER NAME," by observing that, "We occasionally speak of Sarrasine as though he existed, as though he had a future, an unconscious, a soul; however, what we are talking about is his *figure* (an impersonal network of symbols combined under the proper name 'Sarrasine'), not his *person* (a moral freedom endowed with motives and an overdetermination of meanings)" (S/Z 94). In the distinction between figure and person, Barthes gestures toward the ambiguous potential for significance that inheres in the proper name, its function as an index of a symbolic network (the sign of further signs) on the one hand and as a reference to a permanent, persistent identity (that cloaks such a network of significations) on the other. While the tension stems from the extent to which the name itself is understood as a function of language or as an entrée to some kind of "real," extralinguistic existence, the entire project of S/Z consists of showing the inescapable, elemental literariness of the latter. But what does fantastically exist, for us as well as for Sarrasine, is the very "impersonal network of symbols" that may not be exactly embodied as much as it is encoded in what Barthes sometimes styles, with capitalized value, as "the Name."

He helps to clarify what I'm proposing here (and harks back to the meaningless but valuable analysis of Sarrasine's name I executed earlier) when he continues in terms that also recall his comments on the dispersed characterization of the old man and specifies that "we are developing connotations, not pursuing investigations; we are not searching for the truth of Sarrasine, but for the systematics of a (transitory) site of the text" (S/Z 94). This is to say that he is approaching the name Sarrasine as a verbal entity, with "connotations" and "transitory" textual dynamics that insist on the ongoing elaboration of—rather than any possible independence from—a larger symbolic network. Accordingly, the sentence structure couples the negation of both the internally focused "investigations" and the constant, stable identity suggested by "truth" and flanks them with assertive descriptions of his interpretive moves, as if to insinuate the empty gap at Sarrasine's center around which the shifting significations assemble both a sense of self and a self of sense. Barthes hollows out the cut of this nominal hole a bit more explicitly when, after giving literary examples that he proposes accentuate either the figural or the personal understanding of the Name, he ends his discussion by appealing to Proust and his narrator's "perilously maintained lack of a name" (S/Z 95). While the name's absence "creates a serious deflation of the realistic illusion," it simultaneously invigorates the textual "systematics" that fantastically replace such deception: he writes, "the Proustian *I* is not of itself a name (in contrast to the substantive character of the novelistic pronoun, XXVIII)" (S/Z 95). In the intratextual reference that once again sends us to an earlier divagation, Barthes's statement disseminates the identity of Proust's narrator across his own argumentative cuts and digressions to display the networked process—the very reflective movement—by which this figure is simultaneously collected and dispersed.

From this perspective, emptied out of any imaginary, biographical referent, the English pronoun *I* finds itself betwixt and between, an undefined value that might obliquely coincide with the slash that both separates and joins *S* and *Z* in this argument, what Barthes rapturously describes as "the surface of the mirror, the wall of hallucination, the verge of antithesis, the abstraction of limit, the obliquity of the signifier, the index of the paradigm, hence of meaning" (*S/Z* 107). The *I*, in other words, transforms into the reflective lineaments that fantastically create the symbolic network we so ambiguously call a "character" and that reveal how relentlessly we work to understand our selves through and perhaps even as a literary text. This has everything to do with the way Barthes insists on splicing the figure of Proust into THE BALZACIAN TEXT. In a divagation toward the end of *S/Z* that bears this title, Barthes returns to Proust on the heels of listing the four other novels in *The Human Comedy* where the Countess de Rochefide appears after hearing Sarrasine's story from the narrator. As an instance of an explicitly textually constituted "life," the figure of the countess becomes a model for the way "the Author himself—that somewhat decrepit deity of the old criticism—can or could some day become a text like any other" (*S/Z* 211). Barthes thus tempers the authorial death he had polemically proclaimed two years earlier and instead imagines a mode of fantastic vitality to the extent that the author "has only to see himself as a being on paper and his life as a *bio-graphy* (in the etymological sense of the word), a writing without referent, substance of a *connection* and not a *filiation*" (*S/Z* 211). It's at this point that the name of Proust emerges to represent the magical conversion of an integrated biography into the segmented bio-graphy, which entails "*returning* the documentary figure of the author into a novelistic, irretrievable, irresponsible figure, caught up in the plural of its own text: a task whose adventure has already been recounted, not by critics, but by authors themselves, a Proust, a Jean Genet" (*S/Z* 211-12).

In his telling use of the indefinite article, Barthes shelters the "documentary figure" of the man who wrote *À la recherche du temps perdu* within a more generalized linguistic phenomenon, one that is not only indexed by the proper name but that also illustrates the bio-graphical resources it affords. Indeed, this claim is effectively a condensed citation of the argument he makes in his 1967 essay "Proust and Names," where he names the Name as what finally permitted Proust "to utter his work"—to write his life not as a referential narrative but as itself "the story of a writing"

(*NCE* 58, 55). The Proustian Name achieves this fantastic effect because, in linking together what Barthes calls "the order of existence" and that "of speech," it reworks the very operation of reference as we traditionally approach it—approaches it less as a reflexion of reality than of signification itself (*NCE* 58). He explains his point by distinguishing between the discourses of Marcel the narrator and of Proust the writer: Marcel, who is "*going* to write," is "at grips with a psychology [of reminiscence], not with a technique," while Proust "struggles with the categories of language, not with those of behavior." Marcel the aspiring writer remains in the order of existence, Proust the working novelist finds himself in the order of speech, and the Name is the "unit of discourse" they share (*NCE* 58). If these categories seem counterintuitive as they align the literary character with "existence" and the human novelist with "speech," it should only underscore the fantastic way the Name works to collapse the difference between these orders by articulating them both at once. In other words, what the Name refers to is precisely the linguistic reflexion through which life itself is written.[19]

In his attempt to explain this discursive feat in more detail, Barthes exfoliates the functioning of the proper name in terms of an extreme "semantic density (one would almost like to be able to say, its *lamination* [*feuilleté*])" (*NCE* 60, 4:70). This compacted layering stems from the fact that "the Proustian Name fully wields the two major dimensions of the sign": far from achieving its significance via its position at the juncture of the two axes of signification, the Name folds them both—in their entirety—into itself (*NCE* 66). From the paradigmatic perspective, that is, the Name "is in itself and in every case the equivalent of an entire dictionary column: the name *Guermantes* immediately covers everything that memory, usage, culture can put into it" (*NCE* 60). Syntagmatically, "each Name contains several 'scenes' appearing at first in a discontinuous, erratic manner, but which ask only to be federated and to form thereby a little narrative" (*NCE* 61). Parsing what he also calls "a voluminous sign, a sign always pregnant with a dense texture of meaning," Barthes's semiological fantasy here approaches the Name as an amplification or reproduction of the sign's operative structure, a kind of reference to the network of meanings as a whole (*NCE* 59). Its function is thus not to determine or delimit a meaning at the single point where the paradigmatic and the syntagmatic registers of language intersect but rather to reflect the "pregnant" potential for meaningfulness by superimposing one axis of signification onto the other—by, we might say, allowing them to reflect each other. In the Name, that is, the multiple associations of the paradigmatic fan out into a series of successive options, while syntagmatic narrative chains become exchangeable for each other. This is what I think we can identify in Barthes's claim that "as sign, the proper name offers itself to an exploration, a decipherment: it is at once a 'milieu' (in the biological sense of the term) into which one must plunge, steeping in all the reveries it bears, and a precious object, compressed, embalmed, which must be opened like a flower" (*NCE* 59). If the "opening" of the "compressed" petals in the image of the flower suggests the unfurling of the paradigm, the "plunge" into multiple "reveries" stages this signifying "milieu" as a deep collection of dreamlike stories. The result is that the Name comes to refer to a particular individual by condensing the bio-graphical network that constitutes the very significance of their life.

However, the Name's special referential behavior is neither spontaneous nor organic. It is not a natural phenomenon—or, as the scare quotes together with the "biological" qualification of "'milieu'" suggest, it is only natural to the extent that it is symbolic. When Barthes thus goes on to claim that "each Name has its semic specter, variable in time, according to the chronology of its reader, who adds or subtracts elements exactly as language does in its diachrony," he points to the ghostly existence onto which the Name fantastically opens and grounds it in a kind of readerly work whose temporal extension, familiar to us from the last chapter, accords with language's own historical nature. The next sentence continues: "The Name is, in effect, *catalyzable*; it can be filled, dilated, the interstices of its semic armature can be infinitely added to," sharpening our sense of this readerly work as a collage activity that is at once accretive and divisive (*NCE* 61). The tension between the accumulation denoted by "filled" and the distension suggested by "dilated" finds resolution in the infinite expansion of "the interstices" to carve out a burgeoning space of linguistic value as such. The Name gives access as much to a set of associations and syntagms as to the very comparative or reflective practice that coordinates these semes and catalyzes the ongoing production of their meaning. To say this is to see how, for Proust, the Name and the Novel work similarly and to hear the nonexistent pun in Barthes's claim that "[the Name's] structure coincides with that of the work itself [*l'oeuvre même*]: to advance gradually into the Name's significations (as the narrator keeps doing) is to be initiated into the world, to learn to decipher its essences" (*NCE* 66, 4:75).

As this initiation leads Marcel "to understanding, in a single impulse, the world and the Book, the Book as world and the world as Book," it also leads us back to Barthes's laborious efforts in *S/Z* to codify the "nauseating mixture of common opinions" by which the readerly, replete, and referential text of realism "appear[s] to establish reality, 'Life'"—that term to which I am so irresponsibly and senselessly referring throughout these pages (*S/Z* 56, 206). Barthes's account of Proust helps us see how this very coding is what instantiates, from instant to instant, the kind of literal, practical reflexion that revives the vital value of life's language. Proust "has historically displaced the old problem of realism, which until his advent was always posed in terms of referents" because, in his work, "the signs of the world (of love, of worldliness) consist of the same stages as its names; between the thing and its appearance develops the dream, just as between the referent and its signifier is interposed the signified" (*NCE* 66–67). This appeal is less to denigrate a realism in favor of a modernism that comes to be itself displaced by a postmodernism—nowhere more than in the writerly work of Barthes himself—than it is to detect a prefiguration of the more precise project pursued in *S/Z* whereby "the five codes create a kind of network, a *topos*, through which the entire text passes (or rather, in passing, becomes text)" (*S/Z* 20). The result is, once again, to approach the emphasis that the later book places on the plurality of textuality in terms of the thick seams of meaning, reminiscent of the dense foliation of the Name, that its codes reflectively and reflexively articulate. Moreover, the image of the dream—which, as Barthes well knew, is also a form of significant work—stages those coded seams as a kind of psychic experience that might not be exactly real but that also can't be said to be fake. Rather, as a fantastic phenomenon that each of us experiences during the night (even if we don't go to bed early), it helps, by comparison, give a place to what we encounter in the signs of life during the day.

And if those signs come to us as "a smothering layer of received ideas" that make life itself a form of "Replete Literature, mortally stalked by the army of stereotypes it contains," the reiteration of those ideas implied and enacted in the practice of reflexion we've been exploring may well be enough to trick ourselves not out of but *deeper into* the process of signification by which we receive them (*S/Z* 206). This reflexion is thus ultimately a form of reading (which Barthes unsurprisingly casts as "a form of work"), or, more precisely, it is a form of *rereading*, suggested as much by the recurrence of the "re-" prefix reverberating throughout this paragraph—and linking "reflexion" and "Replete Literature" in particular—as by the more general presumption of a portentous anteriority entailed in the very notion of "received ideas" (*S/Z* 10). Hinted at here is the way the reflexivity of this reflective rereading cuts open the smothering repletion of life's constitutive stereotypes, an effect Barthes affirms when, in what is surely one of every professor's favorite divagations, he writes that "rereading is here suggested from the outset, for it alone saves the text from repetition (those who fail to reread are obliged to read the same story everywhere)" (*S/Z* 16). The enchanting irony in these lines offers a final instantiation of the value of reflexion as rereading and repetition diverge from themselves, from their received meanings, through their encounter with each other and take on a rigorously ambiguous originality that we might also think of as a fantastically originary ambiguity. To reflect on our lives with a literary text then is, in a sense, to "*immediately* reread the text... in order to obtain, as though under the effect of a drug (that of recommencement, of difference), not the *real* text, but a plural text: the same and new" (*S/Z* 16). As that impossible "*immediately*," whose italics underscore nothing other than its textual and even typographical mediation, drunkenly hallucinates the indistinction of literature and life, it certainly does not produce "the *real* text"—or it does so only insofar as it describes the fantastic network of "the same and new" in which literary reflexion practically allows us to live.

We tend to repeat what hurts us, things,
 and ghosts of things,
The actual green of summer, and summer's
 half-truth.
We tend to repeat ourselves.

8. Untitled (May 2021). Author's handmade collage.

Citation and Its Image [CHAPTER FOUR]

Working through these readings, I have begun to have the uneasy sense that I am basically repeating myself. On top of this, I am dogged by the possibility that my painstaking articulations are guilelessly reciting ideas overfamiliar to the discipline of literary study, that my interest in the semiological texture of the world and the linguistic construction of life is nothing more than a rehashing of tired poststructuralist pieties out of sync with the fashions and fortunes of contemporary critical discourse. Whether this is or is not finally the case (the answer, I am betting, is both), I have been managing this theoretical anxiety by constantly reminding myself of the central place rereading has in Barthes's thinking. Indeed, when he demands, toward the beginning of *S/Z*, "one last freedom: that of reading the text as if it had been already read," he describes concisely if hypothetically the historical position in which my encounter with his oeuvre is taking place (*S/Z* 15). Insofar as Barthes has *actually* already been read—by master explicators, novice students, and the foregoing discussions alike—his work offers me the opportunity to inhabit the very repetition I fear and to occupy the "smothering layer of received ideas" that, as I write today, arguably include his own analytical interventions and theoretical arguments (*S/Z* 206). If these discussions restate ideas that I have received over the span of what I could fantastically call my reading life, it is in an attempt to continue interanimating both those terms and, which might be the same, to proscribe the suffocating paralysis that would result from keeping them apart.

I address this general intellectual apprehension at this particular point to announce the way this chapter is itself very much about an active kind of readerly repetition, one that seeks to invigorate and even substantiate the reflexive relationship we have to the "received ideas" by which life itself is written. Reengaging the homological reflexion in which the previous chapter found its animating value, it works through an expanded understanding of Literature's distinction that Barthes begins to lay out in a set of remarks, titled "Style and Its Image," for the 1969 Bellagio colloquium. Writing at the tail end of his work on "Sarrasine," he slightly tweaks the emphases we've seen drive both *Writing Degree Zero* and *S/Z* and affirms that, "even before speaking of style in the individual sense in which we ordinarily understand the word, there is *literary* language [*le langage littéraire*], a truly collective writing whose systematic features should be itemized (and not only its historical features, as has been done hitherto)" (*Rustle* 97, 3:978). In addition to tracking the different ways that Literature has signaled itself over time, Barthes searches out a more aggressively formalist tack here, and his subsequent specification of "syntagmatic *patterns*, typical fragments of sentences, formulas, if you like, whose origin is not identifiable but which make up part of the collective memory of literature" approaches literariness by way of the particular linguistic constructions that underwrite it (*Rustle* 97).

The refinement of his attention is motivated here by his interest in complicating the main images or mythologies by which we traditionally view style, one of which he describes as the opposition of *Norm/Deviance* that sees style as an exception to or variation on an evidently standard, everyday speech. In this regard, what I proposed in the last chapter as literature's linguistic self-consciousness becomes synonymous with style itself, becomes "the space of style, and because it is specifically this space, then assumes a shamanic function" (*Rustle* 92). But when he reminds us that the "norm" is not nearly as stable or straightforward as one might assume, he implicitly extends this literary magic beyond the *cordon sanitaire* to which the ritualistic reference to Lévi-Strauss seems to restrict it. It's not just that "stylistic codes of reference or difference are numerous, and the spoken language is always only one of these codes (which, moreover, there is no reason to privilege as the *princeps* language)," as he puts it a few pages later (*Rustle* 95). It's also that, as he begins to elaborate on the "formulas" that comprise Literature, he describes a situation in which the language of the everyday takes on a fantastically literary inflection: "Having worked for some time on a tale by Balzac," he writes with an obvious nod to *S/Z*, "I often catch myself spontaneously carrying over into the circumstances of daily life fragments of sentences, formulations spontaneously taken from the Balzacian text" (*Rustle* 97). The fantastic experience he is recounting, which could be said to epitomize the fantastic at its most obviously or canonically literary, offers us an initiatory image of the significantly quixotic linguistic practice this chapter will be working to bring into focus. That is, these lines depict nothing other than an imaginary relationship, in a necessarily loose psychoanalytic sense, to literature *as a linguistic phenomenon* (a theoretical impossibility that it is the practical work of the word *fantastic* to signify).[1] This is at least the implication I want to see in Barthes's striking uses of "spontaneously" to qualify his comportment here. In an instance of uncharacteristically graceless repetition, this great demystifier of spontaneity's mystification nevertheless seems to be insisting on it, as if no amount of careful critical analysis can keep him from parroting discursive stereotypes. And while we have understood something like this since his alienated conclusion to "Myth Today," here it is specifically *through* his critical analysis that he is inculcated with these formulaic conventions.

This fantastic kind of critical imaginary is what Barthes seems to be envisioning when he goes on to distinguish two moments or two aspects of this spontaneous experience: "it is not the memorial (banal) character of the phenomenon which interests me here, but the evidence that I am *writing* daily life (it is true, in my head) through these formulas inherited from an anterior writing" (*Rustle* 97–98). He immediately rephrases his point in less discriminating terms—"or again, more precisely, life is the very thing which comes *already* constituted as a literary writing: *nascent* writing is a *past* writing"—but the more concrete account of his behavior does not seem content to rest in an exclusively passive or at least not an indolent relationship to this linguistic inheritance (98). Rather, we see him dreaming up a practice of language that activates this anteriority and puts its readerly formulas to writerly work. Indeed, to the extent that his characterization of life as "*already* constituted as a literary writing" effectively serves as a citation of *S/Z*'s argument (and, importantly, not the last we will see), it illustrates the same practice of using "*past* writing" to script a present situation that animates his spontaneous "carrying over" of the Balzacian text into his everyday life. What I mean is that citation itself begins to appear here as a particular intellectual activity, a particular kind of verbal repetition that both recognizes and re-cognizes the words that spontaneously come his way. This claim certainly accords with the larger arguments he is pursuing regarding style's functioning, his "conviction that style is essentially a citational procedure, a body of formulas, a memory (almost in the cybernetic sense of the word), an inheritance based on culture and not on expressivity" (*Rustle* 99). And even more than this, it revises our sense of an image as such, which we can begin to see functioning not as a kind of immediate, monolithic ideal to assume but as a discreet collection of discrete verbal structures to operate. From the fantastic viewpoint of citation, the image that constitutes this imaginary relationship to language and literature is one of literal articulation (to circle back to our introductory discussions of Loyola and Arcimboldo). So it is not really figuratively that Barthes confesses a few years later, "I have a disease; I see language" (*RB* 161).

In this chapter, we will thus be very deliberately looking at a second, complementary cross section of Barthes's illustrious literary criticism to work out the practice of citation whose segmented image he is developing here, the fantastic formulation of one's life or at least isolated experiences in terms and in forms purloined from a literary text. Barthes is careful to distinguish this aspect of his critical vision from the "philological" question of linguistic "sources," which, he says, "has been raised almost exclusively on the level of the content" (*Rustle* 97). Rather, the repeated focus on linguistic formulas imagines the intersection of Barthes's life and Balzac's story to involve as much the representations in the text (the events, the characters, the setting) as the representational activity *of* the text (the phrases, the sentences, the tropes) that give the former their fantastic existence (97). Describing the basis of what, in this context, he significantly calls "the stylistic work [*le travail stylistique*]," he once again enjoins a more schematic "search for models, for patterns: sentential structures, syntagmatic clichés, divisions and clausulae of sentences" (*Rustle* 98–99, 3:980). What catches my eye in this sequence of verbal forms is sequence itself, as both the forward march of the phrases and the "syntagmatic" attributes he accentuates oppose the otherwise static emphasis in the idea of a "model" or even a "pattern." As one effect of articulating the image, this tension suggests that the characteristic prominence of the signifier over the signified in Barthes's citational fantasy is here meant to galvanize our conventional or formalized sense of the world.

Furthermore, in an incipient synthesis of the previous chapters' arguments, citation achieves this by exercising the particular forms of magical linguistic practice they have been anatomizing. The rhythmically successive phrasing Barthes repeatedly uses to parse citation's performance calls back to and in a way executes the cutting work of notation as part of what facilitates the literary reflexion whose structural operation we outlined in the last chapter. If the upshot of these analyses has been to mediate the pressing immediacy of our own lived experience and to open up the constructive force of the cultural models that comprehend it, citation grabs traces of that fantastic force as, once more, a writerly form of readerly analysis. "*To write*," Barthes asserts, "is to let these models come to one and to *transform* them (in the sense this word has acquired in linguistics)" (*Rustle* 97). Without digressing into the intricate workings of transformational grammar, we can nonetheless discern an insistence on treating the literary citation not as a direct expression of one's life but as its interpretive scheme.

My decision to christen this fantastic interpretive activity citation—rather than "allusion," "reference," or "quotation"—is itself an illustration of the transformative linguistic practice that it names, one I include because it drives home the fundamentally verbal character of this phenomenon. That is, the specific term citation finds something like its source in a readerly transformation of Barthes's "tauromachian" account of the word *cited* toward the beginning of *S/Z*. He explains, with dramatic flair, "*citar* is the stamp of the heel, the torero's arched stance which summons the bull to the banderilleros. Similarly, one cites the signified (wealth) to make it come forth, while avoiding it in the discourse" (*S/Z* 22). At this moment he is trying to clarify the process by which a particular meaning and a particular image of the world is presented by Balzac's story as natural or universal; the point is that the story never directly says "the characters are wealthy" but rather sprinkles "anodyne data, seemingly lost in the *natural* flow of the discourse," details that never announce themselves as signifiers but give the impression of wealth as a matter of course (*S/Z* 22). It seems to me, however, that something similar, or at least something homologous, is happening regarding citation itself in Barthes's own discourse here. What gets lost in the flow of his commentary is precisely the linguistic wealth that citation disburses, the surplus stock of meanings it makes available nowhere more vividly than in the bullfighting imagery he calls on. Though the bull seems meant to figure the signified that the discourse, like the torero, avoids confronting directly, its metaphoric and metonymic connotations nevertheless also index the irrepressible energy of the signifier that citation archly "summons." This energy—and the precariously unpredictable, inconclusive work of manipulating it—is what the word *citation* is meant to activate in this chapter's argument. When Barthes goes on to describe how "the semes appear to float freely, to form a galaxy of trifling data in which we read no order of importance," I thus hear as much the machinery of ideological mystification as I do the machinations of undetermined and indeterminate meaning (*S/Z* 22). If such a claim is in rather direct opposition to his reasoning, it also illustrates one of the central affordances of unleashing this energy: that no meaning is ever the final one, no reading ever the last.

The image of citation as I'm approaching it here finds its most compelling dramatizations in two surprisingly similar works that, straddling *S/Z*, each summon the power literary language gives us to read the world in transformative ways. On one side, there is the trio of essays that Barthes published as *On Racine*, which sparked a cultural controversy over the "*nouvelle critique*" that has made it not so much famous as infamous (especially for Anglophone readers like me who are almost wholly unfamiliar with French classical tragedy). On the other, there is the more personal and obviously citational *A Lover's Discourse: Fragments*, which offers us arguably the most extensive exhibition of citation as an analytical method. These resonant discussions allow me to intertwine a collective or sociocultural and an individual or subjective illustration of citation as the fantastic point where literature and life become explicitly, performatively, and most of all affirmatively indistinguishable—where, as we diagrammed in our reading of *S/Z*, a network of meaningful structures coordinate the common basis for literature and life's legibility. The larger cultural manifestation of this kind of lived textuality is what Barthes seems to be insinuating when he opens *On Racine* by maintaining that "the work must be truly a form, must truly designate a meaning in question" and then insisting that "the world must answer the work's question assertively, must endow with its own substance the meaning proposed" (*Racine* ix). Evoking a provocatively presentist interpretation of Racine's plays that came to cause him so much trouble in the ensuing years, Barthes considers the literary text as a formal framework, a kind of cipher, for the "substance" of our own worldly experience. Fourteen years later, we see *A Lover's Discourse* embarking on a parallel, if both more fragmentary and more private, project that uses references from a selection of texts to dissect the experience of being in love as a coded set of verbal "figures" (*LD* 3). "Each of us," he goes on to declare, "can fill in this code according to his own history" (*LD* 5). In their particular ways, both explorations give voice to citation as the linguistic practice that inhabits and potentially enlivens the static forms and cultural clichés shaping our sense of the world.

* * *

The first lines of "Racine Spoken," the second essay in Barthes's collection on the playwright, read as follows:

> It appears that today's public consumes Racine in a purely anthological fashion. In *Phèdre* it is the character of Phaedra one comes to see, and even more than Phaedra, the actress herself: how will she "do" it? Some critics of our stage actually date their careers by the Phaedras they have seen. The text itself is received as an ensemble of raw materials, from which pleasure takes its choice: musical lines, famous *tirades* stand out against a background of obscurity and boredom: it is for this actress, these lines, these *tirades* that we go to the theatre; the rest we put up with, in the name of culture, in the name of the past, in the name of a poetic thrill patiently waited for because it has been localized by centuries of the Racinian myth (*Racine* 141).

The obviously censorious attitude toward the public's "anthological" consumption of Racine sets into relief the specific role citation will play in

Barthes's discussion of these tragedies. In contrast to a selection of mythologically significant passages or figures in which the fact of their collection eclipses almost everything else about them, citation for *On Racine* functions both more scrupulously and more holistically as a fantastic schematic for opening up an entire cultural setting or social condition. To that end, it will be neither character nor actress taking center stage in this interpretive performance; the spotlight falls rather on the dramatic effects of language itself, especially the elemental discontinuities and divergences of verbal articulation, to discern a spectacularly analytical image of the world it presents. The latter is what Barthes formulates in the "Racinian anthropology" he develops in the book's first essay "Racinian Man," which he describes as "dealing with the image of man confined [*la rencontre d'un homme enfermé*]" (*Racine* vii–viii, 2:53). While the confinement he is referring to is that of the tragic situation, a static arrangement constituted by the weight of the inherited past to which we will return momentarily, the appeal to the "centuries of the Racinian myth" that have determined the public's particular piecemeal relationship to these plays suggests a comparable set of confining cultural circumstances that connect Barthes's literary arguments here to his contemporaneous critiques of bourgeois ideology. Though the first edition of *Mythologies* was published in 1957, six years before *On Racine*'s appearance as a collection, he continued submitting mythological analyses to *Les Lettres nouvelles* until late 1959. Meanwhile, "Racine Spoken" first appeared in the March 1958 number of *Théâtre populaire*, with parts of "Racinian Man" following in 1959 before coming out in full as the preface to the edition of Racine's plays published in 1960 by the Club Français du Livre. This chronological coincidence gives historical support to the more fantastic claim I'm making—namely, that *On Racine* explores and exploits the formal aspects of Racine's plays as a citational framework for realizing—and rereading—the structures of cultural mythology shared across the centuries.

    Barthes elaborates the specifically literary form of myth in which the contemporary public finds itself confined by analyzing "Racinian delivery, as it is commonly practiced today"; he describes how "the bourgeois actor ceaselessly intervenes in the flow of the language, 'brings out' a word, suspends an effect, constantly signifies that what he is saying now is important, has a certain hidden meaning. This is what is called *speaking* a text" (*Racine* 142). Barthes's own disjointed phrasing here illustrates the fossilizing effect of this diction, one that transforms the fluid "flow" of language into a series of "suspended" tableaux governed by a meaning assumed to be exterior and antecedent to the vocalization. The actor thus speaks "according to the ineradicable prejudice that regards words as *translating* thought," a naive privileging of a stable signified over the differential dynamics of the signifier that we might consider to be the motor of all mythologizations (*Racine* 142). In vocabulary that will be familiar to us from our discussion of linguistic work, Barthes explains that "this parceling out of meanings had as its goal the facilitation of the listener's intellectual labor: the actor undertakes to do his thinking for him" and goes on to figure this situation even more sensationally as "a singular relation of authority . . . the public is the child, the actor a mother substitute, preparing the food, offering fare already predigested, which the public consumes quite passively" (*Racine* 143). This frankly disgusting imagery literalizes the "anthological" relationship to Racine's work as a form of regurgitated consumption that doesn't just swallow the same "famous *tirades*" or stock excerpts but that also imbibes the very interpretive juices by which those extractions are digested. Such delivery ensures that these texts express the same sense over and over again as the nuances of their actual language dissolve into the chewed cud of homogenized comprehension.

This closed circle of received meaning is very close to what Barthes identifies in his excavation of the tragic situation organizing Racine's plays, "Racinian Man" reflecting a literary homology of the organizing conventions that constitute a common culture. Explaining his conception of the tragic hero as "a man confined, a man who cannot *get out* without dying," he uses the psychoanalytic model of the "family romance" to map the fundamental paradigm or "exemplary constellation" into which Racine's "some fifty tragic characters" can be parsed. As he puts it, "we are dealing, essentially, with masks, with figures that differ from each other not according to their public status but according to their place in the general configuration that keeps them confined" (*Racine* 8-9). The fact that death is the only escape from this "configuration" indicates the extent to which life or living is, in this case, synonymous with structure and paralysis (what *S/Z* scrutinizes in terms of realism's and reality's stereotyped codes). This psychodramatic confinement also has a historical component that begins to echo, or at least to espouse, the linguistic predigestion we've just seen characterize the Racinian myth: discussing the figure of the Father in Racine, Barthes writes, "It is not necessarily Blood or sex that constitutes him, nor even Power; his being is his anteriority: what comes after him is descended from him, ineluctably committed to a problematics of loyalty" (*Racine* 38). As what always comes before, the Father figures tradition itself, the institutions and customs that dogmatically determine the world in which the tragic hero finds himself—and determine it as something fixed and unchanging to be carried on. When Barthes thus goes on and claims "what has been *is*, that is the code of Racinian time," his focus on code points up language and literary convention as part and parcel of the smothering environment he is diagramming (*Racine* 38).

Furthermore, when this carceral condition receives its most capacious schematization early on in his discussion as "the order of language, which is the only tragic order," it begins to gesture toward the capacity for energetic engagement that Barthes's formal analysis of the plays offers to the struggle with cultural or mythological confinement (*Racine* 5). Barthes explores the most drastic effect of this linguistic prison-house in his discussion of the tragic reversal, which he develops as "the fundamental figure of Racinian theatre" (*Racine* 41). For Racine's plays, Barthes claims, the kind of familiar dramatic reversal in which, for example, "the captive [is] crowned, or the tyrant deposed" functions not as a "'story'" or narrative but as "in fact a form, an obsessive image that is adapted to a varying content" (*Racine* 42). The use of the word "form" here does double duty as a term of both literary and psychological analysis insofar as it describes a structure shared across Racine's tragedies as well as a mindset habitually inhabited by the tragic hero. As the hero thus "assimilates himself spontaneously to this form, feels that he is becoming pure and continual form himself," he anticipates, in something of a different key, Barthes's behavior with Balzac and asserts the fantastic link between literary construction and a conception or perception of the world that citation avidly seeks to appropriate (*Racine* 45). At this moment, however, reversal is an agent of confinement as we have been discussing it, not so much a process of change as a structural inevitability or foregone conclusion. And if, in his ideological critiques, such cultural imprisonment is characterized as "universal nature" or what is taken as "natural," here it is called "Destiny," a category whose similarly mythological valence stems from the fact that it "always seizes on a situation already organized, provided with a meaning, a figure (a *face*)" (*Racine* 42).

It's at this moment, precisely as a footnote to this relentless prefiguration, that Barthes gives us some of the typical phrases by which it comes together and implies the practical forces of language itself: "This *solidification* of the experienced situation is expressed in such formulas as: *contre moi tout s'assemble* [everything unites against me]; *tout a changé de face* [everything has changed its aspect], etc." (*Racine* 42). There is a tension here between the immobilizing "*solidification*" he is illustrating, indexed by the terse *tout* or "everything," and the inescapably discontinuous formulation imposed on it by verbal articulation as such. Putting this experience of solidity into words, even if just to identify it *as* an experience, already begins to cut it up, to subject it to analysis, to give it texture: to open it *to reading*.[2] We could, for instance, take the word *face* or "aspect" as an indication of the superficiality or inconsequentiality of the changed meaning; or, more subtly, we could hear the spatial suggestion in the phrase "against me" imply the possibility of a distanced, discriminating perspective on this "everything." These claims are tenuous, but the point is more *that* we can make them than what is ultimately, for now, made of them. And it's in this light that Barthes's framing of these phrases as "formulas" reads not as a fixed paradigm to be thoughtlessly discharged but as a suite of operations to be thoughtfully executed: methodical procedures, maybe even a kind of magic spell, for dissecting and scrutinizing one's otherwise "solid" situation. Though the speaker might not have such a reflective relationship to their words (this is part of what makes them "confined"), Barthes's excision of these phrases from the larger text of the plays indicates the first analytical steps involved in the practice of citation on which the possibility of readerly relief (if not full-blown release) from the strictures of predetermined meaning is predicated.

Indeed, the operation of citation is shown up by the location of this comment in a footnote, the rhetorical space of citationality as such. This is particularly suggestive here because one of the peculiarities of "Racinian Man" is Barthes's strange handling of quotations from both the plays and other thinkers, which appear almost exclusively in footnotes rather than in the main text of his argument. Claude Coste persuasively sees this move as part of what makes *On Racine* as much about Racine as about Barthes himself, "an intellectual biography that does not speak its name" and that "holds the thought of others (Racinian verse or theoretical prose) to the periphery of the page, as pushed into the background."[3] Anticipating the practical orientation to literature that I'm working out, the purpose of this tacit personalization is in part to stage his own struggle with received ideas in terms of the confined tragic hero he is analyzing, whom Coste describes, with an accidental but apt pun on citation, as "these heroes who seek to escape from the laws of the group and society [*du groupe et de la cité*]."[4] And if I read the letter of Barthes's citational practice somewhat differently from Coste, it is in the same spirit of impossible, fantastic liberation (which Coste himself acknowledges as either "the liberty of the fantasy or the fantasy of liberty").[5] The effect of the footnotes, which sometimes take up over half of the page, seems to be as much about distancing this other thought as it is about displaying this other language (see fig. 9). We could say that, by providing a *literal image* of citation, the footnotes work to complicate any kind of predigested or "anthological" consumption of the plays by carving out an impersonal, fantastic space in which language itself might begin to speak, might loosen itself from its speaker and their intentions, might lend itself to additional, unexpected, even inaccurate meanings. Another way to put this would be to say that the citational space of the footnotes sets off language as a continual signifying process rather than a complete signified product. This is a more systematic and more keenly verbal illustration of one, admittedly provisional escape that ated. God raises up or casts down—that is the monotonous movement of creation. Examples of these inversions are countless. It is as if Racine constructed his entire theatre on this model, which is, etymologically speaking, the *peripeteia,* and only afterwards invested it with what is called psychology. This is evidently a very old theme, that of the captive crowned, or the tyrant deposed, but in Racine this theme is not a "story," it has no epic density; it is in fact a form, an obsessive image that is adapted to a varying content. The reversal affects a totality: the hero has the feeling that *everything* is caught up in this rocking motion: the whole world oscillates, there is no alloy in the minting of Destiny, precisely because Destiny always seizes on a situation already organized, provided with a meaning, a figure (a *face*).[2] The reversal affects a universe already created by an intelligence. The direction of the reversal is always depressive (except in the "sacred" tragedies): it casts things down from their height, and its image is the fall [3] (Racine's is probably a *descensional* imagination, as the *Cantique spirituel* no. 3 suggests:[4] the reader will re-

---

[2] This *solidification* of the experienced situation is expressed in such formulas as: *contre moi tout s'assemble* [everything unites against me]; *tout a changé de face* [everything has changed its aspect], etc.

[3] The theory of the fall is given by Aman's wife, Zares:

Où tendez-vous plus haut? Je frémis quand je voi
Les abimes profonds qui s'offrent devant moi:
La chute désormais ne peut être qu'horrible. (Es. III,1)

Why do you seek to rise still higher? I tremble, seeing the deep gulfs that yawn before me: henceforth, the fall can only be dreadful.

[4] Referring to the two men in the self:

L'un tout esprit, et tout céleste,
Veut qu'au Ciel sans cesse attaché,
Et des biens éternels touché,
Je compte pour rien tout le reste
Et l'autre par son poids funeste
Me tient vers la terre penché. (*Cantique spirituel,* no. 3)

One, all spirit and celestial, bids me bind myself to Heaven, concerned with eternal things, and count the rest for nought,

---

9. Roland Barthes, *On Racine,* trans. Richard Howard (New York: Performing Arts Journal Publications, 1983), p. 42. Author's annotated copy. Originally published in English by Hill and Wang (1964).

Barthes allows the tragic hero, itself a quiet citation of the magic we saw him practicing marginally in *Mythologies*: 'the hero *schemes* with tragedy [*le héros ruse avec la tragédie*]' (*Racine* 16, 2:70)."[6]

What Barthes's idiosyncratic use of the footnotes further accomplishes, however, is to extend the practical ruse of this citational scheme to us as readers of his commentary and Racine in tandem. Separated from the captivating flow of Barthes's prose, Racine's verses float in our visual field ready to facilitate our own interpretive activation of the dramatic dynamics he is discussing, influenced but not dominated by his claims. Lacking the kind of explanatory close reading that characterizes so much of my own discourse here, our first task is to decipher the connection between the point he is making and the poetry that is supposed to exemplify and support it. In a more obvious and overt way than traditional in-text quotation and explication, Barthes's footnotes thus repeatedly ask us to practice the kind of meaningful reflexion between a citation from a literary text and a specific idea or experience that he will carry over from criticism proper into everyday life more broadly. This is more so the case considering the oddly prosaic, even banal correlation that most of the footnotes have with his arguments. Footnote 3 on the page I've reproduced, to take an example at random, provides three lines from Racine's *Esther* that are meant to illustrate the mostly "depressive" direction of the tragic reversal, whose "image is the fall" (*Racine* 42). But, far from offering a fully elaborated "theory" as Barthes alleges, the quotation does little more than mention or name the phenomenon of *la chute*; in other words, it simply repeats his point in different diction (*Racine* 42n3). To access such a theory, we must develop it ourselves through a conscientious analysis of the ways Racine's wording is working. Begging the question of what difference literary formulation makes, citations like this incite the kind of linguistic activity to which literature as such gives shape.

To say this is to see citation less as a harnessing of literary form per se than as a practice whereby the formative energy of a literary text is made available for the evaluation and resignification of the world.[7] And while we will dissect this literary energy with more precision and indeed more formality in the next section, the general effect of citation inheres for now in the way it puts language and its signifying operations on display. We could even say that citation as we've begun to discuss it stages on the page what Barthes calls "the key to Racinian tragedy"—namely, that "to speak is to do, the *logos* takes over the functions of *praxis* and substitutes for it" (*Racine* 58). His point refers to the way the plays' events are practically synonymous with the characters' reporting of them, but citation's excision of select verses works to emphasize the action of the plays' articulation over the articulation of their action. It thus coincides with and, in its way, contributes to his concluding claim for tragedy as "an art of spectacle," which is finally where "Racinian Man" brings the plays into explicit relation to myth (*Racine* 60). If myth "starts from contradictions and tends toward their mediation," tragedy, on the other hand, "immobilizes contradictions, refuses mediation, keeps the conflict open," which describes the paralyzed struggle against tradition in which the tragic hero stays trapped (*Racine* 60). Though Barthes goes on in typical dialectical fashion to assert the mythic nature of myth's rejection—"*tragedy is the myth of the failure of myth*," he writes—his closing assertion that "tragedy remains a *spectacle*, that is, a reconciliation with the world [*un accord avec le monde*]" gestures toward the alternative relationship with this mythic confinement opened up by these plays' spectacular language (*Racine* 60, 2:106). In the word *accord*, that is, I'd like to hear less the legal or even financial resonances of "reconciliation" than the more grammatical or syntactical suggestion of "agreement," the verbal inflections that, in French especially, allow one word to coordinate with another. For these kinds of small but meaningful adjustments are ultimately what citation allows us to introduce into our image of the world.

* * *

Barthes offers a more technical, or at least a more elaborated, discussion of the kind of inflection whose potential I'm locating in citation when he returns to these ideas a few years later. As a rejoinder to the polemical critiques leveled at *On Racine* (which we will examine in due course), he published *Criticism and Truth* in 1966 as an attempt to more explicitly spell out the intellectual implications that his earlier arguments have for literary study. Of the many claims he makes, almost all of which revolve around the plurality of meaning that becomes a hallmark of his later work, the most intriguing as well as the most germane for our purposes is his fantastic positing of what he calls "a *literature faculty*" (*Criticism* 75). Modeled after Noam Chomsky's idea of a language faculty, which describes our inborn understanding not of a particular language but of linguistic rules, constraints, and principles more generally, the capability Barthes is imagining here involves "an energy of discourse, which has nothing to do with 'genius,' for it is made up not of inspiration or personal will-power but of rules built up by many people besides the author. It is not images, ideas or lines of verse which the mythical voice of the Muse breathes into the writer, it is the great logic of symbols and great empty forms which allow him to speak and to operate [*c'est la grand logique des symboles, ce sont les grandes formes vides qui permettent de parler et d'opérer*]" (*Criticism* 75, 2:789).

Those last lines, where he's fantasizing about the fundamental intellectual aptitude that literary representation would require and that a particular cultural tradition would exploit, are particularly rich as they hint at a special kind of symbolic thought. Indeed, instead of his more customary vocabulary of the "sign," his use of the word "symbol," with its shades of convention and associations with religious belief, suggests the established capacity for a second-order thinking that takes everyday signs and raises them to a higher, more performative power. Furthermore, Barthes's appeal to a generalized discursive "energy" and the unspecific, depersonalized action suggested by "to operate" disarticulate this power from any exclusive tie to writing itself, as if writing a literary composition is only one way of engaging this intellectual faculty. Indeed, the more specific comments he makes on criticism extend this kind of capacious symbolic work to the reader, as he asks, in provocative, fantastic wording, "does he not feel that he is re-entering into contact with a certain *beyond* of the text, as if the primary language of the work gave rise within him to other words and taught him to speak a second language? That is what is called *dreaming*" (*Criticism* 69). This dreamlike "*beyond* of the text" calls out to the elemental structures or symbolic logic of the "literature faculty" by which received language is treated as raw material for readerly re-formation. We could even say that the specific "images, ideas or lines of verse" he distinguishes from the writer's more abstract literary power function, for the reader, as the medium for further, "secondary" signification.

If these comments begin to describe in more theoretical terms the practical operation of citation exhibited in the preceding sections, it is because citation works to activate or summon the "literature faculty" as a way of providing us a symbolic perspective on our worldly experience. Barthes identifies the stakes of such a perspective when he describes his analytical method in terms that shrewdly speak to the kind of confined situation that links *On Racine* and *Mythologies*: "To do a second writing of the first writing of a work is indeed to open the way to unforeseeable relaying of meaning, the endless play of mirrors, and it is this room for manoeuvre which is suspect" (*Criticism* 33). While the endlessness of meaning's relay, on which he places increasing emphasis in the ensuing few years, has come down to us as the primary lesson of his thinking, I'd like to train our attention for the moment on the space between the "mirrors" where such "second writing" takes place, the fantastic "room" in which the maneuvering of meaning transpires. Doing so returns us to the interpretive space that Barthes's footnotes in *On Racine* exhibit so emphatically and, extending beyond his specific experiment in formatting, allows us to explore the way literary form gives some legible shape to that citational space and the discursive energy it unleashes. In his continued discussion of the dramatic reversal, for instance, he addresses the rigorous formalization of Racine's verses and zeroes in on the way "this reversive operation has its own rhetoric: antithesis, and its versified figure: *la frappe* [the strike][9] (obviously the alexandrine admirably serves the dimorphous organization of the Racinian world[10])" (*Criticism* 44, superscripts original). Tracing a homology among the structure of an entire dramatic world, the rhetorical device organizing more particular oppositions within it, and the traditional poetic line by which it is created, this multifootnoted line exfoliates the specific symbolic logic that runs through the plays and formally animates their language. More specifically, Barthes subtly suggests the expansive disruption introduced by this formalization—the way it opens up what otherwise seems so rigidly fixed—when he telescopes his attention for a moment to the basic unit of classical tragedy and pinpoints the fantastic origin of these formations not just in the alexandrine but in the medial caesura that divides its two sets of six syllables.

The expansionary energy of language's essential discontinuity is what *la frappe* formally indexes, the relatively even rhythm of French leading not, as we say in English, to the "fall" of a stress on a particular syllable but to a more vigorous "strike."[8] The footnote Barthes appends to this term correlates the divided page layout of his discussion to the split structure of the alexandrine and gestures toward the similarly energizing effect that citation as such is meant to afford. It's thus not by chance that the footnote itself cites a comment Paul Claudel makes, "apropos of Racine," on the way the verb *frapper* refers to the minting or "striking" of a coin as well as the clear delineation of a thought (*une pensée bien frappée*) (*Racine* 44n9). The English translation omits the charming use of *frapper* to describe chilling champagne, but the associations indicate the power of the alexandrine's structure to stamp the tragic hero and his world into the confinement of their defined and determinate shapes. Even so, the inventory of the word's various meanings implies the prolix potential of this poetic feature, as if such forceful determination is simultaneously a kind of significant dissemination—a multiplication rather than just a demarcation of meaning. This is how we might understand the curious and somewhat startling aperçu by which Claudel gathers the word's semantic nuances together: "something I should call the detonation of the obvious [*la détonation de l'évidence*]" (*Racine* 44n9, 2:94n9). The phrase is certainly striking, as it explains the imposition of verbal form through an image of explosion (which Catherine Malabou has deftly theorized in terms of form's general "plasticity").[9] But we need not push the reading all the way to this shattering extreme to get a sense of the vibratory charge sparked by the alexandrine's formal *frappe*, a tension between coming apart and holding together that also informs the effect of citation. Stamping the self-evident with the force of a literary formulation, citation imparts a kind of distinct dispersal that sets it off—that makes it work and that makes it noticeable, that makes the workings of its signification noticeable.

We will explore this working in all its granularity when we turn to *A Lover's Discourse* in a moment, but my focus on the alexandrine should not suggest that the symbolic dynamic sparked by citation is limited to the well-wrought language of traditional poetic forms. In Barthes's mouth, rather, this kind of spaciousness is also an effect of words themselves, a condition that receives a significantly less explosive formulation in what Claude Coste calls "l'affaire 'respirer.'"[10] The "affair" to which he is referring involves the famously polemical critique that Raymond Picard published in response to *On Racine*, which takes special umbrage at Barthes's reading of the verb *respirer* in *Brittanicus*. One of Picard's points revolves around the fact that, in the seventeenth century, *respirer*'s dominant meaning was "to relax, to have a bit of respite" rather than the more literal suggestion of breathing to which Barthes appeals when he claims, referring to a line spoken by Nero, that "what this asphyxiated creature craves, as a drowned man gasps for air, is *respiration*."[11] As Picard notes, Barthes's comment is a more specific illustration of an earlier statement regarding the tragic hero's general confinement by the past: "The suffering that the link [of fidelity to tradition] induces is actually an apnoea; asphyxiated, the Racinian hero *wants* to precipitate himself outside his fidelity" (*Racine* 48). Contesting the "pneumatic coloration" informing Barthes's comments—and particularly rejecting the metaphorical extension of *respirer* into the figure of an "apnoea"—Picard bluntly states, "I advise him to consult the dictionaries."[12] This demand for a staunch fidelity to philology unwittingly but revealingly repeats the confined situation Barthes is diagnosing, the stranglehold of tradition from which neither tragic hero nor literary critic can ever fully escape. Coste explains this predicament well when, paraphrasing a point Barthes makes in his seminar on *Sarrasine*, he writes, "dictionaries come under a more or less accepted ideological partiality, which takes nothing away—quite the contrary—from the necessity of consulting them."[13] However, the despotism of the dictionary refines our sense of the freedom that Barthes's reading is nonetheless trying to develop and that citation is aiming to access: not a wholesale liberation from confinement but a more moderate, because moderated, space *within* such confinement where one might at the very least be able to breathe.

Breathing is an ideal image for such restricted freedom (and one Barthes also employs in his 1963 essay "Literature and Signification"), as the expansion and contraction of the lungs within the constraints of the chest cavity embody this tension and associate it with the very support of life.[14] The semantic elasticity that his comments draw from the verb *respirer* are also, in a sense, an attempt to allow the word itself to live and breathe, to oscillate among its various meanings without stifling any of its resonances. More than this, as a lexical version of the alexandrine's metrical *frappe*—an opening bound and actually created by a set of expressive parameters—the development of these various connotations inflects the abstract space of this freedom into a more demarcated shape. That is, to the same extent that *respirer* expands beyond the single dictionary definition on which Picard insists, it also finds its extension curbed by the wide-ranging complex of associations and differentiations in which it takes its place. In a somewhat more expressly circumscribed mode than we saw in the last chapter's theoretical discussion of verbal value, this place receives its airy determination through the particularities of the text in which the word appears. Coste reminds us that, in addition to situating a word in the context provided by the dictionary, "one must not forget the other context that the rest of the work constitutes, in which the meaning constructs itself, step by step, by a network of correspondences."[15] Recalling the argument *S/Z* exhibits so spectacularly, such a network is part of what Barthes is talking about when, rebutting the (seemingly perennial) accusation that his reading strategy allows the critic to say anything at all about a work, he claims his submission to "the formal constraints of meaning" and, two pages later, to "the logic of the signifier" (*Criticism* 81, 83).[16] With the operation of the "literature faculty" rustling behind these phrases, they distill my discussion of Racine's language into the more general symbolic principles that we've been watching citation make available.

For all my careful analysis, however, we have yet to glimpse the efficacious application of citation's symbolic potential in any concrete way. Even Barthes's writing of his life through the Balzacian text with which we began stopped short of showing us any real-world consequences of his fantastic references. It is not really until *A Lover's Discourse: Fragments* and its "'dramatic' method" that we explicitly see the citational dynamics I've been exploring working beyond the delimited framework of a literary text and its critical commentary (*LD* 3). Barthes signals this as soon as he begins to explain how the "figures" or "fragments of discourse" that constitute the amorous speech of the lover "take shape insofar as we can recognize, in passing discourse, something that has been read, heard, felt. The figure is outlined (like a sign) and memorable (like an image or a tale). A figure is established if at least someone can say: '*That's so true! I recognize that scene of language*'" (*LD* 3-4). Even as these lines recall the "received ideas" or "common opinions" that bring on such condemnation in *S/Z*, they resolutely recast them in terms of recognition and frame the "something that has been read, heard, felt" as a kind of language to be deployed as much as a set of stereotypes to be denounced (*LD* 206).[17] This double status is why the figures function, like the citations that help determine them, as both sign and image, which *A Lover's Discourse* substantiates by using its marginal references and citation-filled footers to continue with *On Racine*'s spectacular exploitation of the page space. And while the final section of this chapter will further flesh out the fantastic freedom afforded by citation's articulation of image and sign, we can get a preview in the figure of "drama," which reprises some of the arguments we've been developing in our discussion of Racine.

The central point in his discussion of drama is to assert it as the privileged, if not the only possible, form of the lover's discourse by opposing it to the novel. He writes, "As Narrative (Novel, Passion), love is a story which is accomplished, in the sacred sense of the word: it is a *program* which must be completed," the oblique reference to the inexorability of Christ's Crucifixion suggesting a divine or at least authorial organization to which the lover must submit (*LD* 93). In contrast, "Enamoration is a *drama*, if we restore to this word the archaic meaning Nietzsche gives it: 'Ancient drama envisioned [*avait en vue*] great declamatory scenes, which excluded action (action took place *before* or *behind* the stage).' Amorous seduction (a pure hypnotic moment) takes place *before* discourse and *behind* the proscenium of consciousness" (*LD* 94, 5:126). The elimination of action in favor of speech in the ancient drama resonates with the spectacular language of Racine's classicism that Barthes's footnotes brought into our view. Even more pointedly, however, is the way this kind of "declamatory" emphasis foregrounds language as not only what gives legible shape to action or experience but what makes action or experience available to consciousness at all, a process that might here be aimed at eliciting the recognition of "amorous seduction" but need not be limited to love. Nietzsche, of course, is one of the signal nodes in the genealogy of this kind of textual thinking, and citing him at this point accentuates the instability of signification and the energy of interpretation in which we've been locating citation's liberating image. These energetics find their most compelling illustration as much in Barthes's own manipulation of *drama*'s "archaic" connotation to counter the programmatic determination of the love story as in the other literary example to which he appeals—namely, Goethe's Werther, who "recounts both the events of his life and the effects of his passion" in the letters he sends to his friend (*LD* 93–94). Emphasizing the extreme triviality of these events, Barthes notes how "it is literature which governs this mixture," so that an event "only exists in its huge reverberation" with a literary form or text, such reflexion turning mundane occurrences into fantastic dramas of signification (*LD* 93).

* * *

The extent to which literature does indeed "govern" the lover's speech is one reason why *A Lover's Discourse* is the consummate text to complement and complete our exploration of citation as *On Racine* has been dramatizing it. Another reason, however, is the way that Barthes's later work reorients the socially generalized condition of ideological confinement in a more individual or more subjective direction, what Barthes calls the discourse's *"extreme solitude"* enacting such cultural compulsion on an interior stage (*LD* 1). This is the place where, turning on the visuality of the page play in both these works, the image of citation also begins to receive a more conceptual analysis as Barthes uncovers the verbal scripts informing love's imaginary composition: "This argument does not refer to the amorous subject and what he is (no one external to this subject, no discourse on love), but to what he says," as he puts it in his explanatory preamble (*LD* 5). The imaginary relationship to language that Barthes simulates is also the place where the liberatory affordances introduced by citation come out most forcefully, integrating the various formalist freedoms we've been developing into a fantastic consciousness of language as such. My reading of *A Lover's Discourse* thus trains its gaze not so much on love per se or even really on love's language in general, which would be simply to repeat, figure by figure, the entire course of the book. Rather, I note particular points (and certainly not all of them) where the lover's discourse reflects on itself as a linguistic practice, speaks about the operation, implications, and effects of its speech in terms that open up the citational dynamic at its heart.

As we've begun to see, literature—especially in its explicitly dramatic mode—offers one of the sites where such linguistic self-reflexion is most in evidence, a phenomenon Barthes extrapolates into everyday life when he takes up the figure of "affirmation." (Resonantly, he also characterizes the overall project of the book as "an *affirmation*" of the lover's discourse in the face of its otherwise "ignored, disparaged, or derided" cultural position [*LD* 1]). Establishing the term's expository framework, he begins, "Against and in spite of everything, the subject affirms love as *value*," his italics indicating the enlivening force coursing through that word as a result of affirmation itself. The four comments that follow orchestrate a number of marginal citations on the basis of which they unpack the bracing persistence of love in the face of its depreciation by more rational worldly enterprises as well as by the doubts and uncertainties of any amorous pursuit. Another line from Goethe's *Werther*, a veritable literary guidebook on love that appears repeatedly throughout the discourse, offers Barthes the opportunity to analyze a quotidian situation and to refigure or, more literally, reread its significance. Initially staging the lover in the midst of a prosaic linguistic practice, he transforms it, via a citation, into something much more fantastic. He ventriloquizes, "This morning, I must get off an 'important' letter right away—one on which the success of a certain undertaking depends; but instead I write a love letter—which I do not send" (*LD* 23). The uselessness, inefficacy, and even stupidity of this incident (to use the word *event* would seem to bestow an importance on it that our culture of productivity would deny) is countered by the affirming statement that Barthes cites from Werther at the bottom of the page: "Oh, dear friend, if to tender one's whole being [*tendre tout son être*] is to give evidence of strength, why should an excessive tension [*une trop grande tension*] be weakness?" (*LD* 23, 5:52). It's not just that the line associates tenderness and strength to imagine a framework in which these seemingly irresponsible actions are given, quite literally, a different value. It's also that it asserts this framework through the logic of the signifier as the verb "tender" roots the very capacity or the very power to give in a kind of soft sensitivity; this logic comes out with yet more force in the French cognate, which extends the word's meaning to that of stretching or even straining. Hearing these ideas brought together in the later phrase "excessive tension," we can transform the extreme and assiduous delicacy for which the lover (like the close reader) is conventionally ridiculed into an explosive potency, a powerful aptitude for an alternative form of agency.

For his part, Barthes comments on the situation in evocative terms that affirm the symbolic strength I'm developing: "What love lays bare in me is *energy*. Everything I do has a meaning (hence I can *live*, without whining), but this meaning is an ineffable finality: it is merely the meaning of my strength. The painful, guilty, melancholy inflections, the whole reactive side of my everyday life is reversed" (*LD* 23). Echoing the expansive invigoration that received its most striking literary illustration in *la frappe*, the emphasis on energy here offers a metaphor for meaning and its enlivening effects. Indeed, the repetition of the very word "meaning" refuses to define it more specifically, holding it open instead as a site of live possibility or potentiality, a space of symbolic respiration that could be said to power the "reversal" of his reactivity. The statement itself works similarly as it either appeals to the indeterminate opacity of an "ineffable finality," on the one hand, or borrows Werther's word "strength," on the other. It is here, of course, that the marginal reference to "*Werther*" appears, as if to suggest that entering into the signifying network of a literary text is the ideal way to appropriate love's energetic force and allow himself to "*live*, without whining"—or, more specifically, to live affirmatively rather than at odds with the strength of his tenderness. He concludes with a statement to this effect that, recalling the isolation of the lover's discourse, also asserts the practical limits of this literary intervention: "Born of literature, able to speak only with the help of its worn codes, yet I am alone with my strength, doomed to *my own philosophy*" (*LD* 23).

While the seclusion of the lover posited here tempers any sweeping, world-changing utopianism, it simultaneously locates the lover's active, "strengthened" engagement of that world. This engagement and its "birth" from literature receives more concrete formulation when Barthes approaches citation in terms that go beyond any particular literary text or even any literary genre. Exploring the "deliberative figure" of the lover's "behavior," he offers three comments that seek to address the worldly, practical questions of "What is to be done? How is he to act?" (*LD* 62). He emphasizes the futility of trying to answer these questions definitively since they refer as much to the actions of the lover as to the uncertainties of signification, writing, "everything which is new, everything which disturbs, is received not as a fact but in the aspect of a sign which must be interpreted. From the lover's point of view, the fact becomes consequential because it is immediately transformed into a sign: it is the sign, not the fact, which is consequential (by its *aura*)" (*LD* 63). As the repetition of "consequential" suggests, the "immediacy" of this semiotic transformation takes place by inserting the fact into a chain or, more vaguely, into an *aura* of associative and progressive (paradigmatic and syntagmatic) connections to be imaginatively pursued. He offers a small scene to illustrate his point: "If the other has given me this new telephone number, what was that the sign of? Was it an invitation to telephone *right away*, for the pleasure of the call, or only *should the occasion arise*, out of necessity?" (63). As the question "What is to be done?" becomes indistinguishable from "What was that the sign of?," as actions become synonymous with signals, Barthes implies that the "behavior" of the lover is always at least partly constituted in symbolic terms. We might even see the telephone number that centers this scene as an image for the ultimately empty ciphers through which further signs—the speech or silence of the call itself—stream. This is particularly significant since, of the three points Barthes makes about "behavior," it is the only one that *lacks* an explicit marginal reference (*Werther* and Zen providing the other two points with their citational coordinates), as if these circumstances are a citation not of any specific literary example but of literature or literary operation *as such*. That is, insofar as literature openly creates a world out of an organized system of words, it also describes the situation in which the lover tries to act, a thick skein of potential meanings where, Barthes writes a few lines later, "*Everything signifies*" (*LD* 63). The literariness of life itself, otherwise shrouded in stereotype and standardized "givens," is here made ardently distinct.[18]

The lover's ongoing creation of a significant and signifying world for themselves is, in the end, what citation aims to fantastically reproduce by its sampling of a literary text, an idea that has been playing itself out since

Barthes's critical identification with the Racinian tragic hero and his confinement in a framework of preestablished meaning. His explicit discussion of "identification" as a figure in the lover's discourse thus not only reinforces the structural connection between these two far-flung texts in Barthes's oeuvre but also, and more valuably, frames the imaginary aspect of citation as a linguistic practice—one that is organized in precisely the terms we explored through our reading of *S/Z*'s literary reflexions. The practical valence of this figure comes out immediately in its heading where Barthes transforms the noun "identification" into an active verbal process: "The subject identifies himself with some person (or character) who occupies the same position as himself in the amorous structure" (*LD* 129). Identification is an action—even, to identify a correspondence with the figure we just discussed, a behavior—that is part of the way the subject introduces significance into the world. Unlike or perhaps in addition to the unifying reflexion of the mirror phase as Lacan describes it, identification "is not a psychological process; it is a pure structural operation: I am the one who has the same place I have [*je suis celui qui a la même place que moi*]" (*LD* 129, 5:167). The grammar of that final first-person statement is telling as the integrity of the *I* splits, by its repetition, into an oppositional face-off that itself opposes the identity suggested by the English pronoun "one." Comparably, the French formulates this situation in a traditional subject-object dyad (*je-moi*) with the very referential action of the demonstrative pronoun *celui* constituting the "substance" of the subject. In both cases, identification is a comparative, relational process that, recalling our in-depth account of reflexion and its value, integrates the subject as itself a reflective extension of a differential network of significations. And Barthes verbalizes it accordingly: "I perceive [*perçois*] not analogies but homologies," the visual suggestion of "perceive" ceding to a more intellectual sense necessary for the apprehension of structural rather than substantive similarities (*LD* 129, 5:167).

In the last comment he makes about the figure "identification," Barthes moves this kind of homological perception squarely into the literary sphere with a reference to the famous phenomenon of "Werther fever" in which young men of the novel's era fashioned themselves after Goethe's title character. But, in Barthes's account, this imitation becomes rather more complex than the simple assumption of an image: "Werther identifies himself with the madman, with the footman," he writes. "As a reader, I can identify myself with Werther," he continues before listing the various historical forms such identification has taken: "suffering, killing themselves, dressing, perfuming themselves, writing as if they were Werther (songs, poems, candy boxes, belt buckles, fans, colognes à la Werther)" (*LD* 131). The identification that Barthes fantastically describes is with the

124 Chapter Four

structural openness of Werther's own practice of identification, his ability to see himself reflected in all manner of different figures—now "the madman," now "the footman." This is the distinction between Barthes's homological image of Werther and the analogical one fixated on by his emulators, the extreme variety of their imitations throwing the monotonous identity of their model into relief. It's no accident then that, further down the margin, Barthes refers to another literary persona, always central to his (and our) thinking, whose own aesthetic identifications provide Werther himself with a homological complement: Proust. Raising the particularities of these feverishly literal life-literature liaisons to a more general or more structural level, Proust's simultaneous status as a historical person and a textual production also has the effect of setting off Werther's singular status as a figure, a network of signs laid out baldly in Barthes's excessive listing: *Werther* rather than Werther.

Before getting to the Proust citation, however, Barthes comments on the textual process by which such figural (as well as figurative) identifications are formed in a way that diagrams what we could think of as the practical creation, if not the very "content," of these citational correspondences. Though he may begin by observing that "In the theory of literature, 'projection' (of the reader into the character) no longer has any currency," his assertion that it is nonetheless "the appropriate register of imaginative readings [*le registre propre des lectures imaginaires*]" stems from the fact that he is imagining such projection taking place as a readerly engagement of language, which is to say, on a properly symbolic register.[19] As he explains, "reading a love story, it is scarcely adequate to say I project myself [*je me projette*]; I cling to [*je colle à*] the image of the lover, shut up with this image in the very enclosure of the book" (*LD* 131, 5:169). As the verb "project," in its psychological sense, describes the attribution of one's own feelings or thoughts to another in a way that occupies or takes the place of one's actual interiority, it implies an accomplished process in which readers refuse to recognize the character as such to the extent that they only see themselves in it. Alternatively, the rhetoric of "clinging," in addition to echoing the glued assembly of my paper collages, maintains a subtle distinction between the I and the image, emphasizes their superficial and anxiously impermanent adherence, and intimates a stubborn externality that can never be fully incorporated. To cling is, in our earlier phrasing, to hold on to what would otherwise come apart. Furthermore, the interiority highlighted here is not that of the reader or even of the character but "the very enclosure of the book," an expressly delimited space of verbal signs and textual dynamics that frame the lover's image in signifying terms. From this perspective, what I am clinging to is nothing other than a chain of signs to which I add "myself" as one more citational link.

Barthes's account of the conditions under or by which this clinging addition takes place illustrates the implication of the quotation marks (themselves the characteristic indicators of citation) I've placed around "myself," since he describes how "everyone knows that such stories are read [*se lisent*] in a state of secession, of retirement, of voluptuous absence: in the toilet" (*LD* 131, 5:169). As the seclusion of the toilet seems to cite the "enclosure of the book," it not only carves out a space of privacy within the larger social world but even voluptuously evacuates the subject as such: there isn't, after all, anyone specific doing the reading in this statement. Shedding the trappings of our public identity, we quite literally expose ourselves to and through the alternative or additional signifying network of "such stories." The lines from *Swann's Way* to which Barthes refers us here expand on the kind of fantastic textual subjectivity I'm positing by allying reading with a set of other activities that realize the subject by vacating it of any definite substance: "this room . . . long served as a refuge for me, because it was the only one where I was allowed to lock the door, a refuge for all my occupations which required an invincible solitude: reading, daydreaming, tears, and pleasure" (*LD* 131). As "daydreaming, tears, and pleasure" describe states of indirect or ancillary self-presence, situations in which we come into contact with ourselves through the mediation of imagery, emotion, or sensation, they imply a similar if more obviously detached dynamic for reading and for language per se that comes out nowhere more clearly than in the image of citation itself. The result is to allow us to articulate ourselves as a verbal hallucination, to identify ourselves with the distance of signification, to grasp ourselves *at a remove*.

This paradox is what Barthes describes in the figure that will draw this chapter to a close, that of "understanding," which not only could be read as an apology for the overall discursive portrait his book is staging but also describes, at its most general and imaginative, the fantastic operation citation has been animating. "Suddenly perceiving the amorous episode as a knot of inexplicable reasons and impaired solutions," he begins, "the subject exclaims: 'I want to understand (what is happening to me)!'" (*LD* 59). The series of figures that constitute the book are meant, quite literally, to give words to the "inexplicable reasons and impaired solutions" that knit love's experiential fabric. As he puts it, "I want to analyze, to know, to express in another language than mine; I want to represent my delirium to myself, I want to 'look in the face' what is dividing me, cutting me off" (*LD* 60). Though the demand here for "another language" might seem to depart from the "'dramatic' method which renounces examples and rests on the single action of a primary language," we could read that phrase to be referring to his reliance on others' languages, the words and sentences he has plucked from his cultural archive to make legible love's delirium

(*LD* 3). This legibility is anything but immediate, as suggested by the insistent focus on "what is dividing me, cutting me off," as if to suggest once again the impossible collaging of division and contiguity—a kind of contiguity *with* division. He seems to envision what the lived experience of this fantastic coincidence might look like in the final comment he makes, when he declares, "I want to change systems: no longer to unmask, no longer to interpret, but to make consciousness itself a drug and thereby to accede to the perfect vision of reality, to the great bright dream, to prophetic love" (*LD* 60). I am less taken by the absolutist aspirations of the closing phrases than, stoner that I am, by the idea of "making consciousness itself a drug" and its desire to see experience as such as a form of stimulating intoxication. How this might occur is unclear, but I take a hint from the word "etymology" that Barthes has placed in the margin and suggest that it is precisely the mobile development of meaning it denotes that might constitute this enlivened kind of consciousness. The citation itself obliquely affirms as much, if only because it displays the process of verbal distinction on which meaning itself depends: "The Greeks opposed *onar*, the vulgar dream, to *hypar*, the prophetic (never believed) dream. Communicated [*Signalé*] by J.-L.B." (*LD* 60, 5:90). In addition to the act of comparison or opposition by which Barthes is both qualifying and exemplifying his visionary fantasy, the final fragment communicates little more than linguistic communication itself, the French *signaler*, "to attract attention," pointing to the fantastic effect of signs that the concluding initials cite so literally.

'she had had the impression that something absolutely material, which had been present around her and around everyone and around everything forever, but imperceptible, was breaking down the outlines of persons and things and revealing itself.' Her heart was beating out of her chest, the neighbourhood dialect had become unintelligible, all at once it was apparent that our bodies were not made to stand up to this onslaught. 'I have to seize the stream that's passing through me, I have to throw it out from me,' she said, in order to calm herself. But even before that night, 'she had often had the sensation of moving for a few fractions of a second into

10. Untitled (April 2021). Author's handmade collage.

Conclusion
The Wisdom of Criticism

I suppose this is your problem too—to make students fantasize in front of images.

"A Problematic of Meaning" (*Gift* 110)

For a long time, especially early in its composition, I kept this book a secret. I was a little nervous to say that I was writing a study of Barthes. In the back of my mind, I could already hear the critiques: how passé, how precious, how pretentious (and they would not be totally wrong). The fact that I was trying to talk about the interpretive entanglement of literature and life and the crafty affordances of closely considering language only seemed to affirm the rearguard romanticism of my project. Yet, as Barthes himself avows in the opening of *Criticism and Truth*, "We should not be surprised that a country should periodically review in this way the things which come down from its past and describe them anew in order to find out *what it can make of them* [*ce qu'il peut en faire*]" (*Criticism* 29, 2:759). Justifying the reconsideration of Racine we examined in the last chapter, he is talking more generally about the fresh perspectives on classical texts provided by critical vocabularies innovated from fields like Marxism, psychoanalysis, and structural linguistics. Even more, his comments also describe this project's return to his work: though my continuation of the American academy's love affair with "French theory" might exceed the national frame in which he stages his historical "review," the emphasis he sagely places on a constructive kind of *making* speaks quite openly to the practical, worldly criticism I have been working to cobble together through my readings of his texts.[1] In this, I have been trying to realize the manifold implications of his claim, made in the book's most focused discussion of criticism as a specific intellectual practice, that "the critic experiences in relation to the book the same conditions governing discourse as the writer experiences in relation to the world" (84). The homology will be familiar to us, and I repeat it here to highlight not only the writerly complexion of critical making but also, and more fundamentally, the discursive constitution of the writer's phenomenal experience—of, in reality, phenomenal experience as such.

Barthes makes the latter point somewhat more evocatively, if not fully fantastically, in the preface to his early collection of *Critical Essays* that appeared a few years before the pointed defense of his interpretive methods from 1966: "The writer does not 'wrest' speech from silence, as we are told in pious literary hagiographies, but inversely, and how much more arduously, more cruelly and less gloriously, detaches a secondary language from the slime of primary languages afforded him by the world, history, his existence, in short by an intelligibility that preexists him" (*Critical* xvii). The clinging, undifferentiated sludge of the sentence's slime imagery paints lived experience as a sticky secretion of indeterminate and assumed meanings, which may be sensible, even intelligible, but is not precisely legible. The last results rather from the "arduous" task of the writer, whose "detachment" refers as much to the cognitive distance made possible by verbal articulation as it does to the systematic divisions and distinctions introduced by words themselves. Let us not, in this regard, fail to note the emphatic use of commas to partition and coordinate his phrasing here. Significantly, when Barthes dashingly returns to this laborious process of detachment in his characterization of how criticism works—"The critic separates meanings, he causes a second language—that is to say, a coherence of signs—to float above the first language of the work [*oeuvre*]," he writes in the later argument—he describes an outlook that begins *with words*, that wisely presumes the primacy of the linguistic in the constitution of a particular experience (*Criticism* 80, 2:792). From this perspective, it's not just that the critic is a writer—as Barthes never stops repeating—but that the writer is, at base, also a critic.

At stake in this transposition is the real secret of this book: a manifestly verbal mindset that criticism enacts most emphatically and that I am no doubt exaggeratedly calling its *wisdom*. My argument's ultimate revelation, which was also its fantastic genesis, involves the ardent acknowledgment and explicit exercise of words' role in sculpting our sense of things. As criticism thus finds itself in, even founds itself on, a consciousness of signification equally esoteric and everyday, it doubles down on the practice of language that has driven the foregoing chapters and that this conclusion aims to formulate in as literal and lifelike terms as possible.[2] Doing so entails returning to Proust (if we've ever really left him), the figure whose rhapsodizing of novel and essay offers a writerly illustration of the readerly way of life that has constituted this book's utopian project since the first. For of course it is Proust who, as the presiding genius of my no less than Barthes's intellectual fantasies, sparked the dream of living literature that I have been trying to interpret. Barthes makes his own Proustian investments explicit in a passage from *The Pleasure of the Text* that will scaffold this concluding account of criticism's wisdom: "Proust's work, for myself at least, is *the* reference work [*l'oeuvre de référence*], the general *mathesis*, the *mandala* of the entire literary cosmogony—as Mme de Sévigné's letters were for the narrator's grandmother, tales of chivalry for Don Quixote, etc." (*Pleasure* 36, 4:240). Offering a thumbnail description of the fantastic relationship to language and literature moving through my argument, these lines touch on the referential dynamic it seeks to animate. If the straightforward reference between signs and objects is what Barthes spends his career contesting, the appeal to the narrator's grandmother's and Don Quixote's bibliomancy imagines this process in more complex terms and brings out the sense of active interpretive exertion that the phrase "work of reference" lacks in French.

Barthes goes on to clarify this effort even as he seems to belie it and elaborates the critical wisdom I have in the classified corners of my mind: "Proust is simply what comes to me, not what I summon up; not an 'authority,' simply a *circular memory*. Which is what the inter-text is: the impossibility of living outside the infinite text—whether this text be Proust or the daily newspaper or the television screen: the book creates the meaning, the meaning creates life" (*Pleasure* 36). The forswearing of both "summoning" and "'authority'" indicates that the activity here is less about recall than it is about reading: for knowing that I must read—*that I am reading*—rather than just receiving "what comes to me" is a kind of wisdom that might facilitate the fantasy of living inside the infinite text and allow me to participate, however conditionally, in the meaningful creation of life itself. Indeed, what the rhythmic chain of phrases that ends these lines makes clear is that life is simply a secret code word for meaning's defining movement. Yet it surely has not gone unnoticed that, for all the appeals my argument makes to life, lived experience, and the world in these pages, the insistently verbal accent I've maintained from the start does not necessarily translate seamlessly or obviously beyond the interpretive reading of a literary or, for that matter, a critical text. (Even in these comments on Proust, Barthes is mostly focused on anticipatory echoes of the later author that he finds in Flaubert's and Stendhal's language.) Which is why, in my closing moves, I take up his commentaries on photography as especially lucid elaborations of a perceptual, if not entirely existential, engagement with signification that fleshes out my expressly bookish focus into something closer to literary living proper. This pictorial turn thus draws together the verbal and visual vectors of my discourse and tightens the spiral of the foregoing chapters and interchapters into a generalized linguistic cognizance that, in its infinite wisdom, criticism both requires and allows us to inhabit.

The specific affordance of focusing on photography to conclude my exposition of the fantastic and the practical criticism that offers its most comprehensive mode of production lodges in its elusive status as "an emanation of *past reality*: a *magic*, not an art," to repeat a line from *Camera Lucida* I quoted at the outset of chapter 1 (*CL* 88). As we will recall from our fleeting discussion of that magic, when Barthes finally isolates the *noeme* or "essence" of photography, he locates it in the singularity of the "'photographic referent'" and the necessity that it "*has been there*" (*CL* 76). He asserts, "What I intentionalize in a photograph (we are not yet speaking of film) is neither Art nor Communication, it is Reference, which is the founding order of Photography," a statement that positions photography as an ideal image of the referential work at the heart of the fantastic's magical interface between literature and life (*CL* 77).[3] Furthermore, if, for a photograph, "the referent *adheres*," as he puts it early on using diction that speaks to the sticky sliminess of preexistent language as well as to the gummed construction of my collages, he also observes that certain photographs elicit in him "an internal agitation, an excitement, a certain labor too, the pressure of the unspeakable which wants to be spoken" (*CL* 6; italics added; 18). What's important for me here is less the affective charge guiding his attraction to one image over another than the emphasis on speech characterizing his response. A photograph may be "an image without a code"—or at least, as we will momentarily discuss, an image without the kind of discontinuous, differential signifying system that usually goes by that name—but for this very reason needs and even desires a linguistic admixture to, as we say, *develop* its meaning (*CL* 88). In this, it is like the world with its slurry of unarticulated significance to which, without words, we are superficially stuck.

The "internal agitation" that provokes what we will significantly discuss as a verbal relay also evokes the textual pleasure we've just seen him find in Proust, the "*circular memory*" by which his life becomes intertextually and meaningfully legible to him. Making this connection is meant to signal the literary possibility latent in Barthes's midcareer semiological analyses of photography, which counter the latter's connection to "a certain mythical notion of Life: the image is re-presentation, i.e., ultimately resurrection, and we know that the intelligible is reputed antipathetic to the experiential" (*Responsibility* 21). The fantasy he's talking about is linked to the analogical nature of the photograph, the fact that "to shift from reality to its photograph, it is not necessary to break down this reality into units and to constitute these units into signs substantially different from the object they represent" (*Responsibility* 5). Accordingly, the semiotic terms in which he explores the question "How does meaning come to the image?" can also, homologically if not analogically, complicate our perceptual relationship with lived reality or "Life" itself (*Responsibility* 22). As the theoretical rigor of his discussion maps, in fine-grained detail, the readerly reception that constitutes the wisdom of criticism, it also provides a final sagacious synthesis of the practice of language in which literature and life fantastically interpenetrate—what, in the argument of *Sade, Fourier, Loyola* that introduced and will conclude my entire project, he describes as "receiving from the text a kind of fantasmatic order [*une sorte d'ordre fantasmatique*]" (*SFL* 8, 3:705). For once, I want to linger with the personal, psychologically oriented term "fantasmatic" rather than immediately abstracting it to the more general *fantastic*, because the false consciousness of ideology is what Barthes's early photography essays are primarily committed to investigating. Focusing on newspaper and advertising photography, he explores how the photograph does actually get coded but on the connotative rather than denotative level—in "the way in which society represents, to a certain extent, what it thinks of the *analogon*" rather than the "*analogon* itself" (*Responsibility* 6). Of the "connotation procedures" he enumerates to parse "the imposition of a second meaning upon the photographic message proper," the one that receives fullest comment is also the one most illustrative of criticism's verbalizing wisdom with all its fantasmatic and ultimately fantastic effects—namely, "the text which accompanies the press photograph" (*Responsibility* 9, 14).

The referential dynamic between text and image that he explores in the form of the caption reiterates, in a more capacious theoretical vocabulary, the operation of citation as we explored it in the previous chapter. The general thrust of Barthes's discussion stresses the "*repressive*" influence the text has on the image: instead of the "'floating chain' of signifieds of which the reader can select some and ignore the rest" that constitutes the polysemous denotation of the image (and, at least ideally, of our visual perception as such), the linguistic supplement allows for the "*anchoring* of every possible (denoted) meaning of the object, by recourse to a nomenclature" (*Responsibility* 28–29). The caption, from this perspective, directs both our attention and our intellection, telling us what to see and what to think about it. Precisely because this is the case, however, I am interested in the way the initial terms by which he institutes this interaction also cast such anchoring as a kind of meaningful inflation: "First, the text constitutes a parasitical message intended to connote the image, i.e., to 'enliven' ['*insuffler*'] it with one or more secondary signifieds," he writes a few years earlier (*Responsibility* 14, 1:1128). Even as the scare quotes ironize the rhetoric of life and invigoration introduced by the English translation,

The Wisdom of Criticism 133

they also, and in the same breath, indicate the lively operation of rhetoric itself that the French *insuffler* and the "parasite" metaphor announce more overtly. Meaning to "inspire" or, less figuratively, "to breathe into," *insuffler* hints at an opening up, even a *spacing*, within what is otherwise impenetrably compact or compressed—an unexpected echo of the laborious detachment achieved by the writer and critic (as well as the verbal "respiration" Barthes used to loosen the tragic confinement in Racine). Complemented by the text's "parasitical" status, this airy opening up seems dependent on a kind of piercing bite that also harks back, in more graphic terms, to the cuts of notation by which my earlier arguments advanced their work. In this reading, what we are noting is as much the "secondary signifieds" that the text imparts to the image as it is the very process, the very partitioning practice, on which signification fundamentally lies.

If the expansionary effect of words on our perception is not exactly what Barthes's argument about textual "anchoring" wants to say, my discussion cites the wisdom of his own literary criticism and exploits the fundamental spaciousness that words introduce by working through the multiple meanings and assorted associations they bring with them. In so doing, it sets off the second, "rarer" function that verbal language has in relation to the image—namely, "relaying" (*Responsibility* 30). As no one teaches us better than Barthes himself, words provide meaning's ballast and buoyancy both, its open stability and its operative switch points. Claiming that the relaying function is found "mainly in cartoons and comic strips" (and also, I'd like to add, in collage art like mine), he explains how it creates a "complementary relation" between the verbal and the visual in which "words are then fragments of a more general syntagm, as are the images, and the message's unity occurs on a higher level: that of the story, the anecdote, the diegesis" (30). What is rather sublime about this deceptively simple appeal to story is the way the dialectical synthesis of word and image it describes stealthily imagines, in the progressive form of a narrative, a shape for the mobility of meaning that underwrites their common functioning. Instead of "a kind of vise which keeps connoted meanings from proliferating," these brief lines rework the referential effect by sketching a "general syntagm" in and through which the proliferation of meaning can pursue itself (28–29). What I mean will come out more graphically and indeed more fantastically if I return to *Camera Lucida*, and the famous account of the *punctum*, which is also one of the few places in Barthes's work where we concretely encounter captions (and even one literary citation!) referentially interacting with photographs.

The complex and charismatic effects that effloresce from the concentrated prick of the *punctum* are by now very familiar, and for my purposes here I am particularly drawn to what Barthes calls "a kind of subtle *beyond*"

134 Conclusion

(*CL* 59). His comment regards a Mapplethorpe photograph of a young man with his arm extended, and the erotics informing his discussion imply a relatively obvious fantasy space in which we might imagine any number of narrative scenarios. But he also stages that *beyond* in more general terms on the previous page: "on account of her necklace," he writes with reference to James Van der Zee's "Family Portrait" from 1926, "the black woman in her Sunday best has had, for me, a whole life external to her portrait" (*CL* 57). Of course, the woman in the portrait has in fact had a "whole life" external to it, but the "for me" announces the extent to which the *punctum* here occasions *another* life for her, another story that, Barthes has explained, he weaves out of the echo between her necklace and his family memories. Yet we should also note that, for this photograph, the *punctum* itself undergoes a kind of narrative development, staging its own form of syntagmatic succession as it shifts from the "belt worn low by the sister (or daughter) . . . and above all her *strapped pumps*" to the "slender ribbon of braided gold" by way of the cordlike horizontal shapes linking them (*CL* 43, 53). The story being told here is as much the flights of fancy that the touching point makes available to Barthes as it is the movement of metonymy that multiplies the image's possible meanings.[4] And while this particular metonymic slide might be taking place exclusively in the visual register, the role played by the captions in pinpointing the *punctum* opens space to wisely plot meaning's associative chronicle via the verbal.

Despite their vital place in displaying Barthes's analysis, the captions have, until recently, remained something of an open textual secret hiding in plain sight.[5] Since, as Barthes proclaims, "the *studium* is ultimately always coded, the *punctum* is not," his argument proceeds by induction rather than deduction; the concrete examples offer an accretive demonstration rather than a conclusive definition of this poignant phenomenon (*CL* 51). To effect these demonstrations of the piercing (and highly personal) detail, however, he has no choice but to rely on the shared code of verbal language, brief fragments filched from the flow of *Camera Lucida*'s argument. "*The* punctum, *for me, is the second boy's crossed arms . . .*" appears, for example, with Nadar's handsome portrait of explorer Savorgnan de Brazza, while the more laconic (and provisional) "*The strapped pumps*" hovers under the Van der Zee portrait we just touched on (*CL* 52, 44). Even if they cannot transmit the affective charge that animates the images for Barthes, these citations nonetheless orient and focus us; they perform their own punctuating operation, an alternative instantiation of the "explicitation, i.e., to a certain degree, a stress" that, in his earlier accounts of the caption, illuminated the ideological coding of connotation (*Responsibility* 15). As the ideological in this later work is absorbed in the *studium*, which "always refers to a classical body of information," a kind of "*average* effect, almost from a certain training," the caption moves from the imaginary realm of the fantasmatic into the linguistic reality of the fantastic: the fundamental discontinuity of its wording breaks up and modulates the visually continuous presentation of the image to produce, or at least reproduce, an "element which rises from the scene, shoots out of it like an arrow" (*CL* 25–26). I acknowledge that the arrow imagery is something of a misdirection since, in this case, the puncture is entering rather than exiting the photographic plane. But the suggestion of pointing is what I want to point out insofar as the arrow describes the work of the caption's referentiality at the same time as the clarity of its cutting pictures the emphatic effect on one part of the image (as well as the fragments' excision from *Camera Lucida*'s larger text). When Barthes unpacks the word *punctum* itself—"sting, speck, cut, little hole—and also a cast of the dice"—his incisive vocabulary and the citation of Mallarmé's typographical derring-do gesture toward a shared field of textual activity articulating the visual and the verbal.[6]

I am not, let me be clear, suggesting a wholesale identification between the caption and the *punctum* but rather pointing to a similar operational structure, a resonant effect that drives home the expansionary readerly reception of perceptual experience criticism makes available. Elizabeth Abel has recently distinguished what she importantly calls the work's "textual *punctum*," which will help me to amplify that resonance in more insistently literary terms (and, as my former dissertation adviser and present-day friend, in fantastically personal ones as well). She focuses on one distinctive caption, appended to G. W. Wilson's photograph of Queen Victoria on horseback from 1863, which "unlike all the other photographs (including many by American photographers), is captioned in English—the only words of English in the French text—in words attributed not to Roland Barthes but to Virginia Woolf: '*Queen Victoria, entirely unesthetic* (Virginia Woolf).'"[7] Tracing "a potential but exorbitant genealogy" between these two lions of lyricism, Abel suggests that Barthes "recruits Woolf to, indeed constitutes her as, a performance of the unruly *punctum*, a modernist protest against the blanketing force of Victorian conventions."[8] In doing so, the arrow-like exactitude of his commentary ("a kilted groom holds the horse's bridle: this is the *punctum*," he writes on the facing page) receives an additional vein of textual mediation, a further verbal reference, that locates a supplementary signifying network in the "little hole" he hollows out. This is less to fill that hole than it is to continue its excavation in more detailed terms. As Abel thus proceeds to place this static image—this image of stasis itself—into a network of narrative echoes from Woolf's oeuvre that effectively and fantastically animate it, she approaches Barthes's parenthetical citation of Woolf's name as we've approached Proust's: not as the index of a historical person but as the allusive entrée into a dynamic literary field structured by nothing more (and nothing less) than words.[9]

Even more to the point are the gnomic words Barthes cites from a 1930 entry in Woolf's diary.[10] "*Queen Victoria, entirely unesthetic*...," suggests not just the monarch's visual unattractiveness but also, leaning hard on etymology, an apparent sense of disembodiment, insensibility, maybe even somehow *invisibility*. (The Greek *aisthētós*: "sensible, perceptible.") "Entirely" abstracted from her flesh and blood, the queen is only symbol, which is, after all, the dignified purpose of the crown, especially in late modern Britain—a kind of living sign if not a live signifier. The disruptive cut of this caption, emphasized in that isolating comma, works less to set off any particular detail in the photograph than to sever its subject from what Barthes would call the biographical alibi and to release it into the referential relays of its signifying networks. Hovering in undefined space—Abel also notes that "the collodion plate has been scratched to efface the background of trees" present in the more famous version of the photograph hanging in the National Galleries of Scotland—she is there for us to read rather than to see, or to see only insofar as it triggers a succession of meaningful associations, including but not limited to the literary citations that Woolf's name makes available.[11] This interpenetration of reading and seeing is how we can understand Barthes's concluding comment on this image whose exceedingly suggestive phrasing begins to move us more purposefully to the chiasmus of the literary and lived at which my whole argument is aimed: "The *punctum* fantastically 'brings out' [*fait fantastiquement sortir*] the Victorian nature (what else to call it?) of the photograph, it endows the photograph with a blind field [*champs aveugle*]" (CL 57, 5:834). Naming the modality in which the *punctum* allows the photograph to surpass itself, "fantastic" here qualifies the very real production of its general meaning, the signification of its "Victorian nature." At the same time, the parenthetical "(what else to call it?)" prolongs that production and stages signification as an ongoing practice if, taking the rhetorical question literally, we hear a call for additional, alternative signifieds that would constellate themselves along metaphoric and metonymic axes.[12] As exactly what we can't or don't *see*, this readerly exfoliation of the photograph's interconnected connotations is what constitutes the "blind field" of which Barthes somewhat cryptically speaks.

Approaching the ostensibly visual phenomenon of the "blind field" in these verbal terms is a prime example of the critical wisdom we've been using the caption to illustrate, the outspoken linguistic elaboration that provides our perceptual experience not just with a general intelligibility but with texture and depth afforded by *legibility* more specifically.

Furthermore, by opening this discussion to what exceeds the frame and framework of the photograph as such, the "blind field" links the *punctum* to one of its theoretical antecedents that will impart this wisdom with a conclusive and concretely cutting articulation. I'm talking here about Barthes's eccentric argument in "The Third Meaning," whose focus on "several Eisenstein stills" places it on the spliced edge between photography and film where the "blind field" also finds itself (41).[13] For though Barthes might claim that "once there is a *punctum*, a blind field is created (is divined)" to magically mobilize the photograph's signifying processes, he originally observes this mobility in the cinema because it "has a power which at first glance the Photograph does not have: the screen (Bazin has remarked) is a not a frame but a hideout; the man or woman who emerges from it continues living: a 'blind field' constantly doubles our partial vision" (*CL* 56–57). I don't pretend to fully understand these elliptical lines, but I do get the fleeting sense that they are describing how the inexorable forward march of the film screens off any possibility of full access or comprehension and lends the images an air of contingency. Precisely because the figures here "continue living" (what strange, fantastic wording), these images subtly gesture toward their potential provisionality and preserve the possibility that they could be or, more credibly, could mean something different. The "blind field" thus seems to function as a kind of reserve in which unactivated alternatives and additional seams of potential significance are secreted. If such a reserve is what, with the Woolf caption, we parsed in terms of particularly literary signifying networks, the temporal condition introduced by Barthes's focus on film offers us the vital milieu in which to bring reading itself to life.

He says as much in the fuller meditation on film that he uses to illustrate the "third" or "obtuse" meaning, which anticipates, in less affective and more semiotic terms, the general operation of the *punctum* and its more specific connection to the caption: "for there are obtuse meanings not everywhere (the signifier is a rare thing, a future figure) but *somewhere* [*quelque part*]: in other *authors* of films (maybe), in a certain way of reading 'life' and hence 'reality' (here understood in its simple opposition to the deliberately fictive)" (*Responsibility* 54, 3:498). "Reading 'life'" here seems primarily to describe the particular framing and cinematic style by which an auteur represents the world of their film, especially since he goes on to discuss a kind of real-life image from a documentary on fascism. But the sweeping vagueness in the emphatic "*somewhere*" and that tempering "(maybe)" also allow us to see "a certain way of reading 'life'" in the general terms I've been finding in the wisdom of criticism, not just as an appositional description of directorial panache but as a more wide-ranging perceptual practice that approaches "reality" as a deliberately or, even better, a *deliberatively* realized representation. And although Barthes's opening account of the "third meaning" unfolds in reference to an image from *Ivan the Terrible*, his further explanation maps the fantastic coincidence of reading and reality that my gloss invokes and that my discussion of the caption began to put into words. He describes an encounter with a kind of pure signifier, an "as yet incomplete sign" or a set of "signifying accidents" that evokes the "blind field" in its evasion of a recognizable signified, going on to insist that "this signifier cannot be identified with the simple *Dasein* of the scene; it exceeds the copy of the referential motif, it compels an interrogative reading—an interrogation bearing precisely on the signifier, not on the signified, on the reading, not on the intellection: it is a 'poetic' apprehension" (*Responsibility* 42-43). As these lines displace both the "referential motif" and the "simple *Dasein* of the scene" from their status as given, as something to be plainly received, they linger in the rhythm of their phrasing and draw out their own enunciation to approximate the "'poetic' apprehension" they're trying to bring into being. Indeed, the emphasis they put on the action of reading and not just the abstraction of the signifier distinguishes them from Barthes's myriad other statements on the semiological construction of experience. What is being fantastically experienced here, what could be said to constitute its own by no means simple *Dasein*, is reading itself, the active, time-intensive process of deciphering "a meaning both persistent and fugitive, apparent and evasive," as he puts it on the next page (*Responsibility* 44).

Approaching this impossible being-there of reading as an engagement of "signifying" or "*signifiance*" in Julia Kristeva's terms, Barthes claims that it "opens onto the infinity of language" (43-44).[14] But his less totalizing attempts at describing it lend themselves to the more practical perspective advanced by the caption's pointedly verbal operation and round out the revitalization of reference in which the fantastic is ultimately rooted: he asserts, for instance, that "the obtuse meaning, then, has something to do with disguise," explaining that "it calls attention to itself as false yet nonetheless refuses to abandon the 'good faith' of its referent" (*Responsibility* 48-49). Here, as the language of disguise couples falsity and reference, it complicates the idea of the latter as a simple, transparent act of pointing to an intelligible object and presents it instead as a "good faith" fabrication of that intelligibility. This readerly dynamic is rather more obvious in the case of the caption, as the words tailor our perception into something like a clearly legible disguise. Far from freezing perception, however, this tailoring participates in "a layering of meaning which always allows the previous one to subsist, as in a geological formation" where any particular take is just one streak in a multifarious and open-ended accumulation of connotations (*Responsibility* 49). Offering a spatialized image that begins to come to grips with the network of proliferating meanings opened by signification, this kind of layering also pictures the perceptual payoff of the criticism whose verbal wisdom we've been anatomizing. Though Barthes insists that "the obtuse meaning will not come into being, will not enter into the critic's metalanguage ... what the obtuse meaning disturbs, sterilizes, is metalanguage (criticism)," I want to distinguish what I've been talking about from his assumptions in these lines, which seem to be that the task of criticism in the face of this additional level of meaning is to identify and explain its significance in a particular visual text (*Responsibility* 55). This is an undertaking that the emphasis on an accretive and never complete process of "signifying" renders completely unworkable.

Instead, I take my cue from the strange splintering the essay itself undergoes on the heels of his critical dismissal, the seemingly surplus postscripts that layer a final formulation of his argument onto what has come before and implicitly, even secretly, recast criticism's readerly wisdom as a purposeful fragmentation and reflective rearticulation of a text's signification—if not exactly its specific significations. This is what I think we can gather from the abrupt turn taken in the last pages, flagged as a specifically verbal remainder, that broaches the fantastic by cutting into the temporal movement informing both film and lived experience more generally: "A word remains to be said about the syntagmatic responsibility of this third meaning [*Reste à dire un mot de la responsabilité syntagmatique de ce troisième sens*]. What is its place in the anecdote's succession, in the logico-temporal system, without which, apparently, it is not possible for a narrative to be understood by the 'mass' of readers and spectators?" (*Responsibility* 57; III: 501). By once again underscoring or prolonging the ongoing formulation of his argument, Barthes' last-minute consideration of the sequential aspect of language and narrative asserts the supplementary temporality in which reading and criticism more broadly take place and intervenes in the common-sense "logico-temporal system" that sees simple, straightforward succession as the necessary and natural condition of experience. Triggered by the way the third meaning's fundamental indefinability short circuits habituated patterns of identification and recognition, this intervention inheres in the curious phrase "syntagmatic responsibility," which animates the "general syntagm" that synthesized word and image in the comic strip. What we have here is both a duty to follow the syntagmatic's fundamentally sequential structure and an *ability to respond* to that structure. Sequence itself might be inescapable, but the progression we pursue is less determined than film or life would make it seem.

By way of explanation, Barthes appeals to the metonymic mobility of meaning that the "word-as-relay" activated in our discussion of the caption and transforms the temporality of traditional narrative into something that almost explicitly approaches the signifying operation of the "blind field." He writes, "the presence of a supplementary, obtuse, third meaning ... profoundly alters the theoretical status of the anecdote. The story (diegesis) is no longer merely a powerful system (an age-old narrative system), but also and contradictorily a simple space, a field of permanences and permutations [*un champ de permanences et de permutations*]" (*Responsibility* 58; III: 502). The essay's turn to narrative here also works as a turning of it: the linearity by which the category of the syntagmatic is customarily conceptualized spreads out into a two-dimensional "field" where temporal progress need not be synonymous with a succession of events. Instead, as suggested by the alliterative echo in the phrase "permanences and permutations," it proceeds according to a kind of internal variation or associative logic that counters the headlong progression of the story by plotting meaningful change within an inflated narrative moment, a kind of verbal rather than anecdotal "diegesis." The tale that unfolds here does so according to the movement along the axes of signification that tracks the very multiplicity of meaning as such. To grasp this dynamic, Barthes cites one of Eisenstein's own phrases and calls for "a *vertical* reading [*une lecture verticale*]," a reading that not only advances along the horizontal stream of words, images, or lived experiences as they transpire in front of us but that also cuts into this ceaseless progression to light on the additional layers of meaning waiting for formulation (*Responsibility* 58; III: 502).

Waiting is perhaps the realest part of the ritual on which this vertical reading hinges (at the end of Chapter 2, I called it "hesitation," as if the subsequent elaborations of reflexion, citation, and ultimately criticism's wisdom have been taking place within or even as a kind of pregnant pause). And this is why Barthes trains his focus, in the very final moments of the essay, on "a theory of the still ... whose possible points of departure must be indicated here, in conclusion" (*Responsibility* 61). His object is to approach the specificity of what he calls "the filmic," which he locates not in "what is supposed to be the cinema's sacred essence: the movement of the images" but in the incessant "signifying" sparked by the third meaning (*Responsibility* 60–61). But for me it is enough to observe with Barthes that "the still dissolves the constraint of filmic time," the flow of film disintegrating here into fragmentary opportunities for interpretive exploration (*Responsibility* 61). Again, this is not so much to pause time as it is to make time for additional or alternative meanings to develop. And, *at the same time*, Barthes refuses to view these other meanings as separate from the film itself. Rather, he emphasizes the still's "diegetic horizon" (which distinguishes it from the "simple photograph") to splice them into the progression of the larger story (60). In doing so, he brings us to the point where this vertical reading projects itself as a concrete activity that informs the existential extension of criticism with which we are concerned. In terms that are almost too apropos, he thus describes how the third meaning "can establish (if followed) only an altogether different *découpage* from the one of shots, sequences, and syntagms (whether technical or narrative): an unheard of *découpage*, counter-logical and yet 'true'" (*Responsibility* 57; III: 501). He is imagining an alternative trajectory within the film's obvious forward movement, one that obtusely proceeds according to metaphoric and metonymic linkages with no basis other than the fantastic *Dasein* of reading. The result, as Barthes concisely puts it, is that "you will have another film," which is to say that this reading folds an additional visual experience into or fabricates an additional cinematic text out of the conventional continuity of the movie's reception (57). A similar kind of readerly fantasy is what I want to claim for the effect of criticism on the sense of our lived experience, a "counter-logical" openness to alternative meanings and additional vectors of significance that it is our responsibility to assemble. For if I leave the French word *découpage* untranslated here (Richard Howard offers "script" despite the availability of "decoupage" itself in English), it is obviously to index the layered construction of my cut-up divagations, fabricated from the fragments of reading I have hesitated over, especially insofar as they vertically interrupt the logical development of my argument's traditional articulation with the acute accents of another. But more than this, as a conceptual echo of the *punctum* and its textual captions, *découpage* distills the wisdom of criticism insofar as it frames lived experience not as an unbroken and unrelieved flow but, like language itself, as a discontinuous and combinatory phenomenon.[15]

And while it may be film, with its "shots, sequences, and syntagms," through which Barthes is approaching such phenomenological discontinuity, the real *découpage* derives from writing—as he makes clear in the account he gives, around the same time as "The Third Meaning," of the "amicable return of the author" in *Sade, Fourier, Loyola* (*SFL* 8). Here, to elucidate the textual or even textualized form of life that he figures in obscure terms of "'biographemes,'" he faithfully refers to Proust—"a marked life, in sum, as Proust succeeded in writing his in his work"—but then proceeds to a much more forcefully graphic description: "or even a film, in the old style, in which there is no dialogue and the flow of images (that *flumen orationis* which perhaps is what makes up the 'obscenities' of writing) is intercut, like the relief of hiccoughs, by the barely written darkness of the intertitles, the casual eruption of *another* signifier" (*SFL* 9). As this image of image-text relations imagines the way words, in the obscenely visual form of "intertitles" that mobilizes our discussion of the caption, segment

142 Conclusion

the onslaught of received perceptions, it carves out the space in which to refract those perceptions through reading. He is talking about our reception of the authors' lives whose names compose his title, but, in the fantasy that his own words have been helping me to dissect, he is also talking more generally about the practice of language animating my elaboration of the fantastic as such. The specifically literary inflection of that practice, whose most articulated image we located in citation, finds a final formulation in what is also a kind of initiating instance that spirals us back, here at the end, to the interpenetration of literature and life with which we began.

And really we had no choice but to begin there, in the fantastic middle of things, since there is never a point before this interpenetration where we would have a virgin sense of "life" unscripted by the language and culture into which we are born. So if I've been looking to Barthes and to literature to teach me how to speak this language in practical terms, it is as an apprentice taking dictation at the feet of a maestro, an image I model not only on the magic lessons I mapped between him and the sorceress but also, and more literally, on the formal or structural echo he establishes between his work and the novels of the Marquis de Sade. (The textual figure of Proust that might be more expected given his persistent place in my discussion could be said, with the wide-ranging sadism of his work, to hover nearby in a displaced citation whose absence this parenthetical is trying to wisely put into words.) Commenting on a moment in *Juliette* where "the scene of vice is preceded and formed by a scene of writing" so that "everything occurs at the *dictation* of fantasy," Barthes complements the technical analysis of dictation as such, which will close out our discussion in a second, with a personal example from his own schooling (*SFL* 163; emphasis added). Repeating the word-world interaction he's probing in Sade, he writes,

> This stupid exercise caught in an ideological matrix (since it has the function of ensuring the mastery of orthography, a class act, if there ever was one), this barren childhood memory is also the powerful trace of an anterior text that is *taken*, thereby reintroducing [*reconduisant*] the fragments of a language into our daily life and opening reality to the infinity of texts: what is "spring," the one we actually await with such impatience (and most usually disappointment) around mid-April, when we conceive of longing for the countryside, begin to buy new clothes, but Jean Aicard's "Spring," which was dictated to us one day in school? (*SFL* 164, 3:844).

I do not know Jean Aicard or his poem, but my whole argument is played out here (complete with its bourgeois blind spots). Only one word calls out for criticism: "reintroducing." Implying repetition and recurrence, "reintroducing" not only stages dictation as a kind of *activation* or even *renewal* (which is one of the meanings of *reconduire*) of a language already known but it does so by implying a cutting, fragmentary insertion that slices the world into something as discretely legible as a calendar.

And this is the point he makes in the line that concludes this reminiscence: "The origin of spring is not the elliptical revolution of our globe, it is a dictation, i.e., a false origin" (*SFL* 164). The "falsity" of this origin is what, following the dictation of the other moments in his oeuvre that I've collated and combed over so carefully, I would of course christen fantastic, a terminological conversion that is more than justified by the Sadean textual dynamics in which Barthes's thinking—and, through reading, my thinking—finds a fantasy of *its* origin. He writes, "The dictation written by Juliette opens up a reversion of texts [*une reversion des textes*]: the image appears to originate a program, the program a text, and the text a practice; however, this practice is itself written, it returns (for the reader) to program, to text, to fantasy" (*SFL* 164, 3:844). I can't tell you how many times I've rehearsed this sentence to figure out what it means. The "reversion of texts" Barthes mentions here disrupts the very idea of origin without necessarily denying it, twisting it into a chiasmic fantasy whose impossible verbal shape is essentially articulated in the string of relays running through the succeeding phrases. Reintroducing the parenthetical place of the reader into a critical activity more obviously aligned with writing, the choppy phrasing in these lines hails reading itself as the mobile site of this textual reversion, the practical program for its fantastic realization. Indeed, as these lines return to the language of practice that my concluding claims for criticism's wisdom have been trying to elevate, they leave us with an active and actual sense of the humble readerly work that secretly sustains the practice of language.

11. Untitled (November 2022 to December 2022). Author's handmade collage.

Acknowledgments

Preparatory to anything else, I want to thank the Microsoft Word thesaurus for helping me, at the most basic and practical level, mean what it is that I say in this work.

Heartfelt thanks also go to everyone who didn't laugh in my face when I first started declaring that I wanted to write a book on Roland Barthes. In particular, Sandra Lim, Ben Shockey, Jess Keiser, and Nate Wolff were all early and enduring affirmers of my starry-eyed aspirations. In taking my collage work seriously, Katy Niner, Wesley Simon, and Chantal Zakari allowed me to expand the horizons of my thinking in ways I am still learning about. Lisi Schoenbach, Lisa Lowe, and Martin Hägglund offered official support by writing letters for fellowship applications, and the Senior Semester Leave Award from Tufts University's Faculty Research Awards Committee (FRAC) was crucial in mapping out this project's overall shape. Sonia Hofkosh's flexible arrangement of my teaching schedule also freed up essential time for writing. Lee Edelman and David Kurnick read drafts of specific sections and assured me that I was onto something significant, while Karen Zumhagen-Yekplé, Josh Kotin, and Nancy Bauer all gave me important general encouragement along the way. Special mention should be made of David Divita, one of my first French teachers, who also served as my consultant for particularly thorny questions about the language. Jen Minnen and Kate Hollander were colleagues whose enthusiasm sustained me while I waited for responses to the full manuscript. Finally, Alan Thomas and Randy Petilos at the University of Chicago Press were responsive, patient, and helpful editors who gave me lots of leeway in imagining how I wanted the light of day to see this work.

In her capacity as dean of Academic Affairs, Bárbara Brizuela provided travel funds to visit the Fonds Roland Barthes in Paris when budgets at Tufts were tight, and the FRAC Grants-in-Aid subvention gave last-minute support for the publication costs. Thomas Cazentre in the manuscripts department at the Bibliothèque nationale was supremely helpful in providing me access to Barthes's paintings, and I am also grateful to Éric Marty for granting me permission to see them and to reproduce one in the book.

More personally, Brooke Harris, Samar Post Jamali, Laura Grey, and Bridget Love all listened to regular, sometimes daily reports on the progress and regress of my writing. Marty Banak and Carol Stedman unwittingly provided short writing retreats at Clay Hill Corners, their blueberry farm in Hartland, Vermont, where I first began thinking about this project, and I am so happy to be their down-the-street neighbor now that I'm finishing it. My partner, Arturo, has been a constant as I flailed my way through the fool's errand of writing a book, tolerating my mood swings, my rigid scheduling, and my self-importance. We lost our first true love when our pit bull mix, Helios, died suddenly in 2022, but the arrival of Stevie Nicks a year later brought canine joy and communication back to our home, both of which continue to teach me about how fantastic it is to live together in a world of signs.

* * *

An earlier version of part of chapter 1 appeared as "The Sorceress's Apprentice: Roland Barthes and the Criticism of Magic," in *New Literary History* 52, no. 1 (Winter 2021): 77–94, and earlier versions of parts of chapter 2 appeared in "Working It: On Notation and *The Fashion System*," in *Barthes Studies* 7 (2021). I thank the editors of these two journals for allowing me to rehearse some of my arguments in their pages.

Notes

Fore-Word

1. The most important and extensive accounts of Barthes's lecture courses are O'Meara's *Roland Barthes at the Collège de France* and Pint's *Perverse Art of Reading*, both of which put special emphasis on the central place, announced in his inaugural lecture *Leçon*, that Barthes gives to fantasy in his late teaching. There has also been much ink spilled on the plans and possibilities of the novel whose fantasmatic preparation made up his two final lecture courses; notable contributions to this question include the following: Knight, "Idle Thoughts"; Roger, "Caritas Incarnate"; Compagnon, "Le Roman de Barthes"; Martin, "Barthes et la 'Vita Nova'"; and Amigo Pino, "Le Roman de temps perdu." Finally, Badmington offers an extensive discussion of Barthes's "posthumous" publications in *Afterlives of Roland Barthes*.

2. Sollers, *Friendship of Roland Barthes*, 41, 42.

3. The archive of critical analyses treating Barthes's relationship with Proust is almost as long as the writing of those authors themselves. A very incomplete selection of notable discussions includes Baldwin, *Roland Barthes*; Barry, "Moment of Truth"; Haustein, "'La Vie comme oeuvre'"; Bowie, "Barthes on Proust"; Kritzman, "Barthes' Way" and "Barthes' Death Sentences and the End of Literature."

4. Macé, *Façons de lire, manières d'être*, 10.

5. Ibid., 10.

6. Ibid., 208–9.

7. Ibid., 15.

8. Macé, "Barthes Romanesque," 175–76.

9. Ibid., 176. Macé's discussion employs the language of practice, especially with regard to the fragments of *A Lover's Discourse*, which I want to push further off the page: "There exists in his work a 'novelistic' practice, in the sense where certain textual attributes [*dispositifs*] produce the effect of a narrative fiction, assume their function of incarnation, and support in the reader a cognitive and affective comportment analogous to those of a novel reader" (182).

10. Macé, *Façons*, 25. In more abstract vocabulary, she later writes, "The reader unceasingly oscillates between the place that is assigned to him by a syntactical attribute

[*un dispositif syntaxique*], and the act [*la conduite*] of reappropriation by which he regards this apparatus as a 'capacity' made available" (227).

11. He immediately follows this admission with the fragment "Probably connected on an analytical, intellectual level, to two anterior notions": the "*pregnant instant*" of Diderot and Lessing and an "affective *gestus*" derived from Brecht (*PN* 107). These terms do not reappear in his discussion here, though they are anticipated in his 1973 essay "Diderot, Brecht, Eisenstein" (*IMT*), which has not, unfortunately, been much help to me in elaborating their import.

12. The obvious references are to Felski's *Limits of Critique* and Best and Marcus's "Surface Reading."

13. Cheah, *What Is a World?*, 5; Kornbluh, *Order of Forms*, 4. As Kornbluh uses Victorian novels alongside contemporaneous developments in abstract mathematics to develop a conception of formalism that "stud[ies] how to compose and to direct—rather than ceaselessly oppose—form, formalization, and forms of sociability," she finds herself taking somewhat unwitting advantage of the vocabulary of the fantastic (4, 1). Exploring the anti-mimetic architectural forms that populate both Henry James's novel theory and Fredric Jameson's theorization of postmodernism, she writes the following sentences that still thrill me to read: "This essentially fantastic and estranging dimension of Jamesian architecture is no mere literary flamboyance—it is instead, I want to suggest, a magnification of the fantastic dimension implicit in the very architectural medium. For architecture at root is less the imposition of a pattern or order upon extant materials and space . . . and more a radical production of fluctuant realities"—a fluctuation that flaunts its relationship to the play of the signifier when, discussing Frank Gehry's Santa Monica house, she describes how "Jameson locates utopia on the threshold of fantastical vestibules, windows in dead walls and doors to nowhere" (41; 51).

14. Landy, *How to Do Things with Fictions*, 10. Landy offers an exceedingly helpful overview of "thirteen ways of looking at a fiction" (running from Aristotle to Sidney, Shelley to Iser) to situate his own pragmatic argument.

15. Ibid., 10.

16. Sloterdijk, *You Must Change Your Life*, 4.

17. Ibid., 140. Though his presiding deity is late Nietzsche, Sloterdijk's reference here is obviously to Wittgenstein, in whose "language game theory" he finds "a training theory based on the—itself undeclared—difference between declared and undeclared asceticisms" (144). When he goes on to say that "for the primal ethical imperative 'You must change your life!' to be followed, therefore, it is initially necessary for the practising to become aware of their exercises as exercises, that is to say as forms of life that engage the practising person," he gives us a sense of what is at stake in my focus on literature, which, as Barthes understands it, is precisely the declared engagement of and play with language (145).

18. Gaillard, "Roland Barthes," 845.

19. I am borrowing my language from Gaillard, who puts it succinctly: "The intellectual is without power; he is not without action . . . he must de-alienate meaning by restoring the history and conventionality everywhere that it has transformed into nature" (ibid., 850). Macé lays out some similar claims using more subject-centered terms in her calls "to give a better place to mediations and to constructed forms of intersubjectivity . . . to reaffirm what is decisive about our consent to what first took hold of us, our

acquiescence to models: the prescription of forms, *stronger* than the reader, confronted in his own desire for another wish" (*Façon* 207).

20. Samoyault, "Barthes hier et aujourd'hui," 896–97.

21. Ibid., 898.

22. Ibid., 900.

23. Inspired, at base, by Barthes, this embrace of production also found scholarly encouragement and enthusiastic example in Elkins's *Crafting Feminism*, particularly in the "Techne" interchapters that take a practical, productive approach to the art forms she places in dialogue with particular literary figures. Additionally, in their comparison of Virginia Woolf and Kate Zambreno, Melanie Micir and Aarthi Vadde resist the idea of "criticism as a science" defined by the professionalization of literary studies in favor of an "amateur" alternative that turns to "low-prestige genres" of the scrapbook (close cousin of the collage!) and the blog to destabilize institutional structures and aesthetic hierarchies; see their "Obliterature" (519). More generally, Loveless's *How to Make Art* and Springgay's *Feltness* have expounded on the intellectual, affective, and social potential of using art practice as a method of inquiry, which pushed me beyond my feelings of insecurity and embarrassment over what sometimes felt like a silly, summer camp-style craft project. Finally, I cannot overstate the place of Eve Kosofsky Sedgwick, with her often Proust-inflected textile work among so much other dazzling critical production, in motivating my turn to this alternative mode of thinking.

Introduction

1. In the preliminary steps she takes to imagine a "translation of connotation," Whitaker offers a more general account of this dynamic. See her "Désir de lire, désir de traduire."

2. Pint, *Perverse Art of Reading*, 28.

3. Ibid., 194. The extent to which Pint's approach plays down the linguistic basis of these "important notions from literary studies" (the conceptual emphasis in the phrasing is itself telling) comes out nowhere more clearly than in his discussion of the detail, which "becomes a fetish through which the perverse reader attempts to return to the point where, for the *infant*, the arbitrariness of the linguistic sign was still unclear and the imaginary sign was still equated with the object" (194, 209). He continues, "So in his later work Barthes provides a much more positive evaluation of this moment where language as a system of signs becomes nearly invisible, and an [*sic*] 'reality effect' arises, than he did in the article of the same title from 1968" (209).

4. Ibid., 153. As I briefly discuss in chap. 3, Barthes gestures toward something very close to this when, distinguishing the genre of *Sarrasine* from the fantastic as it was developed in Germany, he refers to what he calls the "*fantasmatic fantastic*" (*Sarrasine* 240). See chapter 3, note 15.

5. Macé, *Façons*, 183.

6. Ibid., 184.

7. Ibid., 205.

8. I am, admittedly, relying on a somewhat unfair and oversimplified characterization of Flaubert's heroine, whose psychic contortions have received several more nuanced discussions that Macé tracks from the pathological account by Jules de Gaultier in 1892 to the more liberatory discussions by Jacques Rancière in 2009; see the section

"Bovarysme des formes," 186–94. As she notes, Barthes himself asserts that "Many—if not all—of us are *Bovarys*" (*PN* 99).

9. Todorov, *Fantastic*, 92. Iser's *Fictive and the Imaginary* offers a more historicized account of fantastic literature that puts the latter in more obvious connection with his titular categories of "the fictive and the imaginary." See, in particular, chap. 4, 171–246.

10. Todorov, 82.

11. Ibid., 82.

12. Ibid., 25.

13. Ibid., 25.

14. Ibid., 89.

15. Ibid., 31. I have made a resonant argument, in terms that focus on the phenomenological materiality of the book as an object, in *Death of the Book*.

16. Ibid., 31.

17. My emphasis on textuality and signification as such might seem to depart from Todorov's insistence that "the text must oblige the reader to consider the world of the characters as a world of living persons" (33) and his explicit warning against the "poetic," which is "to be read quite literally, on the level of the verbal chain they constitute, not even on that of their reference" (60). My project is to reconcile and integrate precisely these oppositions—"the world of living persons" and "the verbal chain"—in a mode of thinking cultivated by the lessons of poststructuralism that Todorov's avowedly structuralist 1970 publication was only able to implicitly or embryonically anticipate.

18. As the original French reads "*le nouveau de Mode semble avoir dans notre société une fonction anthropologique bien définie et qui tient à son ambiguïté*," I deviate from the published English translation that renders the last phrase "which derives from its ambiguity" (perhaps a misreading of *tenir à* as *tenir de*).

19. The distinction I am drawing finds further support in Laplanche and Pontalis's discussion of the "Phantasy (Fantasy)" in *Language of Psycho-analysis*, which was published in the same year as *The Fashion System*. Though Barthes's relationship to psychoanalysis is neither consistent nor especially rigorous, their definition of this term as the "imaginary scene in which the subject is a protagonist, representing the fulfilment of a wish (in the last analysis, an unconscious wish) in a manner that is distorted to a greater or lesser extent by defensive processes" clearly evokes the more individual valence I'm locating in his original French. Furthermore, their specific comment on *fantasme* as the French equivalent of the *Phantasie* of Freud's German notes that the term "was revived by psycho-analysis" and "refers to a specific imaginary production, not to the world of phantasy and imaginative activity in general" (313).

20. See "Reality Effect" in *Rustle of Language*, 141–48.

21. Malabou, *Heidegger Change*, 11.

22. Ibid., 13.

23. Ibid., 12.

24. Ibid., 5; Malabou, *Le Change Heidegger*, 14.

25. Malabou, *Heidegger Change*, 5.

26. Ibid., 12.

27. Ibid., 12.

28. Malabou also compellingly describes the procedure of her argument about the Heidegger change as "an invention resulting from a decision of reading—my own" (1).

This interpretive act consists of what she calls the "empowerment" (*Ermächtigung*) of three unremarkable German words for change (*Wandel, Wandlung,* and *Verwandlung*) that run through Heidegger's writing, a triad that "has been left waiting its *exegetical switching-on*" (2). If the exegetical empowerment of this inventive reading practice is also driving my thinking here, her aim of "*changing, transforming, and metamorphosing the interpretation of Heidegger's thought in its entirety*" also offers a somewhat extravagant image of my own ambition to give us a Barthes who, fantastically, seems both the same as and other than the writer that so many of us love (4).

29. Ibid., 12–13.

30. In this, I am following Sheringham, who has tracked the evolution of Barthes's interest in the everyday in his *Everyday Life*. Though Sheringham sees the 1970s as the decade in which Barthes engages with life rather than just signification and textuality, I am tracing this interest throughout the whole of his work.

31. Malabou, "Pierre Loves Horranges," 99.

32. Ibid., 99, 100.

33. See, in particular, pt. 1 as well as Spivak's discussion of Heidegger in her magisterial preface in Derrida, *Of Grammatology*. I thank David Denrich for referring this text to me in the back of Starlight Bar on Avenue A in 2002.

34. Gallop offers one of the few reengagements of this important work, though her interest is in rehabilitating a more complex understanding of the author whose "amicable return" Barthes asserts as part of the "pleasure" of the text (*Deaths of the Author*, 8). Her inspired reading opens up an understanding of our relationship to the literal deaths of author—and, more broadly, to temporality itself—in a way that intersects with the arguments I have made in *Death of the Book*. Here, however, I am more interested in revitalizing the readerly experience of textual linguistics birthed through Barthes's authorial execution.

35. Macé, *Façons*, 199–200.

36. There is a divergence between the English translation by Richard Miller and Barthes's French that is a bit weightier than the alterations I've been navigating up to now. That is, the English reads, as I have quoted, "fragments of the unintelligible," while the French reads, quite oppositely, "*fragments d'intelligible*" (3:704). As the thrust of "unintelligible" plays an important role in my discussion, I have been at pains to reconcile this terminological discrepancy. At the risk of textually invalidating the claims I make here and further on, however, I have left "unintelligible"—in part because Barthes's own understanding of "intelligibility" is by no means straightforward. This is not to go so far as to suggest, in high deconstructive style, that intelligibility and unintelligibility are fully indistinguishable. Rather, it is to appeal to the way Barthes's investigation into signification is deeply invested in forestalling the easy, immediate sense of meaning that constitutes stereotypes and mythologies and that the textual dynamics he is talking about at this moment especially work to complicate.

37. Macé, *Façons*, 210.

38. For further personal and intellectual context, see Davidson's "Introduction" in Hadot, *Philosophy as a Way of Life*.

39. Hadot, *Philosophy as a Way of Life*, 64.

40. O'Meara, *Lectures*, 109. O'Meara revisits this topic, with a similar focus on Barthes's late writing, in "Barthes and the Lessons of Ancient Philosophy," *Interdisciplinary Barthes*.

41. Hadot, *Philosophy as a Way of Life*, 210.

42. There is a tension in Hadot's account of ancient philosophy between an assertion of continual practice that is "designed to ensure spiritual progress toward the ideal state of wisdom" and the "norms" on which a particular understanding of that ideal is based (59). For instance, Skepticism and Epicureanism both outline spiritual practices, but these practices are organized by differing conceptions of what constitutes "wisdom." Thus, though he emphasizes "a movement, a progression, though a never-ending one, toward this transcendent state," he also cites "the memorization and assimilation of the fundamental dogmas and rules of a school," which undercut the mobility and openness introduced by the idea of practice (59). Noting this tension as something that Barthes's practical thinking consciously tries to occupy, I have neither the expertise nor the space to examine it in more detail, but Macé's emphasis on "the ambivalence of Barthes' relation to forms and codes" tackles this question more directly (183).

43. See his "Ancient Spiritual Exercises" in *Philosophy as a Way of Life*, 126–44.

44. The operation of *différance* should be apparent here, if this differentiation and deferral weren't the very conditions for appearance itself; see Derrida, *Speech and Phenomena*. My train of thought is perhaps closer, however, to Malabou's engagement with and elaboration of Derrida's work with the trace in her development of "plasticity." See her *Future of Hegel* and *Plasticity at the Dusk of Writing*. For a fuller discussion of these ideas, see my "Medium Thickness."

45. See the reproduction of the note in *Album*, 199. Frank's helpful introduction to a recent collection of Caillois's writing gives further intellectual and historical context; see *Edge of Surrealism*. Stafford discusses Barthes's earlier critique of Caillois's "analogical" approach to Marxism as an evacuation of historical specificity; see his *Roland Barthes Writing the Political*, 86–87 and 135–37.

46. Caillois, "Natural Fantastic," 349.

47. Ibid., 354. Barthes also appeals to this strange activity in a discussion of "simulation" that provides him part of his methodology in *Preparation of the Novel*, writing "the object produced by and for the Simulation: a *maquette* (*machietta*), a little stain, sketch; there would be some philosophizing to do around the notion of the work, of certain works as *marks* (*macula*) to be made out, cf. the mark on Leonardo da Vinci's wall," a reference to the latter's *Treatise on Painting* that describes something similar to what Caillois is talking about. Sartre offers a more rigorous accounting of this phenomenon in *Imaginary*, particularly the sections on "Faces in the Fire, Spots on Walls, Rocks in Human Form" and "Hypnagogic Images, Scenes and Persons Seen in Coffee Grounds, in a Crystal Ball" (35–50). From these excessive references, I find this whole fantastic complex nothing short of fascinating.

48. Caillois, "Natural Fantastic," 355.

49. Ibid., 356, 357.

Chapter 1

1. See the opening chapter of During, *Modern Enchantments*, and Landy, "Modern Magic." Bennett's *Enchantment of Modern Life* constructs a resonant argument from a different theoretical perspective.

2. In *Premodern Condition*, Holsinger has offered a wider-ranging account of

Barthes's investment (and that of his colleagues at *Tel Quel*) in medieval culture and pays particular attention to the persistence of the "exegetical culture" of the Middle Ages in the careful analytical fragmentation that Barthes performs in *S/Z* (153).

3. See chaps. 9 and 10 of *Structural Anthropology*.

4. Gaillard, "*Roland Barthes*," 845.

5. Ibid., 847–48.

6. The quoted phrase is During's, which he uses to describe the persistence of "modern" or "secular" magic in contemporary cultural production, not least those of the aesthetic avant-garde (27). In a chapter discussing literature and magic, he addresses the work of Hoffman, Poe, and Roussel, with some side glances at Kafka (see 178–214). Similarly, Landy's "Modern Magic" offers a hypnotizing reading of Mallarmé, while Paige's "Permanent Re-enchantments" in the same volume nuances our understanding of magic's "modernity" by tracing it back to the (French) literature of the late seventeenth century and its invention of the idea of fiction, the "dramatic redefinition of the relation of reality to the imagination" that paves the way for the more obviously "magical" genres of the eighteenth century like the gothic and the fantastic itself (161).

7. Lombardo, "History and Form," 73.

8. This duality of magic finds another illustration in *Mythologies*' ambivalent treatment of Einstein's brain, which works as a site of both a demystified mechanical labor and a kind of gnostic genius. Fenves offers a thorough discussion of the singularity of this mythology in his "'Einstein's Brain' in Three Parts."

9. This ideological resurgence is multifarious and begins even before the institutionalization of this critical methodology. For example, Moudileno unpacks the ambivalent assumptions and oversights about Africa and the African body in Barthes's comments on the "young Negro in a French uniform" on the cover of a *Paris-Match* issue (*Mythologies* 116). See her "Barthes's Black Soldier."

10. Joly, "*Du Symbole au Ninisme*," 65.

11. Joly helpfully reminds us of the idea of asymbolia that Barthes introduces in *Criticism and Truth* (66). In that work, he discusses the "old" criticism's inability to "perceive or manipulate symbols, that is, co-existence of meaning" (*Criticism* 57). See also his account of "monosemy," an insistence that a language or message has only one meaning, which results in a discourse that is, significantly, "entirely tautological" (*Gift* 98).

12. Langlet, "*Inactualité des Mythologies?*," 128.

13. Zenkine, "*Les indices du mythe*," 26. A particularly clear example of this tendency is Barthes's well-known discussion of "The New Citroën," which he categorizes as "a purely magical object" in the first line of that essay (*Mythologies* 88).

14. Michelet, *Satanism and Witchcraft*, 16. By no means an expert in the Middle Ages, I am not necessarily validating the accuracy of Michelet's account of the period but using it instead to elaborate on the place that the sorceress's magical practice holds in Barthes's intellectual imaginary.

15. Ibid., 16.

16. Ibid., 55, 78.

17. Ibid., 58–59. "Simple" in this instance refers to a medicinal drug that has only one ingredient.

18. Compare this to the claim Barthes makes in a footnote of "Myth Today" to find a "non-signifying field" in the natural phenomenon of the sea: "Here I am, before the

sea; it is true that it bears no message. But on the beach, what material for semiology!" (*Mythologies* 112). Thanks to Jeff Kahn for reminding me of this line.

19. Gaillard, "*Roland Barthes*," 848. Or, as Barthes put it in "The Kitchen of Meaning" from 1964, "we must henceforth foresee a new quality of phenomena: meaning" (*Semiotic* 158).

20. Michelet, *Satanism and Witchcraft*, xv.

21. Ibid., 95.

22. Ibid., 95–96.

23. Ibid., 96.

24. Ibid., 93 (trans. modified); Michelet, *La Sorcière*, 134.

25. Michelet, *La Sorcière*, 134.

26. Michelet, *Satanism and Witchcraft*, 92–93. In his virtuosic account of the way "charm" survives in a "postmagical" world, Tucker offers a more detailed exploration of the complementary operation of "ineffability" and "irreference" that this example is dramatizing; see his "After Magic."

27. Michelet, *Satanism and Witchcraft*, xv.

28. As he writes in *Criticism and Truth* of the Picard affair, "What is worth of note in this operation [of attacking the 'new criticism' Barthes represented] is not so much that it sets up old against the new, it is rather that, in an unmasked reaction, it casts a taboo upon a certain kind of discourse about a book: what is not tolerated is that language should talk about language" (*Criticism* 33).

29. Careful attention will detect a *u* in the word "*sourcier*" that does not occur in the word "*sorcier*" to which the other quotations refer, indicating that Barthes is here referring to what, in English, we would call a "water diviner" or "dowser" who uses their rod ("*baguette*") to discover subterranean water sources. Since this might be considered as a more specific form of the kind of sensitivity to signs that I am more generally calling magic, Howard's translation of "*sourcier*" as "magician" speaks to my point even if it elides this particular nuance.

Chapter 2

1. Saint-Amand ("Barthes' Laziness") and Benhaïm ("Barthes on the Beach") have addressed work in Barthes, and both approach it in a dialectic with laziness, as a social compulsion that Barthes seeks to attenuate and even escape through writing and literature. Though work's entanglement with leisure explicitly figures in my discussion (echoing Benhaïm's discussion of laziness as itself an action or a form of work), I am more interested here in the basic effort of articulation imposed on us by our status as linguistic beings.

2. In this, Barthes's work on Fashion anticipates his later arguments in "The Discourse of History." He writes, "Once language intervenes (and when does it not intervene?), a fact can be defined only tautologically: the *noted* issues from the *notable*, but the *notable* is—since Herodotus, where the word loses its mythic acceptation—only what is worthy of memory, i.e., worthy to be *noted*. Hence, we arrive at the paradox which governs the entire pertinence of historical discourse (in relation to other types of discourse): fact never has anything but a linguistic existence (as the term of discourse), yet everything happens as if this linguistic existence were merely a pure and simple 'copy' of *another* existence, situated in an extra-structural field, the 'real'" (*Rustle* 168).

As we will see, this 'copying' is what our interrogation of notation and its work seeks to forestall.

3. One notable exception to this disregard of *The Fashion System* is Sheringham's discussion of it within the context of Barthes's interest in everyday life. He describes how "the existential or lived ('vécu') dimension of modes of signification" might have "fully crystallized" in *Empire of Signs* (177), but it was anticipated and in a way enabled by *The Fashion System*, which shows how "the everyday existence of these phenomena [like Fashion] is more closely allied to their semiological—perpetual present—dimension than to their objective historical aspect" (183). For discussion of *The Fashion System* within the development of cultural studies more generally, see Calefato, "On Myths and Fashion," and for a critique of Barthes's framework, see Carter, "Stuff and Nonsense." In *Structuralist Poetics*, Culler also notes some "serious methodological problems" in Barthes's attempt to adopt the model of linguistics (39).

4. Butor, "La Fascinatrice," 385.

5. Ibid., 386.

6. Translation modified: in the original French, the end of the sentence reads "*et vient enfin toucher et pour ainsi dire imprégner le vêtement (le cardigan)*" (2:961).

7. For example, Barthes refers to a caption such as "*the soft Shetland dress with a belt worn high and with a rose stuck in it*" and explains, "we are told certain parts (the material, the belt, the detail) and spared others (the sleeves, the collar, the shape, the color), as if the woman wearing this garment went about dressed only in a rose and softness" (*Fashion* 15). I love this point of his.

8. To say this is not to imply that this linguistic life is somehow preceded by a raw, meaningless reality into which notation makes its oppositional cuts, as much as it is to make explicit that our very access to reality as such—its very fantastic realness—depends on them.

9. Expanding on his assertion of the "theoretical autonomy" of the real and the written vestimentary codes, he writes, "if we treat the units of the written garment as verbal units, the only structure we reach in such a garment is that of the French (or English) language; we analyze the meaning of the sentence, not the meaning of the garment; and if we treat them as objects, as real elements of the garment, we cannot make any sense out of their arrangement, since this sense is the 'speech' of the magazine which produces it. We stay too near or go too far; in both cases we lack the central relation, which is that of the vestimentary code as actualized by the magazine, i.e., one that is simultaneously real in its aim and written in its substance" (*Fashion* 41, 45). He ultimately posits a "mixed" or "pseudo-real" code, a "half-verbal, half-algorithmic utterance" that "will take its units from language and its functions from a logic general enough to enable it to preempt certain relations of the real garment" (*Fashion* 47). This is perhaps the most rigorous parsing of the real unreality that constitutes the fantastic, though the way its extreme abstraction keeps it from really speaking either to language or phenomenological experience makes it also the least helpful formulation.

10. In the famous lecture on Proust that presages these comments in his course, he writes, "I put myself in the position of a subject who *makes* something, and no longer of the subject who speaks *about* something . . . the world no longer comes to me as an object, but as a writing, i.e., a practice" (*Rustle* 289). Shirking off the conception of the world as a pregiven and static "object," he outspokenly asserts it instead as a discursive "practice," an ongoing, temporally dynamic process in which his own writing might,

at least momentarily, take its place. The arduous exertion entailed in the new life he is imagining becomes explicit when, resisting the pretentiousness entailed in comparing himself to Proust, he insists, "I am not identifying myself with the prestigious author of a monumental work but with the worker [*pas à l'auteur prestigieux d'une oeuvre monumentale, mais à l'ouvrier*]—now tormented, now exalted, in any case modest—who wanted to undertake a task" (*Rustle* 277–78, 5:459).

11. Sagner Buurma and Heffernan, "Notation after 'The Reality Effect,'" 84.

12. Ibid., 97.

13. We will recall Macé's discussion of "the novelistic" (*le romanesque*) as "first of all an existential notion, almost phenomenological" insofar as it describes a "system of perception before being a model of writing" that is linked to "a manner of cutting up the real" (*Romanesque* 175–76). The echoes with my collage practice should be clear.

14. This observation echoes the comment found in the transcription of the lecture course by Nathalie Lacroix justifying the "pendantry" of his appeal to the Latin term *notatio* here: "because you know that, unfortunately, in French the words in '-tion' end up designating the product of the act and not the act. A notation is finally a note. But for me, I would like to retain the active value of the act of noting, and it's for that that I call it *Notatio*" (*Préparation* 47).

15. In the lecture's delivery, he expands further on his point in somewhat less syntactically performative terms and explains, "I would say that *life*, in the stupidly banal meaning of the word, in the meaning it can have for someone who writes, is the river of language that traverses us, that surrounds us, *life* is that" (*Préparation* 47).

16. Barthes makes a similar assertion when he discusses the rhetorical system of Fashion in the book's conclusion, using diction that speaks more directly to the strange status of the fantastic: "to the extent that Fashion rhetoric affabulates, it recaptures a certain reality of the world *against* its terminological system, which itself remains (literally) improbable: here a curious interchange occurs between the real and the imaginary, the possible and the utopian . . . on its literal level, what is real in Fashion is purely assertive (what we mean by improbable). Confronted with this 'unreality' on the terminological level, Fashion rhetoric is paradoxically more 'real' insofar as it is absorbed by a coherent ideology, dependent on an entire social reality" (*Fashion* 284).

17. Compare this point with the argument he makes in his "At the Music Hall" mythology, where he argues that "the music hall is the aesthetic form of work. Here each number is presented either as the exercise or product of labor. . . . The effort is perceived at its apogee, at that almost impossible moment when it is about to be engulfed in the perfection of its achievement" (*Eiffel* 125). His subsequent claim that "the music hall requires a profound enchantment whereby it erases all rugosity from labor and leaves only its finished design" depends on the "immediate time" of the music hall, which "remove[s] the gesture from its sweetish pulp of duration"—a duration we are working to read back into the very process of signification itself.

18. In this, I think we can hear an anticipation of the "Lesson in Writing" that Barthes finds in Japanese Bunraku puppet theater: "What is expelled from the stage is hysteria, that is theater itself, and what is put in its place is the action necessary for the production of the spectacle—work is substituted for interiority" (*IMT* 173–74).

19. In the aptly titled essay "Musica Practica," Barthes locates a "sensuous intelligibility" in the act of playing music rather than just listening—what I am trying to approach through the significant performance of my collages as much as through my ar-

gument's significant practice of language (*Responsibility* 264). I discuss the practical intertwining of signification and sensation from a more theoretical perspective in my article "Medium Thickness."

20. As he puts it in a 1975 interview, "It's just that work is boring, which should never be denied" (*Grain* 222).

21. Stafford, "Roland Barthes's *Travels in China*," 296. In his essay "Bored with Barthes," which is partly devoted to developing Barthes as a "professor of boredom," Badmington describes the "sensual objects" that catch Barthes's eye during presentations and interestingly notes the way that Barthes vacillates over whether clothing can play such a role—including it at one point only to remove it later on (314-15).

22. Lowe, *Critical Terrains*, 160.

23. Notice the echo between this claim and Barthes's account in "Myth Today" that myth "economizes intelligence: it understands reality more cheaply," which emphasizes the elision of language's work, effort, labor, exertion (often at the hands of language itself) (*Mythologies* 153).

24. The thorny question of *Empire of Signs*'s Orientalism has also been a perennial topic of discussion, and Knight provides a well-contextualized analysis in light of his other writing addressing travel, fantasy, and language in her chapter "A Reader Not a Visitor" from *Barthes and Utopia: Space, Travel, Writing*. A more varied dossier of opinions can be found in *Roland Barthes*, ed. Neil Badmington, vol. 4, 109-220.

25. Coste, "*Roland Barthes par Roland Barthes*," 44-45. Coste here recasts the distinction from Barthes's 1960 essay "Authors and Writers [*Ecrivains et écrivants*]" into the somewhat more legible *auteur*/*écrivain* opposition. The terminological shifts are a bit dizzying: the English "author" initially translates the more writerly "*écrivain*" but, in the wake of Barthes's later arguments, shifts to name the more stable, authoritarian place of the *auteur*. What I want to underscore here, in this concluding *note*, are the toilsome terms by which Barthes describes the more dispersive, writerly function as "the man who *labors*, who works up his utterance [*qui travaille sa parole*] . . . and functionally absorbs himself in this labor, this work [*ce travail*]" (*Critical* 144, 2:404).

Chapter 3

1. Barthes repeatedly returns to this idea; for instance, in "From Science to Literature" from 1967, he writes, "Technically, according to Roman Jakobson's definition, the 'poetic' (i.e., the literary) designates that type of message which takes for object its own form, and not its contents" and claims that for literature, "langue can no longer be the convenient instrument or the sumptuous décor of a social, emotional, or poetic 'reality' which preexists it and which it is responsible, in a subsidiary way, for expressing, provided it abides by a few rules of style: no, language is the *being* of literature, its very world" (*Rustle* 5, 4). See also "A Magnificent Gift" (1971), which focuses more intently on the linguistic emphasis that Jakobson bestowed on modern literary study (*Rustle* 159-61).

2. In her expectedly penetrating review of Barthes's work from 1971, Kristeva relies on phrasing that anticipates the framing and movement of my own argument in this chapter and throughout the book more generally, stating that Barthes "is the precursor and founder of modern literary studies precisely because he located literary practice at the intersection of subject and history; because he studied this practice as

symptom of the ideological tearings in the social fabric; and because he sought, within texts, the precise mechanism that symbolically (semiotically) controls this tearing" (*Desire* 93).

3. For a condensed account of this context, see Sontag's helpful preface to *Writing Degree Zero*, esp. ix-xvi. O'Meara gives the fullest discussion of Barthes's work in "Literary Semiology" in her *Roland Barthes at the Collège de France*.

4. Lavers, *Structuralism and After*, 54.

5. Though the famous example is the relationship between *sheep* and *mutton*, Saussure provides a somewhat clearer explanation in the example of money. A one-dollar bill wouldn't have any conceptual meaning if we couldn't compare it a five-dollar bill or a twenty-dollar bill. What we habitually think of as the particular values of these basically similar notes—independent of whatever goods they might be exchanged for—exists on the basis of the differences they have with one another. What money represents is this kind of abstract differential relation that gets activated or put to use in the purchase of commodities.

6. Thibault, *Re-reading Saussure*, 165.

7. Ibid., 198 (italics added).

8. Ibid., 164.

9. Ibid., 165. Compare, in this regard, the more literary version of this point, which Barthes makes in his otherwise rather bloodless "Introduction to the Structural Analysis of Narratives": "Narration can actually receive its meaning only from the world that makes use of it: beyond the narrational level begins the world, *i.e.*, other systems (social, economic, ideological), whose terms are no longer only narratives but elements of another substance (historical phenomena, determinations, behaviors, etc.)" (*Semiotic* 127).

10. Other examples include the reference codes, which are "made in a collective and anonymous voice originating in traditional human experience" that they simultaneously reaffirm, or the sequentiality of the proairetic code, which "exists when and because it can be given a name" even though "its basis is . . . more empirical than rational" (*S/Z* 18, 19).

11. Jameson, "Ideology of the Text," 136.

12. Ibid., 136.

13. Jameson comments on the "formal specificity (and the historical peculiarity) of this *novella*" in terms of its revival of the classical or Renaissance framed tale, the anachronism of which evokes "the simultaneity, in many distinct cultures, of 'realistic' or 'naturalistic' forms of representation and the growth of commerce or the development of a money economy and a system of cash exchange" (Ibid., 141, 144). Homology, indeed.

14. In the "Textual Analysis of a Tale by Edgar Allan Poe" that repeats many of *S/Z*'s points in more summary form, Barthes comments on the speaking corpse in the story by pointing out the "gaping contradiction between Death and Language; the contrary of Life here is not Death (which is a stereotype), it is Language: it is undecidable if M. Valdemar is living or dead; what is certain is that he is speaking, without our being able to relate his speech to Death or to Life" (*Semiotic* 284). In this sense, the fantastic—a word to which Barthes also refers in his discussion of Poe's story (*Semiotic* 269)—is exactly what is able to transgress our most basic existential categories.

15. He explains this extraworldly gloss of "fantastic" in the notes for the seminar

where he first tackles Balzac's story and refers to a line in Balzac's story where the old man is imprecisely figured as "a vampire, a ghoul, an artificial man, a type of Faust or Robin Hood" as an instance of "what is outside the limits of nature (vampirism, magic), outside of the world, outside of man" (*Sarrasine* 241). He hears a hint of irony in this litany of otherworldly figures and imputes a critique of the "German fantastic" popular at the time to extend the term beyond the question of genre: he thus imagines "Balzac opposing to the sham fantastic of Germany . . . the true fantastic, the serious fantastic, that of castration totally exposed, so to speak, castration without reference to a cultural code of the fantastic, without any support but its own code (castrating/castrated), as if Balzac opposed to the cultural fantastic the *fantasmatic fantastic*" (240). In this transgression of the fantasmatic and the fantastic distinction that I worked out in the introduction, we have a kind of fantastic that takes its place *in this world* and that anticipates the textualized subjectivity figured by Proust.

16. As for a discussion of castration *elle-même*, I can do no better than point to Johnson's justifiably well-known reading of *S/Z*, "Critical Difference." This might also be the place to acknowledge the important place *S/Z* has had in critical discussions of gender and sexuality: in addition to the essays in vols. 3 and 4 of Badmington's *Roland Barthes*, see also Zhuo's "Gender Neutral."

17. The original French (in the *Oeuvres complètes*) specifies the semiological connotation of "Selenity (the light of the lamp is soft like that of the moon) [*Sélénité (la lumière de la lampe est douce comme celle de la lune)*]" (3:176).

18. Though the original French has "*dans le texte*" (3:177), Miller introduces an additional "our," which I am maintaining since it increases the referential ambiguity through which textuality itself operates.

19. See also Barthes's discussion of the name in his essay "Pierre Loti: *Aziyadé*" (the gash of the Z continuing to slice its way into this 1971 essay) where he details the "invention" of Loti as "quite a bold stroke." He continues, "if it is a commonplace to sign the narrative of what happens to you and thereby to give your name to one of your characters (this is what happens in the private diary), it is not one to invert the bestowal of the proper name; yet this is what Viaud has done: he has given to himself, the author, the name of his hero," a move whose result is that "a hole is made, a person is lost, by means much more cunning than mere pseudonymy" (*NCE 107*, 106).

Chapter 4

1. This is also the place where my argument intersects most explicitly with Macé's discussion of how, in Barthes, "it is each sentence that presents itself as a gestural invitation, the request or the promise for activation of a manner of conducting oneself" (*Façons* 182). But again we will see how much more emphasis my argument places on the readerly engagement of language as itself a kind of behavior that conditions this mode of being in the world.

2. Compare, for instance, Macé's point, speaking specifically of the *Recherche* as "the instrument of a figural reading of life," that "the work furnishes a language, some possibilities of speech and thus of life" (*Façons* 210).

3. Coste, *Barthes' Stupidity*, 132, 134.
4. Ibid., 132 (emphasis added).
5. Ibid., 136.

6. We will recall the famous footnote discussed in chap. 1: "Even here, in these mythologies, I have used trickery [*j'ai rusé*]" (*Mythologies* 158, 1:868).

7. "Our culture has long wondered what it was that passed from the author into a work," he writes in a 1964 postscript to Cayrol's *Les Corps étrangers*; "here we see that, even more than his life or his time, it is the writer's *strength* [*force*] which passes into his work. In other words, literature is itself a moral dimension of the book: to be able to write a story is the final meaning of the story" (*Rustle* 186, 2:596).

8. My thanks to Audrey Wasser for guiding me through this thicket of French prosodic vocabulary.

9. See her *Future of Hegel* and *Plasticity at the Dusk of Writing*, as well as my "Medium Thickness."

10. Coste, *Stupidity*, 126.

11. Picard, "New Criticism or New Fraud?," 30; the line from *On Racine* can be found on p. 88.

12. Ibid., 30.

13. Coste, *Stupidity*, 128.

14. He writes, "each time we do not *close* the description, each time we write ambiguously enough to suspend meaning, each time we proceed as if the world signified though without saying *what*, then writing releases a question, it troubles what exists, though without ever performing what does not yet exist, it gives the world an energy: in short, literature does not permit us to walk, but it permits us to breathe" (*Critical* 267).

15. Coste, *Stupidity*, 130.

16. According to Picard: "Mr. Barthes transposes the *You cannot tell the truth about nature* of contemporary thought into *You cannot tell the truth about Racine*, and from *Anything can happen* of modern indeterminism he draws a sort of *You can say anything*... No, you cannot just say anything. Racine's words have a literal meaning which was obligatory for the spectators and readers of the seventeenth century, and which cannot be ignored without a game of chance being made of the language" (33).

17. Referring to *A Lover's Discourse*, Macé describes how "the sentences of a text are immediately invested by this reader from an existential situation; they *resonate*, they provocatively retain a sudden sentiment of accuracy, that is to say of new possibilities of speech for an interiority that would otherwise be mute" (*Façons* 199-200).

18. For a resonant argument that places more emphasis on love than on signification as such, see Emre, "Love as Aesthetic Education."

19. I translate "*registre*" more literally here than Howard's "tonality."

Conclusion

1. On the history of Franco-American theoretical relations, see Cusset, *French Theory*.

2. For a more philosophical and broadly historicized account of criticism—which nonetheless places a similar emphasis on language in its constitution—see Wasser, "Critical Thinking."

3. In his article "Text, Image, Reference," Gratton persuasively argues that Barthes's "return to reference" in this late work is by no means straightforward and that, rather, it "can never be separated from a certain loss or absence" (356). In particular, he discusses the restless movement of Barthes's language in *Camera Lucida* as a performance

of the disjunct between text and image, the way the former can never reach the purported adequacy of the latter. He tellingly concludes with a comment on the phrase *monter un rapport*—"to work at, to set up, to stage" a relation between image and text that Barthes uses in an interview instead of the more referentialist *montrer un rapport* (364).

4. The metonymic movement here is even more complex and wide-ranging than I'm able to detail: when Olin argues that "slender ribbon of braided gold" doesn't actually appear in the Van der Zee photograph at all (where it is "a string of pearls") but in a photograph of Barthes's aunt from *Roland Barthes by Roland Barthes*, she suggests that the *punctum* itself can be constituted by a play between presence and absence in a way that implicitly, almost literally, textualizes this visual detail (79). See "Touching Photographs" in *Photography Degree Zero*.

5. In addition to the discussion by Abel that I go on to engage, see two articles from the December 2020 special issue of *Mosaic* dedicated to *Camera Lucida*: Yacavone, "Photograph as Trace," which digs into the text-image dynamics created by the specific journalistic contexts in which Barthes encountered the photographs he includes in *Camera Lucida*, and Bill Scalia's "Icon Machine," which somewhat more tangentially engages the caption's contribution to the extreme subjectivity of the *punctum* as part of a larger argument regarding the photograph's transcendence of itself.

6. Compare his statement in "Literature Today" from 1961: "language is already, anterior to any literary treatment, a system of meaning: even before being literature, it implies particularity of substances (the words), discontinuity, selection, categorization, special logic. I am in my room, I *see* my room; but already isn't *seeing* my room *speaking* it to myself? And even if this were not so, what am I to *say* about what I *see*? A bed? A window? A color? Already I wildly disrupt that continuity which is before my eyes" (*Critical* 159–60).

7. Abel, *Odd Affinities*, 124. The lines from *Camera Lucida* can be found on p. 56.

8. Ibid., 124, 126.

9. As she writes with brio and affection: "We can easily envision Woolf joining imaginatively in these insurrectionary capers, given her propensity to unseat figures of authority from their saddles, especially in the context represented by Queen Victoria as Empress of India: Percival tumbling from his horse in India in *The Waves*, or the narrator's maiden aunt from hers, to the narrator's economic gain, in *A Room of One's Own*" (127). For my part, all this talk of horseplay also has its Proustian echo in the equestrian accident that kills Albertine.

10. See Woolf, *Writer's Diary*, 160.

11. Abel, *Odd Affinities*, 258n13.

12. The parenthetical's original French draws has a similarly emphatic effect using different words: the idiom "(*c'est le cas de le dire*)," which is often translated "you can say that again" or "that's for sure!" (literally, "that's the case of saying it"), draws attention to the performance as well as the content of the statement, indeed to its performance of speech itself as *part of* its content.

13. I am certainly not the first to make this connection: see, among others, Attridge, "Roland Barthes's Obtuse, Sharp Meaning" and Fried, "Barthes's *Punctum*."

14. See Kristeva, "Towards a Semiology of Paragraphs."

15. See also his 1962 review of Butor's *Mobile*, which takes issue with the criticism with its own "discontinuous" presentation of text and images: "For what is hidden be-

hind this condemnation of discontinuity is obviously the myth of life itself: the Book must flow because fundamentally, despite centuries of intellectualism, our criticism wants literature to be, always, a spontaneous, gracious activity conceded by a god, a muse, and if the god or muse happens to be a little reticent, one must at least 'conceal one's labor': to write is to secrete words within that great category of the continuous which is narrative" (*Critical* 173).

Bibliography

Abel, Elizabeth. *Odd Affinities: Virginia Woolf's Shadow Genealogies*. Chicago: University of Chicago Press, 2024.

Amigo Pino, Claudia. "Le Roman de temps perdu: Le mythe de Proust et la recherche de Barthes." *Recherche & Travaux* 77 (2010): 45–56.

Attridge, Derek. "Roland Barthes's Obtuse, Sharp Meaning and the Responsibilities of Commentary." In *Writing the Image after Roland Barthes*, edited by Jean-Michel Rabaté. Philadelphia: University of Pennsylvania Press, 1997.

Badmington, Neil. *The Afterlives of Roland Barthes*. London: Bloomsbury, 2016.

Badmington, Neil. "Bored with Barthes: Ennui in China." *Textual Practice* 30, no. 2 (2016): 305–25.

Badmington, Neil, ed. *Roland Barthes: Critical Evaluations in Cultural Theory*. 4 vols. New York: Routledge, 2010.

Baldwin, Thomas. *Roland Barthes: The Proust Variations*. Liverpool: Liverpool University Press, 2019.

Barry, Elizabeth. "The Moment of Truth: Proust, Barthes, and the Contingency of Old Age." *Textual Practice* 32, no. 3 (March 2018): 489–508.

Barthes, Roland. *Album: Unpublished Correspondence and Texts*. Edited by Éric Marty. Translated by Jody Gladding. New York: Columbia University Press, 2018.

Barthes, Roland. *Camera Lucida: Reflections on Photography*. Translated by Richard Howard. New York: Hill and Wang, 1981.

Barthes, Roland. *Critical Essays*. Translated by Richard Howard. Evanston, IL: Northwestern University Press, 1972.

Barthes, Roland. *Criticism and Truth*. Translated by Katrine Pilcher Keuneman. Minneapolis: University of Minnesota Press, 1987.

Barthes, Roland. *The Eiffel Tower and Other Mythologies*. Translated by Richard Howard. Berkeley: University of California Press, 1997.

Barthes, Roland. *Elements of Semiology*. Translated by Annette Lavers and Colin Smith. New York: Hill and Wang, 1967.

Barthes, Roland. *Empire of Signs*. Translated by Richard Howard. New York: Hill and Wang, 1982.

Barthes, Roland. *The Fashion System*. Translated by Matthew Ward and Richard Howard. Berkeley: University of California Press, 1983.

Bibliography

Barthes, Roland. *The Grain of the Voice: Interviews 1962-1980*. Translated by Linda Coverdale. Berkeley: University of California Press, 1991.

Barthes, Roland. *Image-Music-Text*. Translated by Stephen Heath. New York: Hill and Wang, 1977.

Barthes, Roland. *The Language of Fashion*. Translated by Andy Stafford. London: Bloomsbury Academic, 2013.

Barthes, Roland. "Lecture in the Inauguration of the Chair of Literary Semiology, January 7, 1977." Translated by Richard Howard. *October* 8 (Spring 1979): 3–16.

Barthes, Roland. *A Lover's Discourse: Fragments*. Translated by Richard Howard. New York: Hill and Wang, 1978.

Barthes, Roland. *"Masculine, Feminine, Neuter" and Other Writings on Literature*. Edited and translated by Chris Turner. London: Seagull, 2016.

Barthes, Roland. *Michelet*. Translated by Richard Howard. New York: Hill and Wang, 1987.

Barthes, Roland. *Mythologies*. Edited and translated by Annette Lavers. New York: Hill and Wang, 1972.

Barthes, Roland. *The Neutral: Lecture Course at the Collège de France (1977–1978)*. Translated by Rosalind E. Krauss and Denis Hollier. New York: Columbia University Press, 2005.

Barthes, Roland. *New Critical Essays*. Translated by Richard Howard. Evanston, IL: Northwestern University Press, 1980.

Barthes, Roland. *Oeuvres complètes*. Edited by Éric Marty. 5 vols. Paris: Seuil, 2002.

Barthes, Roland. "On Gide and His Journal." In *A Barthes Reader*, edited by Susan Sontag, 3–17. London: Jonathan Cape, 1982.

Barthes, Roland. *On Racine*. Translated by Richard Howard. New York: Performing Arts Journal, 1983.

Barthes, Roland. *The Pleasure of the Text*. Translated by Richard Miller. New York: Hill and Wang, 1975.

Barthes, Roland. *La préparation du roman: Cours au Collège de France 1978–1979 et 1979–1980*. Transcription of the recordings by Nathalie Lacroix. Paris: Seuil, 2015.

Barthes, Roland. *The Preparation of the Novel: Lecture Courses and Seminars at the Collège de France (1978–1979 and 1979–1980)*. Translated by Kate Briggs. New York: Columbia University Press, 2011.

Barthes, Roland. *The Responsibility of Forms: Critical Essays on Music, Art, and Representation*. Translated by Richard Howard. Berkeley: University of California Press, 1985.

Barthes, Roland. *Roland Barthes by Roland Barthes*. Translated by Richard Howard. Berkeley: University of California Press, 1994.

Barthes, Roland. *The Rustle of Language*. Translated by Richard Howard. Berkeley: University of California Press, 1989.

Barthes, Roland. *Sade, Fourier, Loyola*. Translated by Richard Miller. New York: Hill and Wang, 1976.

Barthes, Roland. *"Sarrasine" de Balzac: Séminaires à l'École pratique de hautes études 1967–1968, 1968–1969*. Edited by Claude Coste and Andy Stafford. Paris: Seuil, 2011.

Barthes, Roland. *The Semiotic Challenge*. Translated by Richard Howard. Berkeley: University of California Press, 1988.

Barthes, Roland. *Signs and Images: Writings on Art, Cinema, and Photography*. Edited and translated by Chris Turner. London: Seagull, 2016.
Barthes, Roland. *"Simply a Particular Contemporary": Interviews, 1970-1979*. Edited and translated by Chris Turner. London: Seagull, 2015.
Barthes, Roland. *S/Z*. Translated by Richard Miller. New York: Hill and Wang, 1974.
Barthes, Roland. *Travels in China*. Edited by Anne Herschberg Pierrot. Translated by Andrew Brown. Malden, MA: Polity, 2012.
Barthes, Roland. *"A Very Fine Gift" and Other Writings on Theory*. Edited and translated by Chris Turner. London: Seagull, 2015.
Barthes, Roland. *Writer Sollers*. Translated by Philip Thody. Minneapolis: University of Minnesota Press, 1987.
Barthes, Roland. *Writing Degree Zero*. Translated by Annette Lavers and Colin Smith. New York: Hill and Wang, 1967.
Benhaïm, André. "Barthes on the Beach." *Yearbook of Comparative Literature* 62 (2019): 162-73.
Bennett, Jane. *The Enchantment of Modern Life: Attachments, Crossings, Ethics*. Princeton, NJ: Princeton University Press, 2001.
Best, Stephen, and Sharon Marcus. "Surface Reading: An Introduction." *Representations* 108, no. 1 (Fall 2009): 1-21.
Bowie, Malcolm. "Barthes on Proust." *Yale Journal of Criticism* 14, no. 2 (Fall 2001): 513-18.
Butor, Michel. "La Fascinatrice." In *Répertoire IV*, 371-97. Paris: Éditions de Minuit, 1974.
Buurma, Rachel Sagner, and Laura Heffernan. "'Notation after 'The Reality Effect': Remaking Reference with Roland Barthes and Sheila Heti." *Representations* 125, no. 1 (Winter 2014): 80-102.
Caillois, Roger. "The Natural Fantastic." In *The Edge of Surrealism: A Roger Caillois Reader*, translated by Claudine Frank and Camille Naish, 348-57. Durham, NC: Duke University Press, 2003.
Calefato, Patrizia. "On Myths and Fashion." *Signs Systems Studies* 36, no. 1 (2008): 71-80.
Carter, Michael. "Stuff and Nonsense: The Limits of the Linguistic Model of Clothing." *Fashion Theory* 16, no. 3 (2012): 343-54.
Cheah, Pheng. *What Is a World? On Postcolonial Literature as World Literature*. Durham, NC: Duke University Press, 2016.
Compagnon, Antoine. "Le Roman de Barthes." *Critique* 59 (November 2003): 789-802.
Coste, Claude. *Bêtise de Barthes*. Paris: Klincksiek, 2011.
Coste, Claude. "*Roland Barthes par Roland Barthes* ou Le démon de la totalité." *Recherches & Travaux* 75 (2009): 35-54.
Culler, Jonathan. *Structuralist Poetics: Structuralism, Linguistics, and the Study of Literature*. New York: Routledge, 2002.
Cusset, François. *French Theory: How Foucault, Derrida, Deleuze, & Co. Transformed the Intellectual Life of the United States*. Translated by Jeff Fort. Minneapolis: University of Minnesota Press, 2008.
Davidson, Arnold I. "Introduction: Pierre Hadot and the Spiritual Phenomenon of Ancient Philosophy." In Pierre Hadot, *Philosophy as a Way of Life*, translated by Michael Chase, 1-45. Malden, MA: Blackwell, 1995.

Derrida, Jacques. *Of Grammatology*. Translated by Gayatri Chakravorty Spivak. Baltimore, MD: Johns Hopkins University Press, 1976.

Derrida, Jacques. *Speech and Phenomena and Other Essays on Husserl's Theory of Signs*. Translated by David B. Allison. Evanston, IL: Northwestern University Press, 1973.

During, Simon. *Modern Enchantments: The Cultural Power of Secular Magic*. Cambridge, MA: Harvard University Press, 2002.

Elkins, Amy E. *Crafting Feminism from Literary Modernism to the Multimedia Present*. New York: Oxford University Press, 2022.

Emre, Merve. "Love as Aesthetic Education." *Raritan* 43, no. 3 (Winter 2024): 4–33.

Felski, Rita. *The Limits of Critique*. Chicago: University of Chicago Press, 2015.

Felski, Rita. *Uses of Literature*. Malden, MA: Wiley-Blackwell, 2008.

Fenves, Peter. "'Einstein's Brain' in Three Parts." *Yearbook of Comparative Literature* 62 (2019): 174–88.

Frank, Claudine. "Introduction." In *The Edge of Surrealism: A Roger Caillois Reader*, translated by Claudine Frank and Camille Naish, 1–53. Durham, NC: Duke University Press, 2003.

Fried, Michael. "Barthes's *Punctum*." In *Photography Degree Zero: Reflections on Roland Barthes's "Camera Lucida"*, edited by Geoffrey Batchen, 141–70. Cambridge, MA: MIT Press, 2009.

Gailliard, Françoise. "Roland Barthes: Parti pris du sens." *MLN* 132, no. 4 (September 2017): 840–50.

Gallop, Jane. *The Deaths of the Author: Reading and Writing in Time*. Durham, NC: Duke University Press, 2011.

Gratton, Johnnie. "Text, Image, Reference in Roland Barthes's *La Chambre Claire*." *Modern Language Review* 91, no. 2 (April 1996): 355–64.

Haustein, Katja. "'La Vie comme oeuvre': Barthes with Proust." In *Anamnesia: Private and Public Memory in Modern French Culture*, edited by Anna-Magdalena Elsner, Peter Collier, and Olga Smith, 174–91. Bern: Peter Lang, 2009.

Holsinger, Bruce. *The Premodern Condition: Medievalism and the Making of Theory*. Chicago: University of Chicago Press, 2005.

Iser, Wolfgang. *The Fictive and the Imaginary: Charting Literary Anthropology*. Baltimore, MD: Johns Hopkins University Press, 1993.

Jameson, Fredric. "The Ideology of the Text." In *Roland Barthes: Critical Evaluations in Cultural Theory*, edited by Neil Badmington, 113–63. Vol. 2. New York: Routledge, 2010.

Johnson, Barbara. "The Critical Difference: Balzac's 'Sarrasine' and Barthes' *S/Z*." In *Roland Barthes: Critical Evaluations in Cultural Theory*, edited by Neil Badmington, 59–68. Vol. 2. New York: Routledge, 2010.

Knight, Diana. *Barthes and Utopia: Space, Travel, Writing*. Oxford: Clarendon, 1997.

Knight, Diana. "Idle Thoughts: Barthes' Vita Nova." *Nottingham French Studies* 36, no. 1 (Spring 1997): 88–98.

Kornbluh, Anna. *The Order of Forms: Realism, Formalism, and Social Space*. Chicago: University of Chicago Press, 2019.

Kristeva, Julia. *Desire in Language: A Semiotic Approach to Literature and Art*. New York: Columbia University Press, 1980.

Kristeva, Julia. "Towards a Semiology of Paragrams." In *The Tel Quel Reader*, edited by Patrick ffrench and Roland-François Lack, 25–49. New York: Routledge, 1998.

Kritzman, Lawrence D. "Barthes' Death Sentences and the End of Literature." *MLN* 132, no. 4 (September 2017): 864–75.
Kritzman, Lawrence D. "Barthes' Way: *Un Amour de Proust*." *Yale Journal of Criticism* 14, no. 2 (Fall 2001): 535–43.
Landy, Joshua. *How to Do Things with Fictions*. Oxford: Oxford University Press, 2012.
Landy, Joshua. "Modern Magic: Jean-Eugène Robert-Houdin and Stéphane Mallarmé." In *The Re-enchantment of the World: Secular Magic in a Rational Age*, edited by Joshua Landy and Michael Saler, 102–29. Stanford, CA: Stanford University Press, 2009.
Langlet, Irène. "Inactualité des *Mythologies*?" In *Barthes, au lieu du roman*, edited by Alexandre Gefen and Marielle Macé, 127–32. Paris: Desjonquères, 2002.
Laplanche, Jean, and Jean-Bertrand Pontalis. *The Language of Psycho-Analysis*. Translated by Donald Nicholson-Smith. New York: W. W. Norton, 1974.
Lavers, Annette. *Structuralism and After*. Cambridge, MA: Harvard University Press, 1982.
Lévi-Strauss, Claude. *Structural Anthropology*. Translated by Claire Jacobson. New York: Basic, 1963.
Lombardo, Patrizia. "History and Form." In *Roland Barthes: Critical Evaluations in Cultural Theory*, edited by Neil Badmington, 57–89. Vol. 1. New York: Routledge, 2010.
Loveless, Natalie. *How to Make Art at the End of the World: A Manifesto for Research-Creation*. Durham, NC: Duke University Press, 2019.
Lowe, Lisa. *Critical Terrains: French and British Orientalisms*. Ithaca, NY: Cornell University Press, 1991.
Lurz, John. *The Death of the Book: Modernist Novels and the Time of Reading*. New York: Fordham University Press, 2016.
Lurz, John. "Medium Thickness: Phenomenology, Plasticity, and the Futures of Form." *Criticism* 61, no. 2 (Spring 2019): 147–66.
Macé, Marielle. "Barthes romanesque." In *Barthes, au lieu du roman*, edited by Alexandre Gefen and Marielle Macé, 173–94. Paris: Desjonquères, 2002.
Macé, Marielle. *Façons de lire, manières d'être*. Paris: Gallimard, 2011.
Malabou, Catherine. *Le Change Heidegger: du fantastique en philosophie*. Paris: Léo Scheer, 2004.
Malabou, Catherine. *The Future of Hegel: Plasticity, Temporality, Dialectic*. Translated by Lisabeth During. New York: Routledge, 2005.
Malabou, Catherine. *The Heidegger Change: On the Fantastic in Philosophy*. Translated by Peter Skafish. Albany: State University of New York Press, 2011.
Malabou, Catherine. "Pierre Loves Horranges: Levinas-Sartre-Nancy: An Approach to the Fantastic in Philosophy." Translated by Steven Miller. *Umbr(a)* 1 (2006): 103–17.
Malabou, Catherine. *Plasticity at the Dusk of Writing: Dialectic, Destruction, Deconstruction*. Translated by Carolyn Shread. New York: Columbia University Press, 2010.
Martin, Jean-Pierre. "Barthes et la 'Vita Nova.'" *Poétique* 156, no. 4 (2008): 495–508.
Michelet, Jules. *Satanism and Witchcraft: A Study in Medieval Superstition*. Translated by A. R. Allinson. Secaucus, NJ: Citadel, 1973.
Michelet, Jules. *La Sorcière*. Paris: Librairie internationale, 1863.

Micir, Melanie and Aarthi Vadde. "Obliterature: Toward and Amateur Criticism." *Modernism/Modernity* 25.3 (September 2018): 517-49.

Moudileno, Lydia. "Barthes's Black Soldier: The Making of a Mythological Celebrity." *Yearbook of Comparative Literature* 62 (2016): 57-72.

Olin, Margaret. "Touching Photographs: Roland Barthes's 'Mistaken' Identification." In *Photography Degree Zero: Reflections on Roland Barthes's "Camera Lucida"*, edited by Geoffrey Batchen, 75-90. Cambridge, MA: MIT Press, 2009.

O'Meara, Lucy. "Barthes and the Lessons of Ancient Philosophy." In *Interdisciplinary Barthes*, edited by Diana Knight. Proceedings of the British Academy 228. Oxford: Oxford University Press, 2020.

O'Meara, Lucy. *Roland Barthes at the Collège de France*. Liverpool: Liverpool University Press, 2012.

Paige, Nicholas. "Permanent Re-enchantments: On Some Literary Uses of the Supernatural from Early Empiricism to Modern Aesthetics." In *The Re-enchantment of the World: Secular Magic in a Rational Age*, edited by Joshua Landy and Michael Saler, 159-80. Stanford, CA: Stanford University Press, 2009.

Picard, Raymond. "New Criticism or New Fraud?" In *Roland Barthes: Critical Evaluations in Cultural Theory*, edited by Neil Badmington, 20-39. Vol. 1. New York: Routledge, 2010.

Pint, Kris. *The Perverse Art of Reading: On the Phantasmatic Semiology in Roland Barthes' Cours au Collège de France*. Amsterdam: Rodopi, 2010.

Roger, Phillipe. "Caritas Incarnate: A Tale of Love and Loss." *Yale Journal of Criticism* 14, no. 2 (Fall 2001): 527-33.

Saint-Amand, Pierre. "Barthes' Laziness." Translated by Jennifer Curtiss Gage. *Yale Journal of Criticism* 14, no. 2 (Fall 2001): 519-26.

Samoyault, Tiphaine. "Barthes hier et aujourd'hui: la critique comme échappée." *MLN* 132, no. 4 (September 2017): 890-901.

Sartre, Jean-Paul. *The Imaginary: A Phenomenological Psychology of the Imagination*. Translated by Jonathan Webber. New York: Routledge, 2004.

Scalia, Bill. "The Icon Machine: Expenditure and Third Meaning in *Camera Lucida*." *Mosaic: An Interdisciplinary Critical Journal* 53, no. 4 (December 2020): 75-93.

Sedgwick, Eve Kosofky. *The Weather in Proust*. Edited by Jonathan Goldberg. Durham, NC: Duke University Press, 2011.

Sheringham, Michael. *Everyday Life: Theories and Practices from Surrealism to the Present*. Oxford: Oxford University Press, 2006.

Sloterdijk, Peter. *You Must Change Your Life: On Anthropotechnics*. Translated by Wieland Hoban. Malden, MA: Polity, 2013.

Sollers, Phillipe. *The Friendship of Roland Barthes*. Translated by Andrew Brown. Malden, MA: Polity, 2017.

Springgay, Stephanie. *Feltness: Research-Creation, Socially Engaged Art, and Affective Pedagogies*. Durham, NC: Duke University Press, 2022.

Stafford, Andy. "Roland Barthes's Travels in China: Writing a Diary of Dissidence within Dissidence?" *Textual Practice* 30, no. 2 (2016): 287-304.

Stafford, Andy. *Roland Barthes Writing the Political: History, Dialectic, Self*. London: Anthem, 2023.

Thibault, Paul J. *Re-reading Saussure: The Dynamics of Signs in Social Life*. London: Routledge, 1997.

Todorov, Tzvetan. *The Fantastic: A Structural Approach to a Literary Genre*. Translated by Richard Howard. Ithaca, NY: Cornell University Press, 1975.

Tucker, Herbert F. "After Magic: Modern Charm in History, Theory, and Practice." *New Literary History* 48, no. 1 (Winter 2017): 103–22.

Wasser, Audrey. "Critical Thinking." *New Literary History* 52, no. 2 (Spring 2021): 191–209.

Whitaker, Jena. "Désir de lire, désir de traduire." *MLN* 132, no. 4 (September 2017): 821–28.

Woolf, Virginia. *A Writer's Diary*. Edited by Leonard Woolf. New York: Harcourt Brace, 1973.

Yacavone, Kathrin. "The Photograph as Trace: Barthes, Benjamin, and the Intermediality of Photographic Discourse." *Mosaic: An Interdisciplinary Critical Journal* 53, no. 4 (December 2020): 75–93.

Zenkine, Serge. "Les indices du mythe." *Recherches et Travaux* 77 (2010): 21–32.

Zhuo, Yue. "Gender Neutral: Rereading Barthes's *S/Z* and the Figure of the Androgyne." *Word and Text: A Journal of Literary Studies and Linguistics* 7 (2017): 119–35.

Zumhagen-Yekplé, Karen. *A Different Order of Difficulty: Literature after Wittgenstein*. Chicago: University of Chicago Press, 2020.

Index

Page numbers in italics refer to figures.

À la recherche du temps perdu (Proust), xv, 95–99
amateurism, xx–xxiii, 149n23. *See also* collage
antithesis. *See* opposition
Arcimboldo, Giuseppe, 20–22, *21*, 24–26

Barthes, Roland, works of: "Arcimboldo, or Magician and Rhétoriqueur," 20–22, 24–26; "At the Music Hall," 156n17; "Authors and Writers," 157n25; "'Blue Is in Fashion This Year': A Note on Research into the Signifying Units in Fashion Clothing," 54; *Camera Lucida*, 32, 131–36; "Cayrol and Erasure," 160n7; *Critical Essays*, preface to, 129; *Criticism and Truth*, 114–18, 128, 154n28; "Culture and Tragedy," xiv; "The Death of the Author," xiv, xvii–xviii; "Diderot, Brecht, Eisenstein," 148n11; "The Discourse of History," 154n2; "Enjoy the Classics," xiv; *Elements of Semiology*, 80, 87; *Empire of Signs*, 72–74; *The Fashion System*, 7–10, 13, 54–60, 63–67, 69–72, 155n9, 156n16; "From Gemstones to Jewelry," 45; "From Science to Literature," 157n1; "Introduction to the Structural Analysis of Narratives," 158n9; "In the Ring," 36–38; "The Indictment Periodically Lodged . . . ," 50; "*Je me suis couché de bonne heure*," 155n10; "The Kitchen of Meaning," 154n19; "Lecture in Inauguration of the Chair of Literary Semiology," 2; "Lesson in Writing," 156n18; "Literature and Signification," 117, 160n14; "Literature Today," xxiii, 161n6; "Literature and Discontinuity," 161n15; *A Lover's Discourse: Fragments*, 106–7, 118–26; "Masculine, Feminine, Neuter," 92; *Michelet*, 35–36; "Michelet, Today," 47–48; "Musica Practica," 156n19; *Mythologies*, 33–34, 36–41, 43, 108, 113, 153n9, 153n18, 157n23; *The Neutral*, xiv; "On Gide and His Journal," 2–4; *On Racine*, 106–19, *112*; "Parallel Lives," xv; "The Photographic Message," 131–32; "Pierre Loti: *Aziyadé*," 159n19; *The Pleasure of the Text*, xxii, 31, 130; "Poujade and the Intellectuals," 49–50, 53–54; *The Preparation of the Novel*, xvi, 60–62, 152n47, 156n14, 156n15; "Proust and Names," 96–99; "Rhetoric of the Image," 131–32; *Roland Barthes by Roland Barthes*, xxi, xxiii, 4–5, 12, 36, 50, 104, 154n29; *Sade, Fourier, Loyola*, xxii, 13–15, 17–19, 132, 141–43; "*La Sorcière*," 33, 41–42, 44–45, 50–51; "Style and Its Image," 103–5;

Barthes, Roland, works of (*continued*):
S/Z, 78, 81, 82-96, 102-4, 106, 109, 158n10; "Textual Analysis of a Tale by Edgar Allan Poe," 158n14; "The Third Meaning," 137-41; *Travels in China*, 67-69; *Writer Sollers*, 48-49; *Writing Degree Zero*, 77-81
being, 11; and language, 48
Butor, Michel, 56

Caillois, Roger, 23-25
caption, 132-36, 161n5. *See also* image
citation, 104-26; as word, 106; in footnotes, 110-14, 116. *See also* form
collage, *xii*, xxi-xxiii, *xxiv*, 18, 22, 25-26, 30, 52, 55, 67, 76, 82, *101*, 124, *127*, 131, 133, *144*, 156n19
connotation, 63-64
Coste, Claude, 75, 117-18
criticism, 129-43, 160n2
cutting, 21-22, 57-58, 60-62, 70, 74, 83-84, 129, 133, 135-36, 141, 143

découpage, 141
denotation, 63-64
Derrida, Jacques, 13
discontinuity, 57, 61-62, 66, 108, 110-11, 135, 141, 143
division, 18, 22, 73, 126. *See also* discontinuity
dream, 89, 99, 115

fantastic, 1-29, 34, 42-43, 46-49, 59, 60-67, 70, 75, 86-87, 90-92, 94-96, 99-100, 103-4, 107, 110-13, 115-17, 119-26, 130, 132, 134-43; as word, xiii, xviii, xxiii; and fantasmatic, 1-2, 10, 15, 18-19, 132, 150n19; and imaginary, 2, 23, 70, 103-4; and fantasy, 2, 4, 142; in Barthes's writing, 4, 9, 15, 18, 22; as genre, 5-7, 89; and ideology, 63-65, 67-69, 99-100
film, 137-41
formula, 15-17, 103-5, 110
form, 103-5, 107, 113, 114, 116-17
fragmentation, 55. *See also* discontinuity

Gide, André, 2-4
gender, 85-86

Hadot, Pierre, 15-16
hesitation, 6, 70
history, 77-80
homology, 82, 91-94, 109, 123, 128

identification, 123-24
image, 57-59, 104, 111-12, 130-39
immediacy, 32, 37, 71, 100, 105. *See also* mediation
In Search of Lost Time. See *À la recherche du temps perdu*

Kristeva, Julia, 138, 157n2

Lévi-Strauss, Claude, 33, 103
life, 8-9, 14, 58-62, 73, 96, 98, 130, 137-38; and art, 90-92, 94
literature, xxiii, 9-10, 14-17, 25, 33, 44, 48-50, 56-57, 60-62, 70-71, 77-80, 82-100, 103-26, 135-36. *See also* form
Loyola, Ignatius, 17-19

Macé, Marielle, xvi-xvii, 3, 14-15, 147n9, 147n10, 149n8, 156n13, 159n1, 159n2, 160n17
magic, 26, 31-35, 40-42, 44-47, 49-50; and immediacy, 37; and myth, 38-39, 41; and speech, 36; and tautology, 39
making, 57, 128
Malabou, Catherine, 10-13, 116, 151n28, 152n44
mediation, 34-35, 43, 45, 50, 105. *See also* immediacy
metalanguage, 35, 41, 42-44, 55
Michelet, Jules, 32-36, 41-44, 46-48, 49
money, 87-89

name. *See* onomastics
network, 81-82, 87-88, 95-96, 135
Nietzsche, Friedrich, xiv, 119
notation, 54-55, 57-58, 61-62, 78, 105, 133; and absence, 67-68
novelistic, xvii

onomastics, 84–85, 94–98; and language, 95, 97–99
opposition, 34, 36, 44, 46, 55, 58, 60, 64, 69, 80–81, 89–90, 126
orientalism, 69

perception, 7, 22, 24, 57–61, 66
photography. *See* image
Picard, Raymond, 49, 117–18. See also *Criticism and Truth*
Poujade, Pierre, 50, 53–54, 63
practice, xvii, xx–xxiii, 14–16, 20, 34, 40–44, 46, 48–50, 55, 57, 60–62, 64–66, 71–75, 77–78, 81, 84, 87, 104, 110–11, 113, 115, 121–24, 128, 130, 140–43. *See also* work
projection, 124
Proust, Marcel, xiv–xvii, 82, 84, 95–99, 124–25, 129–30, 141
punctum, 133–36, 161n4, 161n13

reading, 15, 22, 87, 99–100, 102, 125, 130, 136–38, 140–43; as experience, xviii, 6–7; as behavior, xviii; necessity of, xxiv
reality, 10, 38, 41, 45, 47, 49, 54, 60, 63, 79, 86. *See also* unreality

reference, 130–31, 160n3
reflexion, 79, 82–100, 105; alternative spelling of, 81
ritual. *See* practice

Sade, Marquis de, 142–43
"Sarrasine," 84–96; genre of, 84, 89
Saussure, Ferdinand de, 80
Sollers, Philippe, xiv, 48–49
sorceress. *See* witch
Sorrows of Young Werther, The (Goethe), 29, 119–24

temporality, 6, 55, 65–66, 68–74, 139–40
time. *See* temporality
Todorov, Tzvetan, 5–7, 70, 150n17
translation, 1

unreality, xxiii, 10, 54

value, 45, 79–84, 87–88, 92–94, 120

witch, 33–34, 41–44, 46–47, 49–50, 53, 77
witch doctor. *See* witch
Woolf, Virginia, 135–36
work, 53–75, 78, 84, 105, 130; and idleness, 53, 63–65